D0723257

New Medical Technologies
and Society

New Medical Technologies and Society

Reordering Life

NIK BROWN & ANDREW WEBSTER

polity

Copyright © Nik Brown and Andrew Webster 2004

The right of Nik Brown and Andrew Webster to be identified as
Authors of this Work has been asserted in accordance with the
UK Copyright, Designs and Patents Act 1988.

First published in 2004 by Polity Press Ltd.

Polity Press
65 Bridge Street
Cambridge CB2 1UR, UK

Polity Press
350 Main Street
Malden, MA 02148, USA

All rights reserved. Except for the quotation of short passages for the
purposes of criticism and review, no part of this publication may be
reproduced, stored in a retrieval system, or transmitted, in any form
or by any means, electronic, mechanical, photocopying, recording or
otherwise, without the prior permission of the publisher.

ISBN: 0-7456 2723-4
ISBN: 0-7456 2724-2 (pb)

A catalogue record for this book is available from the British Library.

Typeset in 10.5 on 12 pt Sabon
by Graphicraft Limited, Hong Kong
Printed and bound in Great Britain
by MPG Books, Bodmin, Cornwall

For further information on Polity, visit our website: www.polity.co.uk

Contents

1

Introduction: New Medical Technologies and Society

This book examines the role and cultural significance of current technological innovation in redefining the meaning of medicine and health.
New medical technologies are increasingly attracting widespread commentary as to the forms of social and cultural change with which
they are associated. For instance, information and communication
technologies (ICTs) and telemedicine are said to be reordering the
relationships between citizen and state, health-care practitioner and
patient. The term 'wired welfare' has now entered sociological and
policy parlance as an expression of the changes accompanying ICT-
mediated care, where the internet in particular is used as a medium
for self-help and access to various forms of social support. Again
within the context of ICTs, the ready availability of medical information via the internet has begun to destabilize the professional boundaries of medical knowledge itself, and has generated new information
for people (whether patients or not) from a much wider range of
sources than in the past. The electronic patient record, increasingly
sophisticated sonography (for ultrasound scans used especially in reproduction) or the more recent use of telemedicine to provide images
of the body at a distance define the body and its representation in
entirely new ways: as Samson (1999) has argued, 'The patient is
rendered as a universalised datum, disconnected from both any tan-
gible, corporeal body and the sentient human being, becoming an
image that can be moved through computer networks anywhere
around the world. Understanding such a patient does not require
human touch' (p. 17). And perhaps the most eloquent illustration of
this are the 'GRID'-based medical devices, including mobile sensors
placed on people (whether they have a status as patients or not) to

relay information automatically to a central clinical site on a daily basis – what might be termed an 'e-panopticon' for medicine.

In regard to the 'new biologies', transpecies transplantation, transgenics and cloning (both 'reproductive' and 'therapeutic') are posing difficult and challenging questions concerning the character of our human/non-human identity. They also raise ethical questions about the rights of donors, recipients and the new entities that are associated with these recent developments in biomedicine. In turn, such technologies generate new risks where, for example, transpecies transplantation is also accompanied by the threat of transpecies (viral) disease. Innovative health technologies have created new uncertainties, for example, with regard to the dilemma presented by new genetic diagnostics, where the diagnosis of a disease-susceptibility (rather than calculable risk) in the absence of treatment provokes new anxieties and concerns for those so diagnosed. Here 'genetic-risk-identity' can be said to be expanding temporally (that is, predictive of personal pathological states that are located far into the future) as well as expanding spatially in its relevance for a growing number of diseases and conditions.

A third area of medical development combines the technologies of ICTs and the biosciences to create what some have seen as the new 'cyborg' hybrids (Haraway 1991, 1997) or 'assemblages' (Michael 2000) that bring together machine and body tissue. The development of bioinformatics, where massive DNA databases are managed through high-capacity information infrastructures, is one notable example of this convergence of the digital and the biological. Others see these combinations as heralding the onset of a new type of 'regenerative medicine', such as artificial skin, bone and even heart. Much of this depends on micro-design (nanotechnology in some cases) and micro-computing allied to molecular biology and biochemistry: spare parts, prosthetic and assistive devices, and intra-body motors and instruments (such as the 'Rotablator' conceived to clean out clogged arteries) make for new machine–body relations that change the terms on which we understand and cope with our embodiment, illness and disease.

Some sense of the technological shifts in medicine can be derived from various sources recounting the historical development of techniques and equipment. These are often presented as the result of combining medicine and engineering in innovative ways. For example, the UK's National Academy of Engineering recently declared:

> It is astounding to compare the medical technology of today with that of 1900. Then, doctors with small black bags came to one's house and,

using a few instruments and their senses, determined one's illness. . . .
Health technologies really began to blossom in the last half of the
century, when engineering and medicine became increasingly interdisciplinary, and the human body was more fully recognized as a complex system of electrical fields, fluid and biomechanics, chemistry, and
motion – ideal for an engineering approach to many of its problems. . . .
Engineers have worked with the medical profession to develop artificial organs, replacement joints, life-enhancing systems, diagnostic and
imaging technologies – remarkable machines, materials, and devices
that save lives and significantly improve the quality of life for millions.
(NAE 2000, 1)

Given the arrival of these new – and apparently wondrously effective
– technologies, it is timely that their sociological implications are
explored. How is sociology able to make analytical sense of these
changes? In what ways do they differ in terms of their social and
technical complexity compared with developments in medical technologies that have appeared in the past? What conceptual resources are
available to social science scholars of contemporary debates in health
technology that can be drawn on to help build a critical commentary
on the implications that new medical technologies (NMTs) have for
society? How might we locate the specific debates about these technologies in a wider sociological understanding of the dynamics of
late modernity? And how far are NMTs shaped by contemporary
changes related to our perceptions of such issues as family, kinship,
identity, risk and trust, the lifecourse (including the meaning of death)
and lifestyle patterns and choices?

In trying to answer these questions, we hope that this book offers
a useful contribution towards the analysis of NMTs not only for
those directly engaged in medicine itself, but also for a wider audience who are interested in understanding the ways in which contemporary technologies can be interrogated through core sociological
inquiry. In doing so we will draw on a variety of traditions, including
social theory, the sociology of science and technology and medical
sociology. We do not intend in this book to develop an argument
surrounding the evaluation of new technologies in the conventional
sense found within fields such as health technology assessment. We
will, however, in our concluding chapter try to derive some broad
implications of our overall analysis as these relate to the way in which
the value or social utility of health technologies is presented. There
has been a long-standing debate about the 'real impact' and efficacy
of new techniques, prompted especially by the work of Thomas
McKeown (1979), who has argued that the benefits of developments

in clinical medicine for population health are overstated (at least in terms of mortality rates). We will try to address such matters towards the end of the book, since we do believe that this text should be able to contribute, critically, to the more specific questions raised in health policy circles about the effectiveness of innovative health technologies. Measures of benefit and effectiveness are always contestible and often indeed contested. In part, this reflects the fact that innovation in NMTs is complex, reflecting a wide range of distinct and competing interests, including the science base, professional medics, patient advocacy groups, private-sector organizations in drug innovation and biomedical engineering, and the broad priorities of public health agencies. Where we can, we shall try to show how these differing interests affect the contemporary pattern of NMTs.

Organization of the 'body' of the book

Medical technologies are designed to understand, diagnose and treat disease, acute and chronic illness, and physical and psychological disorders, as well as to try to prevent such pathologies arising in the first place. Though disease and illness can strike people unexpectedly, our very notion of why this unfortunate state of affairs arises depends on a view we have that links morbidity and mortality to broad stages of the body's and the mind's temporality: medical classification systems provide us with lists of illnesses that are more closely associated with the body at certain times during life – diseases of childhood and of the elderly, and the different diseases of men and women in 'mid-life', etc. Not surprisingly, public health services and state provision are orchestrated around the needs of these broad categories of people within national (and international) populations, while epidemiologists keep track of shifting illness patterns as demographic and wider environmental changes affect the locus, scale and significance of different pathologies.

In short, conventional medicine assumes that there is a typical body that has a typical lifecourse, one that allows medical science to construct standardized models of 'normal' and 'abnormal' bodies, acute or less threatening illness, the onset of the death-sequence (Mulkay 1993) as well as the point at which human 'life' might be said to have begun in the embryo (the so-called primitive streak; see Warnock 1990) or stem cells cultured *in vitro*.

These broad criteria through which the status and health of our bodies and minds can be assessed according to expectations linked to the lifecourse allow clinicians to diagnose, prescribe, and decide when to intervene and when to refer a patient to others, to offer prognoses and to use their discretion in such a way that the particular illness or disease is seen to be 'managed' effectively. Clinical judgement and assumptions about 'best practice' are also heavily tied up with wider *social* norms about health expectations that change during a person's lifecourse. While clinicians are expected to devote whatever technical and clinical resources they can to preventing 'untimely' death in the very young, the same may be much less true of managing prolonged illness among the elderly. Over generations, of course, this may change as a result of, say, better nutrition, because the life (and health) expectancies of an earlier generation were less good than those of a later one. As Laslett (1989) has argued, this may well mean that in practice future generations of older people will enjoy a 'compression of morbidity' (p. 136), inasmuch as they will remain relatively healthy but experience a fairly rapid and ultimately fatal illness towards the end of their lives. Against this optimistic view, an alternative perspective argues that, as the longevity of the ageing population is extended, so their levels of chronic morbidity will increase.

This focus on the lifecourse as a series of processes and events surrounding reproduction, death, transition and change over different periodizations of life provides an organizing framework for the 'body' – in both a biological and a textual sense – of this book. This has two advantages for us: first, it helps us to marshal a wide range of material into relatively discrete – but, as we shall see towards the end, linked – arenas within which medical technologies are used; second, it helps us to show how, as a result of the impact of these same technologies, the conventional periods of the lifecourse and the boundaries of the body are being redefined, dissolved, and given new meanings. As a consequence, the boundaries of medicine and the social position occupied by professional clinicians are also changing. In our concluding chapter we explore the implications of our analysis for the reordering of life.

So, the book is organized around the 'lifecourse', that is, the idea of a successive movement through conception, birthing, childhood, adulthood and death. Following the first two chapters that set out the broad theoretical terrain on which the book is based, subsequent chapters deal in turn with reproduction, the body's maintenance, technologies of replacement and finally technologies of death and dying.

There are of course a number of limitations with the conventional 'lifecourse' model. Two are worth noting here, together with our response to them. The first is that the lifecourse model is entirely temporally naïve. That is, it assumes that time is an unproblematic and always uniform temporal passageway through which lives progress, sequentially, from one stage to the next. As Armstrong observes, following other analysts of time, this kind of thinking obscures the way in which lived time is itself artefactual (Armstrong 2000). Time is a product of ordering. It is not a cause of the body's ordering. If we are properly to understand the temporal organization of the body, it is necessary not only to explore the conventional periodizations of the body but also to explore the newly emerging forms of action and agency through which the traditional notion of the lifecourse is being altered. This we shall endeavour to do in each of the substantive chapters.

The second problem, derived from the first, is that the notion of the 'lifecourse' tends to mirror assumptions made more widely that there are clear periods – such as 'childhood' – that have a biological reference point in regards to the body's natural development. As has been argued, these notions of biologically defined stages are socially (and so historically) constructed and thereby vary between and within cultures: as Ariès (1973) argues, 'the idea of childhood did not exist' (p. 125) in medieval times. Much of our position echoes the comment made by Armstrong when he observes:

> The birth and death of the body have been the traditional markers of the temporal space of the life span. However, the twentieth century is remarkable for the extent to which this temporal line has been remapped, its space sub-divided, scrutinized, and reconstituted as a web of temporal movements, its outer boundaries increasingly blurred. (2000, 248)

With these caveats in mind, our use of the 'lifecourse' is primarily as a heuristic device through which we can throw light on the changes that NMTs create in regard to our understanding and management of the body. This organizational device provides us with a platform through which we can explore the body–technology–medicine nexus without thereby necessarily assuming that it unfolds in some sort of gradual linear way. Moreover, this strategy also enables us to avoid organizing the book around a list of medical technologies which would, thereby, simply prejudge the most significant, the most novel, the most transformative. In serving for us these heuristic purposes, we do not want to deny that, existentially, the lifecourse is a powerful experience at a personal level, where we are aware of our bodies' multiform processes of growth and decay. But, as the chapters ahead illustrate, the lifecourse is being reshaped, opened up temporally and spatially, not only in an attempt to address physical deterioration but also to redefine the boundaries of life itself (as in stem cell research).

Our general argument and conclusion is that NMTs are instrumental in the production of a new temporal ordering of the body through, for example, the creation of eternal cell lines, sequenced DNA, transplanted tissues, stored organs, semen, ovarian eggs and so on. In this way, the 'course' of life now both *pre*cedes (in a temporal sense) and *pro*ceeds from or goes beyond (in a cultural sense) the traditional boundaries of what once counted as 'life'. Just as importantly, this reshaping also produces new entities whose moral bearing is highly contested. Dispute over the moral status of early embryos is a ready example, but so too is that of personal biological data, as numerous legal challenges to the research and utility rights to patient records will attest. When these kinds of contests arise, they demonstrate a debate over the radical reorganization of life, humanness and its course.

First, however, we shall try to summarize the principal contributions that those working in the sociological tradition have made towards our understanding of medical technologies. In doing so, we need to try to answer the question What is so *different* about new medical technologies today? In answering this, of course, we are simultaneously asking What is different about the societal shaping, mediation and use of medical technologies? For technologies are always *socio*-technologies. In saying this, then, we do not subscribe to some linear, deterministic account of the 'impact' of medical technologies, as though this were a) the same wherever it was experienced, and b) unfolded according to some evolving (and progressively 'better') set of medical models and techniques. We shall show that these technologies are informed by the context of use and that their 'trajectory' is far from straightforward. It is also the case, of course, that many technologies do not displace older ones: far from it, for in medicine one of the chronic complaints of those who have to assess, appraise and decide whether to invest in new techniques is that they tend simply to expand the range of patients and conditions that fall within medicine's orbit and/or duplicate existing medical interventions.

Understanding NMTs

There are a number of sociologies, often overlapping and highly porous, that have sought to make sense of the connections across technology, the body, illness and social change. Those most important for our purposes are contributions from within theories of socio-historical change, the sociology of the body and the field of medical sociology.

Each of these analytical perspectives can be said to offer distinctive and useful conceptual resources with which to understand NMTs. Apart from considering the general contributions these fields have made, we have a particular interest, as sociologists working within science and technology studies (STS), to determine the relationship between STS and these other approaches, particularly in regards to how it can benefit and learn from these related analytical traditions. At the same time, we want to show how an STS analysis can inform and strengthen these other approaches. Before we do this, however, it is important to set down some general questions about contemporary medical technologies that focus especially on their novel character-istics. These questions will help us then explore various fields for useful answers.

Our first question is: how far are NMTs representative of some-thing uniquely distinctive about the way we engage with, order and (through clinical intervention) reshape our bodies and our biologies today? Does this reflect a wider set of social and cultural changes in the understanding of our bodies and our identity? It may well do so, since medicine has always been closely interwoven with the wider values, beliefs and forms of knowledge found in the society of which it is a part: contrast, for example, the models of the body associated with Chinese holistic philosophy, African Azande spiritualism and the physicalist approaches of nineteenth-century Anglo-Saxon medicine. Moreover the cultural dynamics of late modern society associated with the emergence of 'reflexive modernization' (Beck 1992; Crook 1999; Giddens 1994) tend to undermine a society-wide subscription to core values, beliefs and knowledge systems. If this is true, then we can ask whether medical technologies are caught up in this shift and so adding to the uncertainties of contemporary society, even though they are apparently better equipped scientifically and technically than ever to answer problems that have existed for centuries, such as how to cope with infectious disease, cancer and so on.

So our first sense of novelty relates to changes in the wider culture within which medicine is embedded. In a reflexive social world we are perhaps much more likely to question the expertise on which medical knowledge is based, to seek alternative routes through which to secure information about health, to be less certain about the calcu-lation of the risks we confront, and to link health to a much wider range of environmental settings and lifestyle choices.

Second, how might we understand the socio-historical periodization of medicine and technology, to help us identify what might be seen as unique to the contemporary characteristics of NMTs? Here novelty relates to contrasts that we can draw with earlier forms of medical knowledge and its clinical use. Some analysts regard contemporary medicine as quite distinct from earlier forms in the past. The difference lies in the way medical knowledge is produced, by whom, and for what 'markets'. For example, the more our medicine depends on high-tech science, the more its tacit, bedside, discretionary knowledge is said to be under threat. Medical expertise may become defined more and more in technical rather than in professional terms. This might in turn suggest a qualitative shift in the relations between expert and lay discourse. Clearly, this might not necessarily be peculiar to medicine, since many other professional bodies of knowledge are undergoing similar shifts related to the introduction of expert systems, computer-aided support tools, and the like. However, inasmuch as this is true, we might legitimately argue for broad and substantial shifts in the grounding of expert knowledge today where its legitimacy and accountability to consumers is based more on its technical than its charismatic or ascribed authority. However, the paradox is that, the more people insist that expertise demonstrates greater precision in its technical judgements, the less experts can persuade through an appeal to technical 'indeterminacy' (Jamous and Pelloile 1970) and professional 'discretion': 'you can never be sure, leave it to the experts' starts to lose its appeal.

Another question relates to the use of the term 'new' by those who are *directly engaged* in the technologies. How, in other words, are medical technologies actually *positioned* or presented as 'new' or, on the other hand, everyday and mundane by their advocates (see Michael 2000)? The reader should note here that the notion of 'the new' is not straightforward. The new is normally used to signify the exotic, the unfamiliar, the displaced and transformed, a change in principle. It is typically used in contrast to familiar patterns of socio-technical order signified by repetition, tradition, reproduction, and the embedded. However, even if we take this contrast as a useful guide to what we should look for, it is clear in practice that what *is* 'new' often provokes highly contested claims and counter-claims and is frequently the focus of argument among advocates seeking to define the relevance and significance of technical and social change. We can see this, for example, in the debate over the novelty, scope and implications of the field of drug discovery known as 'pharmacogenetics' (see Chapter 4). Some in industry regard and present this as a revolutionary change in the way drugs will be administered to patients, while others see it as merely an extension of existing practice (Hedgecoe and Martin 2003). As analysts, we cannot assume that one of these stories is right and the other wrong, but have to try to understand why the field is positioned as radical or, in contrast, as 'more of the same'.

In understanding this we have to try to distinguish between the claim that something is 'new', made as a rhetorical *attribution* of medical technology, and the notion that 'the new' refers to the socio-material *property of* medical technology (see Brown 1999, 1997; Brown and Michael 2003; Marvin 1988). For example, much of the discourse around gene therapy in the early 1990s concerned the novelty of a technology that promised to revolutionize the treatment of disease. Since then, because of technical setbacks and a number of fatally adverse reactions during trials in the US and Europe, gene therapy has been repositioned primarily as a 'tool' to help refine existing research and clinical techniques, and its proponents are more modest in their claims for its existing and potential benefits. In this case, then, novelty can be seen to be as much a *rhetorical* attribution made of gene therapy as it is something to do with the *actual* properties of the technology itself. As difficulties are overcome, we may well see another repositioning towards more dramatic claims. Similar shifts around the boundary line between the radical and the mundane have been seen elsewhere, as in the positioning of GM crops by plant researchers and the seeds industry. In the 1980s genetic modification was presented as the solution to an array of problems associated with conventional plant varieties. Today, twenty years later, many molecular breeders stress the routine line – 'this is only what happens in nature' – to defuse public anxieties over genetics (Plein 1991).

Finally, it is common to find both analyst and policy-maker speaking of 'new' medical technologies and doing so in regard to fields such as genetics and ICTs, precisely because both fields seem to point to a *cluster* of developments that *share* something 'new' in common. On the face of it, one might say that this cannot reside in their technical properties since these are materially quite different. However, while the language and terms of DNA-based genetics are quite distinct from the digital language and terms of the world of ICTs, they do have common features as information platforms, and, indeed, both forms of knowledge are, as a result, increasingly interwoven. The mapping of the Human Genome Project (completed 'in draft' in February 2001 and finalized in April 2003) relied on an alliance of genetic and IT-based expertise and data handling, especially through competence in bioinformatics (Brown and Rappert 2000). But the informational complexity of these technologies also has convoluted social dimensions: what these fields share, as a cluster of new medical technologies, has then to be seen in *socio*-technical terms extending out to organizational demands and global interdependencies.

Our exploration of these issues will be undertaken primarily through the adoption of the STS perspective mentioned above. That is, technology should be seen to mediate social relations, while these too are inscribed by the technologies, instruments and machines that surround us and shape our everyday life. Even so, the relationship between the old and the new has been a constant backdrop to broader sociologies of change (such as the change from traditional to modern society), with some accounts examining the specific role of technology in this process. These accounts swing between those that might place more emphasis on the determining effects of technology and others that stress the shaping of technology by social processes. Here, as we noted above, we wish to avoid adopting anything that might be construed as technological determinism, since this would be to presume that technologies possess a stable and singular identity and materiality that has a linear and identical 'impact' wherever they are introduced. Rather, we explore the dynamic interaction between the technical and the social in giving meaning to, mobilizing, and so defining the role of NMTs in reshaping the boundaries of the lifecourse. Through this approach we focus on change in such areas as the boundaries of the body, the characterization of disease and illness, the institutional and organizational structures and processes through which health and life is ordered, the forms and sources of knowledge on which both lay person and expert draw to account for health and illness, and so on.

Our overall aim in exploring these issues is to understand changes in the body–medicine–technology relation. Let us first sketch out how this has been addressed by the sociological perspectives noted above.

Theories of socio-historical change

The work we want to discuss here relates to those writers who have sought to account for the broad patterns of historical change in medicine and its associated technologies and techniques. We do not necessarily intend to cover the vast literature on the long and complex history of medicine or the emergence of specific medical devices. Our aim is to discuss material that has tried to identify significant shifts in the character of medical technology in order to see whether this analysis helps us gain a better understanding of the meaning of NMTs today and in the future.

A number of historians of medicine have offered very valuable accounts of such broad periodizations, notably Pickstone with his various contributions over the past decade (e.g. Pickstone 1992, 1993, 2000a; and Cooter and Pickstone 2000). Pickstone argues that science, technology and medicine can be characterized in terms of four historically successive but overlapping ideal types, what he has called 'socio-cognitive types': biographical medicine, analytical medicine, experimental medicine and techno-medicine (1993, 2000a). The last of these types represents the contemporary form, one that originated around 'the end of the nineteenth century, when certain laboratory products (or processes) became commodities, so partially reconstructing the social relations of science, technology and medicine to include industrial research laboratories, linked to universities, to state laboratories and to other institutions, in ways which have since become familiar in more and more areas of [science, technology and medicine]' (1993, 434).

Such technological shifts shape and are shaped by wider social changes in the socio-economic and political contexts within which medicine is found. Focusing on the 'political economy' of medicine, Pickstone distinguishes three broadly sequential changes in the socio-economic priorities and drivers of medicine over the twentieth century. These drivers have successively emphasized a 'productionist', a 'communitarian' and a 'consumerist' type of medicine. While elements of all three may coexist today, over the past century the emphasis has shifted from first to last. Productionist medicine, predominant in the first part of the period, gave priority to the health and reproductive powers of the workforce; communitarian medicine stresses in contrast the shared public-service medicine of a providential or welfare state, while the consumerist medicine of today highlights the way in which medicine is positioned as 'a commodity, chosen by individuals, usually in free markets' (2000b, 3).

Consumerist medicine is reflected in the growth of private medical insurance, in the increasing demand from consumers for a wider range of choice over medical treatments that should be available (often associated with the arrival of the 'expert patient' equipped with multiple – often internet-based – sources of information), in the privatization of formerly public services, in the development of internal markets within nationalized health-care systems, and perhaps most significantly in the blurring of health, lifestyles and fitness through, for example, psychopharmaceuticals, etc.

Pickstone argues that, of the three, the last two (communitarian and consumerist) are most likely to predominate in the future in varying degrees of balance in advanced industrial states (though not, of course, in poorer countries, increasingly marginalized from the West). The combination of the two types of medicine is of significance here since together they encourage a mix of large-scale (indeed globalized) as well as smaller, niche markets for NMTs that cut across public and private divides. For example, the state as well as private consumers may buy into new, experimental drugs for the treatment of disease, though the state as the provider of public funds may set limits on the degree to which it will do so. This in turn presumes and encourages the growth of private-sector, fee-based health care. Patient advocacy groups or charities might seek to move the boundary where state support begins and ends, of course, while the pace and scope of developments have led to the creation of health technology assessment agencies in Europe, the US and elsewhere charged with the task of measuring, anticipating and rationing the effects (both clinical and economic) of a wide range of innovation.

We can begin to see how Pickstone's analysis draws our attention to the relation between changing institutional boundaries, resourcing and markets and the creation of conditions conducive to NMTs. The consumerism and fee-based payments associated with medicine in advanced states (such as the US) not only foster increasing specialization, as consumers seek out the latest medical devices and techniques tailored to their individual needs, they also create a situation where the logic of mass public health care enshrined in practices such as national vaccination regimes is challenged. This encourages individuals to seek their own health technology solutions to existing or anticipated health problems – not only in regard to public immunization strategies (as illustrated by the UK controversy in 2002 over the triple (MMR) vaccine compared with single shots for mumps, measels and rubella) but for all health-care problems. Consumers of health as individuals inevitably shape the pattern of medical technology provision as a result of shifts in demand and of changes in the sources through which (public or private) health services can be delivered, such as the internet. These processes have been especially marked in the United States, giving rise to a huge array of medical technologies to meet ever more diverse consumer demands (see Reiser 1978).

Mention of the internet links to another strong theme in the history of medicine, the role of informatics. Foss and Rothenberg (1987) suggest that the 'first medical revolution entailed the move of chemistry into drug research, while the second medical revolution involves the move from biomedicine to informedicine.' Taking this further, Drews (1995) has argued that drug research has moved from the chemical paradigm to the informational paradigm. And, as Cooter and Pickstone note themselves, 'at the dawn of the twenty-first century, the language of information technology has become common in biomedicine, when for most of the twentieth century the dominant metaphors were drawn from engineering and warfare' (2000, xv). As we shall see in much more detail in later chapters, such information is both informatics- and gene-based and, as noted above, we can regard biology and biomedicine as increasingly information sciences in themselves. Moldrup and Morgall (2001) go as far as to suggest that the changes wrought by genetics on medicine are akin to the 'impact of the periodic table on physics' (p. 60).

Apart from these accounts that portray shifts in medicine in terms of grand paradigmatic change, other historians concentrate on more specific technical developments or focus on modification in particular medical regimes, notably those that are drugs- and equipment-based. Exemplifying the first of these approaches, Le Fanu (1999) offers a classification of medical technology in terms of three categories: what he calls 'life-sustaining', 'diagnostic' and 'surgical'. The first might refer to the intensive-care ward, life-support machines and prosthetics, such as pacemakers; the second refers to devices related to diagnosis, testing and screening, such as scanners, cardiograms, NMR (nuclear magnetic resonance) and so on; the final category is extensive in its compass and would include implants, transplants, different forms of organ or tissue replacement and engineering, plastic surgery, and so on. Le Fanu places great emphasis on the arrival and development of increasingly sophisticated *optical* devices (such as endoscopes) that allow medics (and surgeons in particular) to see within the body and to target, remove or treat very precise pathological sites. He suggests that the story surrounding optics is a paradigm for the broad impact of technology on medicine: the body becomes more accessible to medical intervention while simultaneously extending the range and variety of clinical problems that can be dealt with more directly. He observes, however, that this 'can be something of a two-edged sword. Technology can make medical intervention almost too easy, leading to inappropriate investigations and treatment' (p. 230).

Indeed, Le Fanu's narrative is not one of unalloyed medical progress. Instead, he argues that contemporary medicine is 'out of control' (1999, 252), inasmuch as it overuses diagnostics, presumes a technical fix to complex disorders, and condemns the terminally ill to a long and protracted process of dying. He has little time for the 'new genetics', which has failed to fulfil the promise it once held out (especially in areas such as gene therapy). We do not, however, share Le Fanu's rather normative position that genetics are 'out of control', for this would be to subscribe to a form of technological determinism.

Even so, Le Fanu's 'rise and fall' argument suggests that what is new about medical technology is also that which for some appears to make it less effective as a means of preventing illness or restoring health. This takes us towards debates surrounding the risks associated with medicine, an issue we consider more fully in Chapter 2.

Another approach, exemplified in the separate contributions of Blume (2000b) and Goodman (2000), maps socio-technical change in medicine in regard to fields (rather than Le Fanu's specific technical arenas) that as industrial sectors have had a major impact on the shape of medical technology and its meaning: pharmaceuticals is especially important here. The modern pharmaceutical industry grew out of the late nineteenth- and early twentieth-century work on synthetic dyes superseded by the discoveries associated with the antibacterial properties of a number of biological and later synthetically derived agents. Perhaps one of the most important 'breaks' in the innovation path came with the move towards molecular biology and the possibility of 'rational drug design', where the empirical trial and error of screening many thousands of chemical compounds for their possible clinical value has gradually been displaced by designed drugs targeted at specific pathologies or diseases. The more recent arrival of pharmacogenomics takes this to its logical conclusion where drugs are 'tailored' to a patient's genotype: such individualization of medical care customized to consumers as patients is a hallmark of health delivery systems today.

Having said that, we should note too that drug development has been dependent on the wider *regulatory* and political climate shaping health supply and demand. In this regard, studies that have mapped the historical and more recent paths of innovation within the field of medical technology have increasingly focused on two conflicting processes. On the one hand, medical innovation has been seen (correctly) as an industrially dynamic sector, an important source of economic growth and competitiveness. Its component sectors, including pharmaceuticals and medical instrumentation, have been highly research intensive and highly profitable (Hale and Towse 1995; SPRU 1996). On the other hand, from the early 1970s on, technological innovation has been identified as a major contributing factor in the escalation of health-care costs (echoing the claim made by Le Fanu above). For twenty years, national health authorities have sought to curb

health-care costs in part through regulating more strictly the introduction and reimbursement of new procedures, drugs and devices
(Klein et al. 1996; Immergut 1992; Harrison and Moran 2000). Frequently, these attempts at regulation have been only modestly successful (Schieber et al. 1994). Even so, more explicitly political questions
about whether these health programmes meet both economic and
social objectives have become commonplace.

Such questions focus our attention not only on the efficacy and
effectiveness of new technologies and medicines – frequently overstated – but also where we are likely to find them deployed – the
clinic. Most commentators – from Jewson (1976) onwards – have
stressed how crucial the hospital has been as a site for the development of medical technologies, more so than is primary care. Hospitals
provide economies of scale that make it possible to serve large (typically city-based) populations and to enable the purchase of high-tech
and high-cost medical devices and systems. They have also been able
to provide access to a readily available supply of (patient) body tissue,
organs, cadavers, blood, and so on that has been crucial for medical
research. Sometimes, of course, body parts have been secured without consent (including at Alder Hey in Liverpool and Crumlin in
Ireland), leading to major public controversy and calls for greater
regulation and improved clinical governance.

Hospitals are complex environments within the medical system,
and their role over time has increasingly been linked to professional
education and training, the reproduction of a medical elite, and the expansion of new technologies and investigative procedures (Granshaw
1992). These functions will no doubt prevail for the foreseeable future,
but those who attend to the impact of NMTs acknowledge that this
is not merely clinical but also organizational. That is, new technologies
are reconfiguring the organizational mode, location and staffing of
health care, disturbing long-established practice and even hierarchies
across the medical professions. Hospitals will persist in one form or
another, but new technologies enable more mobile and distributed
sites for medical diagnosis and delivery and broaden the clinical and
non-clinical sources of expertise that provide it. As Edwards and
McKee note:

> Many of the organisational changes [to the hospital] are being driven
> by the emergence of new technologies. These will have an especially
> lasting impact on activities such as imaging and pathology. Whereas
> previously technology drove centralisation, the likelihood is that near-
> patient testing kits, mobile radiology facilities and telemedicine will
> facilitate further dispersion of services. (2002, 2)

What do these various broad accounts of the historical shifts in the pattern of medical technology tell us, especially in regard to our primary interest in the novelty of NMTs? There are perhaps four lessons we can draw from this brief overview:

- first, the development of NMTs during the construction of orthodox medicine over the past two hundred years or more has not been a linear process; on the contrary, it is marked by a series of breaks and shifts in foci, as technical and institutional drivers reflecting scientific, economic and professional interests have constructed complex paths through which NMTs have developed
- second, the more recent technical changes of note relate to the emergence of informedicine and the 'new' genetics, and these are seen as paradigmatic shifts in the form and content of medical science and practice
- third, the pattern of development has fostered a growing individualization and commodification of health and its delivery, while the body has become – as a site for medical intervention – more available, accessible, mobile and dematerialized
- finally, despite the obsession (Blume 2000b) with 'miracle technology', these developments have not been entirely beneficial to overall levels of health but, as Beck (1992) notes, generate side effects that pose new risks for society today: 'Because of its success, medicine also discharges people into illness, which it is able to diagnose with its high technology' (p. 205).

These contributions to the historical shifts in medicine point to the many ways in which the body has been reconfigured as a site for medical intervention; indeed, according to Palladino (2001), such is the diversity that there appears to be no stable 'body' that presents itself to the analyst; he asks, 'I cannot help but begin to wonder about what exactly is a body?' (p. 544). This is the central question of those working in the sociology of the body, to which we now turn.

Sociology of the body

It might be expected that the body has been of central interest to sociology since the beginnings of the discipline. Yet the early sociologists and most of those who developed their work through to the relatively recent past rarely examined the body as a physical or material object: typically, sociologists have tended to speak of the individual as a social actor rather than as an *embodied* one. The way in which social perception has been handled is instructive here: perception in sociology has not meant 'What do I sense?', 'What do I feel?', but 'What do I think?'

This has changed dramatically over recent years, inspired in particular by contributions from feminist theory which, through its critique of gender relations, put the body, as a biological and sensate site for investigation, onto the sociological map. There are a number of areas of interest found in the contemporary sociology of the body (see Shilling 1993; Featherstone et al. 1991), which include gendered bodies, bodies and sexuality, bodies as sites of display and modification, disabled bodies (Shakespeare 1998), ageing bodies, the civilizing of bodies (Elias 1994), the disciplining of bodies within organized (such as occupational) settings (McKie and Watson 2000), and even the 'everyday' body (Nettleton and Watson 1998). Space prevents us discussing these areas of investigation, and our primary interest here relates to work on what can be called the 'medicalized body', and in particular the medical-technical body.

Our focus here is on work that has explored the socially constructed sense of the body as 'anatomy' and as a site for medical and scientific intervention and invention. Most attention has been on the way in which the body has been subject over the centuries to the power of medical classification, supervision and regulation (Foucault 1976). The social breadth of medical regulation is paralleled and strengthened by the depth to which medicine penetrates the body, as it has moved deeper and deeper into body structures – from surface anatomy, through X-rays, to intra-body physiology, and now to genetics, leading to the geneticization (Lippman 1992) of our bodies and even, indeed, our identities. As Waldby (1998) observes, the development of medical technologies can be seen as 'a history of the struggle to render the opaque, self-enclosed volume of the body transparent, to see inside to the interior space of pathology' (p. 373).

This biomedical model of the body, on which has been built the disciplines of anatomy, physiology and pathology, seeks not only to understand and classify illness and disease but in doing so to determine the limits of normality and abnormality which lead to medical intervention. Notions of normality have also been highly gendered: Gallagher and Laqueur (1987) have shown how the human body for early anatomists well into the eighteenth century was regarded as an ungendered, generic body. The male body was indisputably the norm. The female body had all the parts of the male: they were simply rearranged, outside in, and so deformed: 'Woman was an inferior man' (p. 80).

Sociological analysis of the body challenges the biomedical model as a way of understanding the meaning of the body and its illnesses, and shows how the body is as much a socially constructed object as it is one which takes on specific anatomical form. As Hughes (2000) says: 'Unlike the biomedical model sociology can deal with all sorts of bodies, largely because it relates to them primarily as either the source or the outcome of meaning' (p. 13).

Similarly, recent work has argued that the relationship between our bodies and nature should not be seen as part of some natural order (or ordering, whether divine or otherwise). Instead, as Macnaghten and Urry (2000) have argued, 'rather than there being a singular nature there are various natures, which differ from and often contradict each other . . . there is no 'pure relation' between the human body and nature' (p. 4). Notwithstanding this, there are those working within the sociology of the body who, while recognizing the socially mediated meaning of the body, seek to stress its materiality to ensure we do not lose sight of its organic, physical and biological attributes (Williams and Bendelow 1998).

For Foucault the rise of industrial capitalism and modernity signifies the rise of new technologies for normalizing the body and self, especially by means of new regimes of ordering mediated through technologies of disciplinary knowledge (physiology, criminology, psychiatry, etc.). These regimes are found in institutions for their enactment (hospitals, prisons, schools, etc.) with their innumerable prescriptions on the body, including 'exercises, timetables, compulsory movements, regular activities, solitary medications' (1979a, 128). 'A normalising society is the historical outcome of a technology of power centred on life' (1979b, 144). As Hewitt (1991) argues: 'The body stands as a metaphor for the anatomical focus and embodiment of power; a materiality that acts as a source and target of power, whether expressed politically, sexually, juridically or in discourse' (p. 230). Waldby (1997) argues that medical technologies are best seen through reference to Foucault's term 'technologies of power'. She argues that such technologies 'organise and exploit the materiality of the body in the interests of both social order and the generation of certain kinds of knowledge' (p. 79).

Foucault (1976) argues that medicalization is a process through which the 'medical gaze' defines the objects under its scrutiny. He uses this phrase to describe both literally and figuratively the sense in which the patient is subject to medical inspection. In this process we yield control of our bodies to medical experts and as such we are in this sense *de-centred from our bodies*: they become objects for others. He argues that the medicalization of the body involves three aspects:

1 *The power to define disease and illness*: Social problems or concerns fall prey to the medical gaze whereas previously these concerns were managed via very different forms of knowledge and
   discourse. For example, mental illness became medicalized during
   the eighteenth century, while before such deviance might have been
   defined in religious terms as the result of possession by witchcraft.
   Religion ceded territory to an emergent psychiatric profession.
2 *The discourse of 'scientific medicine'*: The biomedical model extends and deepens its understanding of and engagement with the
   body as a result of the development of medical science expressed
   and reproduced through an increasingly differentiated and complex
   knowledge base, professional practices and institutional structures
   that expand and police the boundaries of scientific (as opposed to
   'quack' or 'alternative') medicine.
3 *The state sponsorship and management of medicine*: Here Foucault draws attention to the wider institutionalization of medicine
   within the state. The agencies of government produce 'medico-
   administrative knowledge' through which the state at a 'biopolitical' level regulates the wider society. Medical power is therefore
   found not only at the level of the individual but also at a collective level through the regulation of bodies by the state and its
   health agencies. One example of this today is the growing number
   of state-sponsored programmes to secure population-wide DNA
   information derived from individuals to build national DNA
   registers (such as the Icelandic population genetic database and
   the UK's Biobank) which will be used to manage and monitor
   disease (Tutton and Corrigan 2004). Conceivably these banks
   (discussed in Chapter 4) might also be used to regulate sections of
   the population who, because of gene–environment interactions,
   are discouraged from living in a certain geographical location or
   doing a certain job. Insurance cover might be withheld if clients
   do not take such advice.

Through Foucault's work, and those who follow in his tradition, we
learn how the body is a site of social contest and power, a site through
which the regulation of sexuality, health and definitions of normality
are secured at both societal and subjective levels. Similar arguments
have been advanced by Turner (1996), who has shown how the body
is at the centre of political struggle (related to gender, generation,
ethnicity) and a vehicle for social performance and degradation as well
as classification. Medicalization of the body is one important means
through which this is achieved, by objectifying the body according to

measures of physical normality and abnormality; medical technologies are the medium through which not only clinical but *social* abnormalities or pathologies are contained.

Critics of the Foucauldian perspective on medicalization (such as Charlton 1993) argue that it leads to a highly deterministic and reductive reading of the medicine–body relation, and fails to accommodate the growing challenge to biomedicine that lay people and other health systems are making. In response, Foucauldians argue that this apparent demedicalization of the body is simply a more sophisticated form of 'the penetration of the clinical gaze into the everyday lives of citizens' (Lupton 1995, 107). The process of medical surveillance is no longer contained or bounded by the clinic, but is just as determining when, for example, we actively choose a more healthy, balanced 'lifestyle' (Armstrong 1995; Bunton et al. 1995). The rise of a 'discourse of rights' centred on health, wellness and reproduction creates new needs and new technical demands warranted by the inalienable rights of individuals to what *medicine* itself had prescribed as necessary. Rights and choice become means for securing the illusion of voluntary compliance to new disciplinary technologies of the body and self (Martin et al. 1988). As Williams puts it:

> 'Surveillance Medicine' has now, it is claimed, eclipsed 'Hospital Medicine': a transition symbolised through a strategic shift to the psycho-social dimensions of disease and the spatio-temporal calculus of risk, crystallised in the new emphasis on 'lifestyles'. (2001, 148)

Accompanying this shift is the growth in technologies of surveillance – such as screening, testing, annual 'check-ups', personal vigilance over diet, and so on. This might, of course, be seen as part of a wider phenomenon, the so-called surveillance society (Lyon 2001), paralleled by the audit culture (Power 1999) or what Barry (2001) has called new 'metrological regimes'. Ironically, these new forms of surveillance and control and the greater range of information these provide tend merely to generate new risks or new uncertainties (Strathern 1996). This has its effect at the local level, for example, for those acting as intermediaries between clinicians and patients in medical practice – such as midwives – who now must deploy and help interpret more and more diagnostic and screening results, whose meaning might be quite difficult to determine: as one midwife observed in Ettore's study on reproductive genetics, 'There is too much information, there is too much technology' (2000, 408).

While not sharing the conceptual perspective adopted by Foucauldians, and indeed often strong critics of it, feminist scholars who have focused on the body provide a similar account of the medicalization process, but here driven by the dynamics of patriarchy and gender. For our purposes here we can focus on two broad areas of work that feminist analysis has conducted, those related to reproduction and to 'women's health'.

Reproduction is said to be highly regulated through those medical technologies associated with contraception (fertility control), the management of labour and childbirth, antenatal technologies and monitoring techniques, and technologies designed to manage infertility and enable pregnancy (such as IVF and surrogacy) (see e.g. Martin 1989, 1994). The effect of these is to place the management of motherhood in the hands of physicians regulated within a social ordering and regime of what is to be regarded as 'normal reproduction'; thus, teenage pregnancy that falls outside of this is deemed to be 'irresponsible motherhood' (Tabberer and Hall 2000).

Feminist writers (e.g. Haraway 1997) have also examined the specificities of women's bodies and health, especially in regards to the increasing medicalization of 'diseases *of* women' (and not merely *in*) women. Hence the public screening programmes for cervical and breast cancer in some health-care systems. A key point here relates to the self-disciplining of women to participate in these programmes where screening is seen as normative behaviour – a 'moral obligation' to participate (Singleton and Michael 1993): this suggests that such action is not simply sensible disease prevention but framed as part of 'being a woman' (Rapp 2000). Howson (1998) argues similarly, in concluding her study on cervical screening, that women's participation in screening is 'an expression of both a social duty and the embrace of social entitlement' (p. 235).

While the Foucauldian and feminist analyses point to the plastic – yet constrained and disciplined – nature of the body, more recently sociologists have begun to examine how the two technologies we noted above – informatics and genetics – are shaping the very meaning of the body. Most importantly, they are disrupting and creating new perceptions of our bodies and how our body–identity relation is, or is not, sustainable.

The body–identity relationship has been said to have been reconfigured by the play of these two technologies. In the informatics context, the emergence of 'cyberanatomies' (Moore and Clarke 2001) has enabled the decomposition and recomposition of the body and its parts for medical science (and trainee medics):

> It is now possible to take the body (the anatomically universal, standard white, physically fit, youthful male) and then segment, digitise,

computerise and transmit it to multiple transnational social worlds, including medical schools, high schools, physical therapy offices and private residences. (2001, 78)

The body that was used to create this virtual anatomy was that of a deceased prisoner: and, as Moore and Clarke go on to observe, 'the fact that a prisoner's body has become part of a global biomedical disciplinary is Foucauldian in the extreme' (ibid.). The globalization of the body is of course tied to the globalization of medicine itself: as Gallagher and Riska (2001) argue, medicine today involves 'a globalised traffic of patients seeking cures in geographically distant advanced centres of medicine; of health professionals seeking superior practice environments and better economic opportunity; of massive streams of pharmaceuticals and medical equipment drawn into global commerce' (p. 2).

As before, in our discussion above of literature on the historical shifts in medical technology, we can derive some key lessons from this short review of the sociology of the body, as follows:

- the biomedical model of the body generates classificatory systems that define normality and abnormality, reproduced and extended by the technologies of disciplinary-based knowledge
- medicalization and the medical gaze are expressions of the technologies of power that regulate the body as a moral and clinical object
- technologies of body surveillance have become more complex and more physically distant from the body, yet reproduce systematic (gendered) inequalities
- the body is subject to processes of decomposition and temporal-spatial distribution, especially as a result of informatics.

These points complement and extend the broad ideas derived from our discussion of the historical shifts in medicine and focus our attention on the technology–power–structural relationships within which established medicine is located. These issues have also figured in our third area for consideration, medical sociology, as we see below.

Medical sociology

Medical sociology (and the sociology of health and illness) has made a huge contribution towards our understanding of the meaning of health, doctor–patient relations, the social and economic rationing of health care, health policy and practice, and so on. Yet, apart from a few notable exceptions (including Elston 1997; Kent and Faulkner 2002; Prout 1996; Timmermans 1998), its contribution to the significance of medical technologies has been somewhat more limited, at least in the sense of research that focuses *explicitly* on the socio-technical. Marking the twenty-fifth anniversary of the journal *Sociology of Health and Illness*, a number of papers observed the relative scarcity of research exploring the way 'tools and technologies are encompassed and embodied within [medical] social action and interaction' (Heath et al. 2003, 76; see also Timmermans and Berg 2003). More recent work on genetics has begun to redress this, but, as with many other fields in mainstream sociology, 'the technical' has been noticeable by its absence from the debate.

Even so, there are some generic areas of work in medical sociology that bear on our engagement with and framing of technology, and one in particular needs to be discussed here. This relates to the doctor–patient or expert–lay relationship within the clinic (and beyond), for it is here that medical technology is experienced, negotiated (in its – diagnostic – results) and challenged by patients. Trust in medical technologies and trust in medical expertise are two sides of the same coin, and the particular import of trust in the medical encounter is captured by Daniel's comment that 'medical practice, in particular, is not possible when trust fails' (1998, 218). However, the advent of the range of informatics- and genetics-based technologies we have been discussing so far has been seen to disturb the trust placed in the authority of medicine. But we should recognize too that the expert–lay relationship has been seen to change within wider society as a result of fundamental shifts in 'late modernity' that influence our engagement with and acceptance of knowledge, expertise and authority. Most importantly, as Giddens (1994) has argued, 'active' forms of trust and 'radical' forms of doubt characterize contemporary life, such that trust can no longer be presumed but has to be actively won by those in expert positions.

Perhaps we can begin our discussion of expert–lay relations in the clinic with the following observation:

> Although the mere outward behaviour of 'sick person takes medicine recommended by expert' is the same in the contemporary world as in, say, the 14th century, the act is enveloped in a far different set of meanings and expectations. (Gallagher and Riska 2001, 11)

One of the most significant changes in this 'act' is the redefining of the relationship between the lay patient and the clinical expert. Many medical sociologists have documented the increasing ambivalence of lay patients towards medicine – often highly critical of, yet also highly dependent on, the intervention of the clinician, and especially prescription medicine. Medical technologies are typically experienced in everyday clinical encounters as familiar low-tech equipment or devices: 'Most of the encounters in medical care systems are more or less routine depending on small-scale technologies, such as laboratory tests, or common diagnostic procedures such as X-ray and sonography' (Mechanic 2002, 464). Where 'high-tech' treatments – such as intensive-care units (ICUs), transplantation or NMR – are involved, the evidence suggests that, while patients might regard these with apprehension, as Williams and Calnan (1996) observe, in general they 'tend to be greeted with a considerable degree of reverence and respect by the lay populace' (p. 257).

The deference to medical expertise in part depends upon the medical profession's strategic management of both uncertainty and certainty in such a way as to reproduce its power. Harvey (1997) has distinguished between 'achieved certainty' and 'achieved uncertainty': both relate to the ways in which the medical expert has the power to determine the relative levels of uncertainty of a patient's medical diagnosis or prognosis. Technologies help to create both – ICUs proclaiming high levels of technical control over an acute condition, for example, while screening programmes are promoted because of high levels of uncertainty as sections of a population are deemed to be 'at risk' (of breast cancer, for example).

Harvey's observations are instructive for us here, since the analysis of NMTs suggests that a new type of uncertainty might be at play – less a form that is 'managed' by the medical expert, but one that creates problems as much for the medic as for her or his patient. Genetic diagnostic tests, especially when concerned with the assessment of levels of *susceptibility* to particular diseases or disorders, seem to be especially problematic: physicians cannot simply deploy, as normally the case, discretion, prior experience or what Berg (1992) calls 'routines' or 'norms' to compensate for their uncertainty. The lack of clear clinical guidelines and yet-to-be-determined standards of normality and abnormality complicate the expert–lay encounter here, as does the need for a wide range of other social actors – the genetic counsellor, the laboratory staff who test the sample, wider kin who are implicated – all are involved in framing and managing the meaning of the test. The long-standing problem of false positives or false negatives in diagnoses is compounded here where the meaning of both 'negative' and 'positive' is blurred, and a form of risk calculus must be undertaken that leaves medic and patient with perhaps as much uncertainty as before. Even where the eventual diagnosis is more promising, patients will carry long-term anxieties about what Lupton calls a 'silent illness' (1995, 92), which may of course generate stress-related disorders.

Patients in these circumstances do not necessarily have symptoms but 'risk profiles', so that risk becomes highly individuated. Risks are also thereby placed more fully on the shoulders of the patients themselves, and, as a result, the investment in clinical expertise alters markedly. Most importantly, the locus of knowledge and sources of advice broaden, and the 'expert patient' appears. Perhaps not surprisingly, the uncertainties generated by NMTs create the search for more secure forms of understanding outside of the orbit of conventional medicine. In part this is reflected in the continued expansion of alternative medical therapies. At the same time, it has led to the search for more robust and nationally approved forms of 'evidence-based' knowledge within the orbit of medicine (not always welcomed by clinicians, who often avow the need to maintain localized clinical judgement and discretion).

The repositioning of expert–lay relations and the demands placed on doctors to deploy therapies and new technologies, not only efficiently but effectively and appropriately, have led governments in many countries to push the medical profession into accepting new regimes of clinical governance. This is also driven by growing concerns over litigation and liability – in the US alone, up to 98,000 hospital deaths are reportedly related to clinical error or negligence (Kohn et al. 2000). At the same time, these developments have led to health authorities in many countries placing more demands on patients, now to be treated as 'partners' in the consultation (e.g. DoH 1998). This may, of course, have all sorts of unintended effects in regard to patient 'adherence' or 'compliance' to therapeutic treatments. But it might also mean that individuals are reskilled in this situation and that, as Williams and Calnan observe:

> far from rejecting modern medical technology, individuals are increasingly coming to 'reappropriate' it for their own rather than professional ends as a potential means of 'liberation' . . . Medical technology may actually be seen as a resource rather than a means of social 'oppression' in controlling the 'natural', 'sick' or 'recalcitrant' body. (1996, 263)

This brief review of the shifts in doctor–patient relations as they pertain to the advent of new technologies that bring new risk regimes complements the contributions from both the previous two fields of research we have discussed. In particular, it suggests we need to:

- explore NMTs across our schematic 'lifecourse' as likely to generate new types of social relationships between doctors and patients as they preoccupy themselves with the reproduction, maintenance or termination of the body
- anticipate a mélange of knowledge sourcing and use within and outside of medicine
- map the redrawing of the boundaries of responsibility and a greater individualization of both the patient and her/his care
- determine how far the state seeks to orchestrate the public and private provision for and so responsibility of government for NMTs.

Conclusion

This chapter has mapped out the approach we intend to take in this book in our sociological investigation of new medical technologies. We began by asking how we might understand the various dimensions of 'the new', of what might make today's medical technologies in different ways distinct from the past. This provided four broad parameters we believe will help us interrogate the novelty of the situation today. We have summarized these in box 1.1.

Box 1.1 Dynamics of medical socio-technologies and the new

Changes in the way medical knowledge and expertise are embedded in wider culture

Emphases on a highly technical and standardized form of codified knowledge

Rhetorical claims to novelty and the socio-technical positioning of NMTs

Clustering of technologies and the appearance of new (often globalized) networks

We have then discussed, selectively and synoptically, ways in which three very broad fields of inquiry – relating to historical change in medicine, the body and medical consultations – can help us examine general patterns of transformation underlying our present-day health-care systems. The various 'lessons' we have derived will inform our more substantive discussion in Chapter 3 and beyond.

Our next chapter explores the contributions made by another, fourth, perspective, science and technology studies (STS), within the sociology of science. STS is especially concerned with exploring the development of new technologies as these systems are mobilized and articulated within wider social and economic arenas. It is particularly interested in the plasticity of these technologies, the range of alternative paths and networks through which they are configured and reconfigured, in other words their mutability. Within this framework there has been a growing literature on the implications of a range of new technologies that have a generic role in the contemporary science system, such as the new biosciences and informatics.

As we have already noted, the combination of the biosciences and ICTs is a key aspect of the technical novelty of NMTs today and the basis upon which we can see how social and bodily boundaries begin to get redefined. Stankiewicz and Granberg (2001) have argued that one reason why these discrete sciences can come together is because of their respective 'molecularization'. That is, today technologies are occupying a 'design space' that is becoming more and more finely grained, and this allows technologies to converge, operating at a similarly micro-scale level. Indeed, a third technology – nanotechnology – operates at this level, and the three are increasingly linked. As high-tech areas, they are to be distinguished from older technologies marked, as they are, by 'rapid combinatorial expansion, a shift to molecular and sub-molecular levels, technological convergence of previously unrelated spaces, a high degree of articulation and codification, great information intensity and the fluidity of [their] boundaries' (p. 2).

In our next chapter we shall examine how such material changes in technologies relate to the social processes through which they are produced. First, though, we need to step back a little and discuss how STS analysis helps us understand how all technologies – including 'medical' ones – express complex socio-technical orderings.

2

Science and Technology Studies: Opening the Black Bag

Introduction

If work in the sociology of health and illness, medical sociology and the sociology of the *body* has regarded the body and our perception of it as the principal site for investigation, science and technology studies (STS) have sought to explore *technology* in a wide range of fields. Yet, until fairly recently, even those in STS working on health technologies had not given as much attention to the body as one might expect. As Casper and Berg (1995) observed, 'The [STS] investigator stood with his or her back to the heart of medicine and studied the "social phenomenon" surrounding it' (p. 397).

Recently, however, this has undergone dramatic change, with a growing number of scholars who have been interested in the complex connections running across technologies, bodies, illness, disease, disciplinarity and knowledge (see e.g. Elston 1997). In their edited volume on medical technologies, Lock, Young and Cambrosio (2000) use the term 'intersections' to describe the complexity of the relationships between 'human actors, the tools, the entities and the bodies that are constitutive of new medical technologies' (p. 1). As a result, the site of medicine – the body – has become subject to a sociological gaze that renders its meaning deeply cultural. Ironically, however, this derives not simply from the inherent socializing agenda of social science, but from the play of biomedicine itself that has created multiple versions of 'the body' for its own clinical inspection. As Waldby (2000) argues:

> The ever-growing intellectual interest in embodiment as a site of culture has been, in part at least, driven by the way in which biomedicine

treats the patient's body as both naturally given and utterly malleable
at every level of scale – the molecular, the cellular, the biochemical and
the macroanatomical. (2000, 465)

At the heart of the STS literature on NMTs are conceptual debates
about the location and character of action, defined much more broadly
than is customary. That is, STS asks how we should regard the *agency*
of different kinds of 'actors' implicated in medicine and the relationships between them. These relationships have been explored through
numerous case studies where knowledge, technology, bodies, medicines, and clinical institutions are examined as participatory 'actors'
in the socio-technical world of health. Indeed, STS has been especially attracted by the compelling allure of NMTs as objects of inquiry
for the very reason that they represent sites where bodies, expertise
and hardware seem to be so clearly interwoven.

Central to these debates are questions of the degree to which the
multiple elements of NMTs can be treated symmetrically. That is,
that the apparent differences between humans and non-humans, cultures and natures, agents and structures, should not be taken for
granted. These differences or 'asymmetries' should be treated as the
objects of analysis rather than the resources for analysis (Latour 1993).
This is perhaps one reason why STS has been so inherently resistant
to easy disciplinary categorization. For example, to offer a 'sociological' account of NMTs is perhaps to give the wrongful impression
that, to us, it is the 'society' alone that is important. So perhaps we
should begin by clarifying what we mean by our sociology and the
social in general. The sociological approach to NMTs that we want
to formulate here is one thoroughly steeped in the overall thrust of
science studies. That is, a social that is completely interwoven with
nature, technology, materiality, and so on. The point, then, is to engage
in a sociology that is acutely sceptical and which interrogates the way
in which these asymmetries come about through the co-construction
and complicity of multiple actors.

Before we explore the work within STS that relates to medical
technologies, however, we need to provide a brief sketch of the broad
theoretical approach that STS takes, since this may be new to some
readers. We introduce the main perspectives found and identify those
core ideas that inform our later analysis.

STS and the socio-technical

The field of science and technology studies has grown rapidly over
the past twenty years and more. There are a number of perspectives

within it that vary in their conceptual approach to science and technology and how these are to be understood as systems of knowledge and practice, and how we are to regard the claims made by them about the material and 'natural' world. In different ways, all challenge the notion that our understanding of the world is a direct mirror of that world. Instead, nature and society are mutually constituted: while we apprehend and make sense of the world through different socio-cultural interpretations, practices and techniques, these interpretations are not simply overlaid on nature. That is, our reading of the world articulates with the materiality of nature – but is not reducible to it.

So, for example, different disciplines in science explore and explain the particular part of the world they are interested in through different classification systems, criteria of what might be said to be 'significant' findings, techniques for measuring and testing claims, and so on. Plant botanists, for example, vary as to whether they classify species according to their morphological (surface appearance and structure) rather than their genetic bases: most of the time, these will be in agreement but some of the time they are not. Nature does not act to tell them what is 'right' when there are disputes over the 'correct' ordering of plant species, but it can act to prefer some readings over others. Where there are differences, however, such anomalies are allowed to remain so long as they do not create major problems for the scientists involved – they do not jeopardize careers, grant-seeking, doing experiments, gaining awards, and so on. When they do so, we are likely to see conflict and controversy in science, and indeed cases of scientific controversy have been most revealing of science's social *and material* embeddedness (see Nelkin 1984; Pinch 1994).

Detailed analysis of these occasions of scientific controversy, along with close observation of the science lab (through 'laboratory studies' such as that of Latour and Woolgar 1979) and analyses of the ways in which scientific knowledge is mobilized and gains credibility beyond the confines of the lab (e.g. Fujimura 1987; MacKenzie 1990; Collins 1990), has shown that *scientific knowledge has to be built*. It requires both technical and social competences and is shaped by the interaction and interests of a variety of actors – not just those scientists immediately involved but also funding agencies, regulatory authorities, lay groups, advocacy groups, political actors, marketing and consumers and the play of the object of scientific interest, whether this has a material, natural or even abstract (such as a theoretical proposition in cosmology) form.

For some, this means that science and technology have been seen to be 'socially constructed', a perspective in STS that became known as SCOT (the social construction of technology) and which has its roots in the work of Bijker, Hughes and Pinch (1987). This also means that things could have been otherwise – the 'social shaping' of science and technology requires us to accept that there is no inherent logic to the direction or path that they take. As Mol (1999, 76) puts it: 'the alternatives for any currently constructed fact or well-diffused artefact were not doomed to lose from the beginning. They got lost somewhere along the way as a matter of contingency.' This is often quite hard for us to accept, as we are surrounded by evolutionary narratives of science, whether in science textbooks, heroic histories or science museums, and the increasing globalization of science and technology gives a strong impression of closure around a set of theories and technologies that appear to converge around a similar set of ideas and artefacts. Global telecommunications systems, for example, depend on shared technological platforms, standardized data systems and solid-state physics.

However, that science is 'socially shaped' and could have been otherwise is most apparent during the emergent, innovative stage of inquiry, at which point multiple routes remain open until the full force of economic, political and technical factors come into play. As the late Roy Porter, historian of science, observed: 'Scientists like to promote the view that science is outside or above politics. This has never been true' (Porter 1987, 14). Moreover, scientific priorities today are – even before the work is done – orchestrated by both political and commercial interests especially, and by a variety of advocacy groups (such as patient organizations, NGOs, and so on) and others as well. The narratives we read of a rational, cumulative science mask such pluralism, contingency and competition between contrasting interests.

Even so, it might still be said that the technologies we have are those that simply work best and are not thereby socially shaped, but technically self-selected. On the contrary, STS argues that science, which is technically effective, has to be demonstrated as such – it cannot speak for itself. It may well be the case that some technologies – such as those we find in global communications systems – exhibit a strong directionality or 'path dependency' as alternative options get closed off by designers and manufacturers. In part, as Williams and Edge (1996) comment, 'earlier technological choices pattern subsequent development' (p. 867), and the selection of a technology may well have been 'logical' in the past but is quite illogical in the present. The QWERTY keyboard, for example, was designed to slow typists down when using manual typewriters, thus preventing mechanical type bars jamming on the print surface. But by the time alternative and potentially faster arrangements of keys became possible because of the shift to electrical typing, QWERTY had already become irreversibly established as the 'locked-in' standard. However, this closure around a relatively stable set of devices and practices does not happen 'automatically' but as a result of negotiation and often conflict over competing corporate, regulatory and public interests.

There are also *localized* versions of technologies that may differ from that promoted as the global standard: these may prevail in a niche market for some time or founder, not because they are necessarily technically less efficient or effective, but because they may relate to *existing* technologies and social practices less well. For example, as we discuss in Chapter 4, those promoting telemedicine have sought to standardize and improve the technology, and to implement it in many countries as a way of both meeting clinical need in remote areas and speeding up consultation processes. Despite this, it has had a mixed reception, among both clinicians and especially across different disciplines: for some disciplines, such as radiology, the use of telemedicine to relay digital radiographs has been welcomed, but for others, such as dermatology, concerns have been expressed about the quality of information on skin disorders conveyed in a digital rather than directly physical form.

Reference to telemedicine and the telecomms systems on which it depends is apposite here, since, just as they only function by virtue of extensive networks, so STS has shown that scientific knowledge itself only 'works' when it is successfully mobilized via networks. In contrast to the SCOT perspective, actor network theory (ANT) developed by Callon, Latour, Law (see e.g. Callon 1986a, 1986b; Latour 1987, 1988; Law 1988, 1991) and others, explores the ways in which networks operate to stabilize the social, technical and natural readings and orderings of the world. Such networks are the 'mechanism by which the social and natural worlds progressively take form' (Callon 1986b, 224). ANT theorists show how central actors enrol others to build networks of different parts, as 'heterogeneous engineers', bringing together a range of human and non-human *actants*. This is not easy, and networks are fragile – perhaps we may say as strong as their weakest link, since to lose the support of one part of the network can lead to its entire collapse. Case studies found in ANT's early literature include analyses of attempts to develop an electric car (Callon 1986a), a new light railway system (Latour 1996) and new aircraft design (Law and Callon 1992).

ANT theorists have continued to build on this work. Some of the most important research has shown how technologies are 'inscribed' with the network relations of which they form a part. As Akrich argues, 'Technical objects thus simultaneously embody and measure a set of relations between heterogeneous elements' (1992, 205). We shall see later in the book how medical technologies carry such inscriptions. Other work focuses on the way technologies only succeed, are only made mobile, through their being translated across different parts of the network: the concept of 'translation' plays an important role in the conceptual language of actor network theory. It suggests that the meaning of technology has no singular, essential nature that defines how it is to be used, how it is to be seen to be 'working' or malfunctioning, what its role in a wider set of technologies is, and so on. Instead, technologies are appropriated and reconfigured by social actors in multiple ways. They need to be translated into localized needs: the social and the technical are in this sense mutually constitutive. Networks do not then 'pass around' technologies, like the party game 'pass the parcel', each actor gradually revealing the essential meaning of the artefact or machine or idea: instead, networks translate and reshape that which passes along and through them. It is for this reason that Latour insists that ANT's notion of a socio-technical network is one that involves a 'series of transformations' rather than, as is often the case in conventional usage of the term, 'transport [of objects, information etc.] without *deformation*' (1999, 15, emphasis in original), without change. At a more fundamental ontological level, the logic of the Latourian position is that there is no single rendition of reality, but, as Mol says, the possibility for multiple realities. As she observes, the laboratory is a site 'where new ways of *doing* reality are crafted. From there they are exported, not so much in the form of "theory" but rather – or at least as much – in the shape of vaccinations, microchips, valves, combustion engines, telephones, genetically manipulated mice and other objects – objects that carry new realities, new ontologies, with them' (Mol 1999, 75).

This focus on socio-technical transformations, especially via different networks, draws our attention to the ways in which links are built up between different actors. Another perspective within STS that emphasizes the need to understand science and technology development in terms of linked, interacting elements adopts a perspective that highlights the *systemic* characteristics of socio-technical development (see e.g. Constant 1999). Much of the work here was originally encouraged by important contributions from Thomas Hughes (1983, 1986), who showed how the history of innovative technologies had to be understood through an analysis of the interplay of technical, economic, financial, social and political interests. Socio-technical systems have to be built and then orchestrated effectively in order for innovation to succeed. For example, Hughes provides a rich account of the development of electricity as a domestic and commercial source of energy in the nineteenth century. Thomas Edison's success in building electricity networks in the US depended on his ability to enrol and orchestrate diverse socio-technical interests to ensure his innovation could compete with gas, the then dominant form of supply. Edison is an excellent example of a 'system-builder', someone who brought together material artefacts and social institutions in order to realize his ambition.

Innovation analysis, another perspective found within the more economic and policy-oriented wing of STS, has built on this earlier work, especially in regard to the analysis of technological trajectories, path dependencies, and the 'co-construction' or co-evolution of new technologies in parallel with new social institutions (see e.g. Stewart and Williams 1998). Innovation is seen to occur at the boundaries of sectors where conventional organizational and disciplinary commitments are broken down (Gibbons et al. 1994; Nowotny et al. 2000; Webster and Rappert 2002) and where the adequacy of conventional knowledge-producing institutions (universities, government research laboratories or corporate labs) is called into question. Moreover, these changes mean that the spatial distribution of knowledge also changes by becoming much less firmly rooted within discrete institutional or organizational arenas (David and Foray 2003).

This means that one must approach innovation in terms of specific innovation environments whose component parts are interdependent – sometimes mutually reinforcing, sometimes in conflict with each other. The innovation ecology is not, however, fully self-coordinating or self-adapting to the threats and opportunities it meets. It is not driven by some 'internal logic' of self-coordination. Nor does it have some foreseeable future: though it is path dependent, the innovation system is *sui generis* a creator of its own uncertain future(s).

Contemporary innovation policies supported at national and international levels (such as by the European Commission) are premised upon particular characterizations of the processes of technological change, as well as acknowledging their uncertainties. Technologies are rarely seen to develop along linear and easily determinable routes. Linear planning and technological forecasting have been widely substituted by narrative and interactive methodologies such as scenario building or foresight studies (Brown et al. 2000; Miles 1997). Planning methods have developed with the intention of accommodating this flexibility to cope with change and uncertainty.

Recent work, most notably by the Dutch STS group at the University of Twente (Geels and Schot 1998; Rip and Schot 2002; Rip 2001), has shown how uncertainties might multiply when we see that innovation is a multilayered process. They argue that emergent innovation seeks to secure a *niche* at the micro-level within a wider socio-technical *regime* that in turn is found within a wider socio-technical landscape at the macro-level. New technologies – or their creators – must try to open up a (protective) niche in which their ideas might make progress in an otherwise highly competitive and hostile environment.

What these various commentaries on innovation and the development of socio-technical systems suggest is that innovative technologies require social and technical investment that is highly risk-laden. We saw in Chapter 1 how sociologists of medicine and health have drawn attention to the risks associated with new technologies and our experience of them. Work on the concept of risk is not peculiar to STS, of course. There is a huge – and still growing – literature in the field of risk analysis. A fault line running through all this work marks the boundary between those who approach risk as quantifiable through the process of rational calculation and those who regard risk as socially constructed, as highly contingent on the circumstances people confront, such that its 'measurement' is never stable or unequivocal. Such a division is, however, unhelpful, and indeed many now advocate approaching risk as being made up of both material and perceptual dimensions, such that the meaning and impact of risk and the way we deal with it will always be socially mediated.

The rational calculation model of risk has its roots in the nineteenth century. One of the most important changes in the development of risk was the emergence at that time of a whole raft of measures and statistical techniques which sought to gauge and so control the processes of social change associated with industrialization and urbanization. The emergence of the national census was very much a creation of this shift. The expansion of large cities, their hygiene and public health needs, the increasing demands for energy and transport infrastructure, new, potentially dangerous forms of factory labour, and so on, led to a growth in accounting, calculation and, perhaps not surprisingly, the insurance industry. Risks became as much actuarial as they were physical, and notions of standardized risk and so compensation began to anchor themselves in the regulatory regimes of nineteenth-century society across Europe and the US.

In the twentieth century this process continued, aided by increasingly sophisticated information sources based on computing technologies and the new sciences of risk assessment. This led to what we can regard as a highly modernist approach to the language of risk assessment, one grounded in a technical, quantitative measure of risk, often based on the effects of something at the level of the individual person rather than at a higher, more systemic level. Moreover, these technical measures of risk fail to consider the cultural processes that come into play when people respond to the risks that confront them, such as how they take the news that there is a genetic predisposition in their family towards a disease. Much of this will depend on cultural judgements about who their 'family' includes, who are to be regarded as their wider kin (through blood lines or those they see most often?), their knowledge of kin and whether they think doing anything in terms of lifestyle changes is actually worth it. Research has indicated that individuals who have had a genetic test may be reluctant to reveal its results to relatives because of the conflict or hostile emotional reactions that may follow (Green et al. 1997).

In broader terms, this critique of risk as a cognitive, rationally calculable matter has been developed through the many contributions made on the subject by Mary Douglas. Her work (such as Douglas [1966] 1994) relates risks and their perception to wider social structures and relationships among social groups. Variation in these relationships produces different risk cultures, such that, as she observes, it is hard to imagine these systematic differences being reducible to the level of individual or personal anxieties: in other words, as Douglas says, it would be 'hard to maintain that the perception of risk is private' (1994, 12). Indeed, Beck (1996) argues that risk is everywhere today, since scientific innovation generates new risks while simultaneously seeking to control them. Many may be quite intangible to most people – such as the broad environmental risks posed by biotechnology, the ozone hole, the possibility of contracting cancer, of losing one's job – but this does not necessarily make them less worrisome. Some of these might be subject to scientific intervention and government regulation, but experts and government regulators are increasingly mistrusted. Trust, just as we said of science and technology, has to be built, to be mobilized through socio-technical networks: technologies are not intrinsically more or less trustworthy. When we begin our exploration of NMTs in the next chapter, this issue of risk will be examined in more detail.

At this point it is worth summarizing the main themes we have outlined above. Through the work of SCOT, ANT, innovation and risk analyses, work in STS has shown how science and technology are deeply social phenomena. More specifically, there are a number of conclusions we can draw from this:

1 Science and technology are socially embedded and crafted; they thrive through being mobilized via complex, heterogeneous networks, but their meaning in such networks is never singular or uniform.

2 There is no pre-given linear path that they take, and they might take different paths simultaneously as they build – in a socio-technical sense – various versions of nature, 'reality' or materiality.

3 Innovations in any field – including medical technologies – have to work within and through existing socio-technical regimes or systems, and are more or less successful because of this: no technology ever 'speaks for itself'.

4 Technological change will be part of a wider socio-technical transformation, since the social and the technical are co-produced.

5 Contemporary society might be characterized as having a risk culture not least because of the new, intangible risks that we create for ourselves through the very innovations that science and technology produce.

These various insights from the field of STS lift the lid on science and technology, not thereby to debunk or dismiss its contribution or indeed its benefit to society. On the contrary, STS analysts are interested in seeing how science and technology might be made accountable through being more 'socially robust'. This is to broaden the terms on which science is built, to move beyond the confines (without losing the value) of professional expertise towards a 'socially distributed expertise' (Nowotny 2002) that is both more accountable and inclusive of a wider range of understandings of the world.

There is, then, a double sense of opening science here: first, by making science and technology more open, more inclusive and more democratic and, second, in part doing so through opening 'the black box' of science. This second sense refers to the ways in which STS strips away the public image of science, its stable façade, to examine what goes on beneath the surface. Latour (1987) talks of the two-sided 'Janus-faced' world of science, the public, reassuring world of hard facts and certainty and the much messier, uncertain, hidden and provisional world of the lab, its experiments, notebooks, disagreements and conflict.

We can use this metaphor of 'opening' in regard to NMTs by suggesting the need to open a metaphorical 'black bag' of medicine, to see how the tools and ideas found therein are much more provisional than the front-of-stage image medical science might like to present. We can also go on to ask whether the newer tools and ideas – those of informatics and genetics, for example – increase the sense in which medical knowledge is more uncertain, more contestable, perhaps because diagnosis is more provisional. While the stethoscope has become something of a cliché for medical authority and status – especially as a conspicuous identity statement worn by junior hospital doctors – it is difficult to imagine the same being true of more recent diagnostic devices, such as computer-aided support tools. You can't wear them, they don't look clinical and they may well complicate and create as many problems for clinical decision-making as they solve. How, then, have the insights and critique of STS been applied to medical technologies?

STS and medical technologies

We noted above that one of the lessons of STS is that science and technology are socially embedded, expressed and created through complex networks. Medical technologies are no exception here. The relation between medical technologies and their mobilization through different networks is an important focus for STS. Their meaning and utility are constructed in multiple ways (as shown in Berg and Mol 1998; Casper and Berg 1995; May and Ellis 2001). Studies on the (re)classification of illnesses through genetics discourses across different networks (Lippman 1994; Kerr and Cunningham-Burley 2000), on the organization and control within the clinical network (Atkinson 1995; Rabinow 1999), or on the construction of alternative futures for technologies as a result of their promotion within different networks (Nelis 2000) document the contested, socially constructed and variable 'pathways' of medical technologies.

Let us explore some examples of STS research to illustrate the five summary points made above, drawing on a variety of studies and medical technologies to do so.

We first suggested that networks are key to the successful mobilization of new technologies, but that the more mobile they become the more subject they are to multiple translations and transformations. There have been various studies that document the translation process at the level of the clinic, such that the patient, his or her body, the disease, are given multiple meanings as they are apprehended by different medical practitioners, measurement techniques or therapies. So, for example, Mol (1998) has shown how the condition known as atherosclerosis is defined in multiple ways depending on which disciplinary language describes it – the clinical, radiological or pathological.

In a similar fashion, Berg (1997) shows how the interaction between patient and practitioner involves an alignment between very different sets of needs and priorities – personal, professional and organizational. Clinical protocols that are supposed to dictate the most efficient and effective care for patients (such as the UK's National Service Frameworks) are far from uniformly applied, but are shaped by much messier – though often understandable – compromises in practice between participants in the clinical encounter. This might be because of the different ways in which those involved in clinical cases negotiate the relative importance of the social, ethical and clinical aspects of a particular set of circumstances to be given more or less weight in shaping clinical decisions. A patient, for example, might insist that their physician does not tell their partner that they are the carrier of a genetic disorder that renders their offspring susceptible to a particular disease. Clinical protocols might suggest that a duty of care to the partner would lead to a breaking of this confidence, but ethical considerations might argue against this: in other words, formal clinical guidelines are often transformed into multiple, contingent interventions.

On a wider canvas, we can see how medical technologies are mobilized across different networks, and as those involved seek to enrol support for the technology, and as the technology is crafted through networks, it takes on very different representations. A very useful illustration of this that is anchored in the ANT perspective is the work on telemedicine by Mort et al. (2004). Telemedicine involves medicine 'at a distance', providing information and acting as a medium of treatment for a growing range of specialists. Mort and his colleagues show how there are two very different networks that have appeared: that of the policy-making constituency, keen advocates of the benefits of telemedicine, and that of the much more critical and hostile network among clinical researchers: 'We find that the policy community discourse around telemedicine employs the most positive and unproblematic perspective, while the accounts of practitioners reflect ambivalence and uncertainty' (Mort et al. 2004, x). The main reason they give for this is that policy-makers endeavour to enlist support for telemedicine primarily in relation to its capacity as a more efficient technology (in relaying information), while researchers are much more wary of it in regard to the *quality* of the information (or clinical evidence) that it can relay. As Mort et al. argue:

> Actors who perceive telemedicine to be about *medicine* appear most likely to express ambivalence about large scale implementation, while

those who perceive it to be about *technology* i.e. a tool for delivery, a vehicle for healthcare, are most likely to become advocates for roll-out. (Ibid., x)

Surrounding these two main groups, we find a range of others – patients, regulators, nurses, and so on – who are recruited by the different networks and whose participation gives more warrant to each position. Mort's study shows that the meaning of telemedicine is far from stable: as Latour argued, it is transformed within and between networks. The point of this study is not merely to point to the mutability of telemedicine, but to show thereby the limitations of current national controlled trials that are being developed to evaluate its merits. These trials presume a standard protocol that can be measured outside of the contingencies of actual clinical practice. Yet the meaning and value of telemedicine has to be understood in terms of such practice and how different networks use different criteria to judge the merits of the technology.

This takes us on to our second point noted above, that is, that there are no pre-given linear paths to the development of a technology. There are a variety of studies that have documented this, especially in regard to innovation analysis (see e.g. Fleck 2000; Williams et al. 1997). In the context of health technology we can draw attention here to the work of Abraham (Abraham and Lewis 2000; Abraham and Lawton Smith 2001), who has sought to explain the multiple and divergent regulatory paths that an ostensibly identical pharmaceutical compound has taken in the US compared with Europe. One might expect that the scientific analysis of a compound, subject to similar testing and regulatory review, has similar if not necessarily identical outcomes as it moves through the process of approval at national level, by the Federal Drugs Administration (FDA) in the US and the European Medicines Evaluation Agency (EMEA) in Europe. Abraham and Lawton Smith (2001) have shown, however, that there are systematic inconsistencies in the regulatory outcomes between the two; that is, drugs approved by the US agency might well be rejected by the European agency. This inconsistency does not reflect more, or less, stringent procedures across the two agencies, but differing definitions of innovation; the same drug compound is regarded as more or less innovative and therefore more or less open to approval as a novel and so patentable 'new chemical entity'. Thus the 'same' compound experiences radically different regulatory careers on the two sides of the Atlantic. There is no single innovation path that determines its position in the pharmaceutical domain. Drugs companies are, of course, well aware of this variability in approval procedures and might well use it strategically by targeting those national (or transnational) agencies more likely to give certain types of drug a more favourable hearing.

Our third argument was that medical technologies are mobilized within and through existing 'socio-technical regimes' and are more or less successful because of this: that is, *no technology ever 'speaks for itself'* but has to be given voice through actors creating a niche for it, by mobilizing resources, by building new links.

This argument finds recent expression in an analysis of the development of informatics and genetics in health research and service delivery (Brown et al. 2000). Were technologies to 'speak for themselves', we would expect that those that were intrinsically superior would be widely adopted by health science and clinical practice in many countries, other things being equal (where the costs of the new technologies could be met, for example). However, the analysis by Brown, Rappert and Webster of prevailing national health research and delivery regimes in Europe shows that the meaning of these technologies and how they are received (as, for example, being more or less risk-laden) and deployed varies considerably from one country to another. More specifically, variations reflect broad cultural and political configurations that engender distinct responses to technologies. As Jasanoff (2002) has observed:

> Although projects of rational planning, classification, regulation and technological progress have been pursued in all Western countries, the result is not a formless political and cultural homogeneity. New technologies continue to produce striking differences in public response and receptivity across countries, with citizens sometimes opting for greater restraint than experts and elected governments. (2002, 366)

In regard to health technologies, additional variation might reflect different countries' policies on the resourcing and rationing of health care. Health systems that are 'free at the point of access', such as that in the UK, will in part allocate health technologies through what has been called *science-based* rationing (Cochrane 1971), through a determination of the 'evidence-based' utility of a new technique (diagnostic device, surgical procedure, drug, etc.) relative to the state of the art. Health technology assessment will review the economic costs of new procedures, but these will be framed within this broader evidence-based overview. A more fee-based system will deploy strongly *economic* rationing via the market, or forms of social or private insurance (as true in the Netherlands and the Scandinavian countries). Nationalized health-care systems, such as that in the UK, can, of course, run parallel to and accommodate the interests of private health care. So, for example, in the UK the National Institute for Clinical Excellence (NICE) determines which drugs may be prescribed in the UK on the National Health Service, but these guidelines do *not* apply to private medical prescriptions (Whalley et al. 2000).

Apart from these differences in the broad funding patterns of health care, however, Brown and his colleagues found that what is especially important in understanding why some NMTs are mobilized and taken up through a health system is the sort of network 'configuration' that is found in a specific medical field of research and practice within any one country.

Configurational relations in medical (and indeed in other) fields can be distinguished in terms of two ideal types, one more 'close-knit' and one more 'loose-knit' in terms of the overall degree of integration and coordination among those that constitute it. A close-knit configuration is made up of a stable, complex network of public and/or private organizations and actors with high levels of alignment, regulation and coordination. A configuration made up of loose, decentred relations displays weak institutional integration, regulation and governance structures.

Brown, Rappert and Webster show how close-knit configurations may be quite resistant to innovation if they generate overly specialized, closed networks: such networks can resist knowledge-sharing since experts tend to have their own knowledge bases, language and approach to problems and opportunities. In contrast, loose-knit forms may be unable to build innovative momentum as they lack sufficient social 'glue' through which it can be built.

Drawing on this analysis, very different networks were found in clinical genetics in the UK, Spain and the Netherlands. First, in the *UK*, health genetics has a strong, resource-intensive network aligning the pharmaceutical, academic, health-care and government constituencies which are closely involved in arrangements for the production and sourcing of data and the development of clinical trials and diagnostic tests. Extensive formal and informal links have produced a complex set of scientific and economic links between public and private sectors (notably universities and firms). At the same time, there is considerable attention being given to enrolling the public and patient groups into the genetics agenda, since they are seen as most likely sources of resistance to the new technology (not least as a result of the migration of risk perception from other fields, such as GM crops).

While this genetics network is strong, it is not too close-knit to be closed off to innovation but, on the contrary, seeks to open up and broaden the investment in new, multifactorial genetics on which future medical innovation is seen to depend.

In the *Netherlands*, in contrast, health genetics and especially diagnostics have, for many years, been the preserve of a historically much more restricted clinical genetics network. These are concentrated around a small number of national centres for testing with the mandate to set the agenda for genetics, thus containing and managing the wider public uncertainties and expectations that are associated with it. This Dutch configuration is, in this way, much too close-knit for the mobilization of new genetics technologies to take place. It is not surprising then that this monopoly has been challenged by the arrival of new interests through new networks keen to explore multifactorial diseases, led especially by researchers in oncology, pathology and specialists in coronary heart disease in academic hospitals throughout the country. This may have the result of opening up the conservative professional domain of clinical genetics and/or creating a discrete novel network through which new genetic agendas can be mobilized.

In *Spain*, the development of genetic services has been a continuous bottom-up process that has lacked strategic centralized planning within health-care services. Most units and centres have emerged as a specialization within other medical fields, notably biochemistry, obstetrics, paediatrics, clinical pathology and haematology. The creation of genetic services and research in health genetics (diagnostics and gene therapy) are the result of the initiatives of key individuals with a personal interest in promoting and pursuing research. These research actors must overcome difficulties due to the lack of health policies to manage or control genetic services and the fact that formal training in clinical genetics must be obtained abroad. Private interest and investment in genetics is minimal. As a result health genetics is a relatively loose-knit configuration of primarily public research groups.

These contrasting sketches of British, Dutch and Spanish genetics networks illustrate how there is no singular route down which medical innovations move. They also indicate that genetic diagnostics does not speak for itself, but is given voice by a variety of different actors. The play of the differing configurations creates different paths along which genetics is mobilized or, indeed, constrained. Such variation also impinges on the ways in which the different countries will evaluate the merits of the new genetics procedures. As such, network analysis would warn us to be wary of any claim that the efficacy or effectiveness of a new medical innovation can be demonstrated through the application of techniques such as randomized controlled trials (RCTs). In practice, the efficacy and utility of new technologies depend on the play of interests found within the existing medical arena in each country. The very *definition* of the field alters from one context to another, and so thereby do the locally deployed measures of effectiveness.

Our fourth claim was that we need to understand technological change as part of a wider process inasmuch as technical changes are framed and express social changes, and as such the two are *co-produced*. One area where this is readily apparent is the field of health informatics, especially in relation to health information management systems deployed to manage clinical and/or administrative information within and between clinical settings such as hospitals. The very rationale of the technology is to create new media for the management of information at an organizational level, in theory ensuring that clinical data is logged, transferred and mobilized much more effectively.

A recent study by McLaughlin, Rosen, Skinner and Webster (1998), on health information systems at Finlay Hospital in the UK, examined the introduction of a new information system in the public health laboratory based in the hospital. The lab undertakes diagnostic tests on patient samples provided by the hospital wards and externally from general practitioners. The results of the tests determine the sort of treatment clinicians will provide – such as antibiotics, antivirals and so on. The laboratory as a whole is actually made up of a number of discrete departments, including bacteriology, virology, haematology, biochemistry, cytology and molecular genetics.

Before the introduction of the new system, the lab operated a mix of paper-based and IT systems that were discrete to each department. The new system was introduced to integrate patient information across the departments to ensure the more effective management of clinical tests. Most importantly, the new system was a modular one based on different elements of the hospital's management of the patient (from initial inquiry through differing treatment stages), whereas the previous system was a sample-based one. The new system meant that all samples had to be registered and linked to patients before any pathology tests could be conducted, whereas previously technicians and clinicians could avoid this as all tests were simply accompanied by a separate paper-based form. In addition, the system set new protocols that the technicians should follow when doing the tests, determining in advance what tests to carry out and how best to respond to subsequent results. Results could be entered and accessed by any of the departments via the IT system. Doctors in the lab – such as consultant bacteriologists – would have to validate the results and sign off whatever treatment was deemed appropriate.

It is clearly evident that the new system would have an impact on the procedures and practices of the laboratory, since this was its explicit goal. However, the actual effect was much more a matter of the users reconfiguring the system at the same time as changing their own occupational and professional practice to accommodate to the new demands it posed. The technical features of the system and the social ordering of the organization *co-evolved*.

That the technical and social are intertwined was evident from the very day the new system was acquired by the lab. The system was originally US designed and as such embodied culturally derived presumptions about laboratory practice that made little sense in the UK. As McLaughlin (1998) and her colleagues report:

> Since the system was designed as an administrative system for US hospitals, its core structure – based on repeat billing of fee-based patient tests – meant that a patient's specimens could be distributed across multiple account numbers.... This caused possible errors and misunderstanding during the implementation phase [at Finlay]. [Its] US heritage also meant that the system was designed to register results electronically, displacing paper-based records; the [Finlay] team did not anticipate that the introduction of the system would mean the abandoning of paper altogether. Moreover, [the system's] US pedigree meant that it did not arrive with the capacity to follow up patients, a legal requirement in some of the laboratories, such as Cytology and Clinical Genetics, where patients may need repeat examinations. (1998, 63)

As a result, the laboratory managers reconfigured the system to meet their local practices and requirements (such as ensuring it could act as a long-term repository for genetic information in case of the need for patient/family follow-up). At the same time, however, technicians found that the new protocols it carried undermined their professional control over the test procedures, and sought ways to reaffirm this while still meeting the efficiency demands of senior management. 'The end result was the involvement of users in a changed system, a changed organisation, and a changed articulation of their professional identity' (1998, 124).

Our final, fifth, argument – following the ideas of writers such as Beck (1992, 1996), Crook (1999) and Lupton (1999) – was that contemporary technologies manufacture new (often intangible) risks.

There has been a growing body of work on risks that are linked to new medical technologies, and much of this from within the field of STS. Prior et al. (2002), for example, have explored the way in which genetics clinics determine patients' risks of breast cancer, showing how the various protocols, referral guidelines and computerized decision-support tools that are designed to facilitate clinical decisions are more like 'rules of thumb', and that considerable negotiation between a wide variety of actors, and much tacit knowledge about how to read data, actually determines the diagnosis made. These actors are not solely the patient and her clinician, but counsellors, laboratory diagnosticians, wider kin, other physicians, and so on. The construction of risk estimates in the cancer clinic also depends on the way in which risk is 'made visible' through a variety of pictorial representations, using charts, diagrams, and tables to help anchor the estimate in what is perceived to be a more certain set of measures. As Prior et al. say:

> in the routine work of the clinic rough observations about family history, anxieties, patterns of disease and so forth (in the referral letter) need to be edited, moulded, re-presented as data before decisions about risk are finalised. Furthermore, in that data making process images play a significant role. (2002, 256)

This work illustrates not only the negotiated route through which diagnosis is made – something that has been long recognized in medical sociology – but how the diagnosis of genetic risks is posing new problems in the clinical encounter for both physician and patient. Genetics is creating a range of new uncertainties relating to how inheritance is expressed and understood across kin and how, in complex multifactorial (non-Mendelian) disorders, risk calculation and some measure of disease susceptibility is increasingly provisional. Ironically, the uncertainties here derive in part from the increasing ability of clinical science to determine signs of some sort of disorder much earlier than in the past. As Prior (2001) observes elsewhere, the growing sophistication (through imaging and genetic diagnostics) of such programmes means that the boundaries of abnormality are being pushed back to find disease at earlier and earlier stages. In general, while this may strengthen the technical (and reductionist) claims of the biomedical model, paradoxically it does not thereby enhance the clinical capacity to act, since therapy is unavailable, economically unwarranted, or uncertain in its efficacy and outcome. As has been suggested elsewhere, rather than bolstering medicine and medical delivery:

high-tech medicine generates forms of diagnosis that are more likely
to depend on the language of *risk* and probabilities than the language
of causality. This is especially so in the context of the 'new genetics'
(principally related to complex multifactoral disease) derived from
molecular biology where genetic diagnostics creates new categories of
presymptomatic 'patients' – those who *may* develop disease in the
future – but for whom it can offer little now. (Webster 2002)

These changes in the relationship between clinical science and clinical
therapy are suggesting not only a generic shift in medicine towards a
regime that is both more predictive yet less therapeutic, but also a
transformation in the relationships between patient and expert and
in our understanding of personhood (see Novas and Rose 2000).
While a chronic condition such as high blood pressure may be framed
by a patient as a disorder that is a) manageable and b) unrelated
to his or her sense of personhood or identity, a diagnosis of either
a dominant (single) gene disorder (such as Huntington's disease,
duchenne muscular dystrophy) or a more complex, multi-gene disorder
(such as some cancers, psychiatric conditions, or heart disease) may
well change the ways in which a person defines their relation to their
body, to others, and to the future. As a result, new identity and lifestyle strategies may be combined with more explicitly clinical or health-
related strategies to cope with the diagnosis. Some people diagnosed
with a single-gene disorder may regard this as an all-embracing condition – even if its symptoms are yet to appear – around which they
orchestrate their (and their personal and familial) life: parents of a
child diagnosed with cystic fibrosis learn to cope with a prognostic
trajectory that will shape their relationship to that child, their other
children and their own lives.

The circumstances of those diagnosed with a more provisional susceptibility to a late onset disorder, such as Alzheimer's disease, might
make for a less fatalistic reading of risk, but might carry its own form
of risk-laden uncertainties that require the adoption of new lifestyle
strategies hedged about by a good deal of self-monitoring. In short,
whether single or complex, gene disorders can create social disorders
(in the sense of disturbing our ability to contain illness within a temporary sick-role) and create new demands and risks for those suffering them.

We can now move on to try to bring together the basic argument
of this chapter with those that we made towards the conclusion of
Chapter 1.

Conclusion: opening the body and the black bag

At the end of Chapter 1 we made a number of claims in regard to those areas to which we need to be especially attentive as we explore the play of NMTs throughout the metaphorical 'lifecourse' used to organize this book. We said there that previous work in related fields emphasized new types of practitioner–client relationship created by NMTs, new sources of information social actors use to make sense of health and illness. Also that NMTs are related to the increasingly individualized tendencies such that the boundaries of state provision and social disciplining of health are changing.

Our review of STS takes these arguments further but does so through a much closer observation of the health–body–technology relationship. We can in fact speak of two types of opening, the opening of the *body* as both an object and a site for social investigation and the opening of the metaphorical *black bag* of medicine.

In regard to the first of these, as we noted in Chapter 1, work in the sociology of the body reveals its contingent, diverse and contested meanings. By linking these insights to those of the sociology of science and technology we can also see how the body's boundaries are opened up. This is not simply by virtue of their internal properties being, literally, revealed to medical inspection, but also in the way the body is made mobile, is broken up, and becomes more, or less, a physical object. Informatics-related technologies have been especially important in creating the *in silica* body, but the relationship between technologies and the body has been seen to be part of a wider transformation where the body as both physical and cultural is constructed through diverse social arenas, where art and science and the narratives they invoke produce a diverse range of body stories. Haraway (1992, 298) argues that 'the various contending biological bodies emerge at the intersection of biological research, writing, and publishing; medical and other business practices; cultural productions of all kinds, including available metaphors and narratives; and technology, such as the visualization technologies that bring color-enhanced killer T cells and intimate photographs of the developing fetus into high-gloss art books, as well as scientific reports.'

As we go on to discuss in Chapter 4, Haraway's work within postmodern feminism eschews earlier feminist, typically essentialist notions of the (female) body subject to an oppressive, patriarchal technology, and instead argues that the body in advanced capitalist societies is simultaneously captured by, yet empowered through, contemporary (information) technology. The body is a 'cyborg', a 'hybrid of machine and organism, a creature of social reality as well as a creature of fiction'. It is quintessentially a product of the information revolution, both natural and artificial, sharing a biological and digital identity where we see 'the translation of the world into a problem of coding'. The body becomes (for feminism) a site that is to be defined not in terms of an essential femininity but through informational texts, one that has multiple possibilities, multiple 'inscriptions', written in a radical and liberating way. Techno-science is not to be demonized but used as a route to a postmodern embodiment.

> Late twentieth-century machines have made thoroughly ambiguous the difference between natural and artificial, mind and body, self-developing and externally designed, and many other distinctions that used to apply to organisms and machines. (Haraway 1991, 152)

One crucial vehicle for the writing of body scripts is, of course, the internet. A person may use the internet to construct multiple texts of his/her body free from the physical constraints of embodiment itself. In this regard, Moore and Clarke (2001) point to the digital mobility of the body, allowing for its multiple re-representations in cyberspace: 'Anatomies can (and we believe should) be viewed as *both* immutable and mutable. They travel "as they are" and that may well be consequential, but meanings ascribed and usages may also vary widely across local cultural/political/historical/economic formations' (p. 58).

This celebration of the body and its meanings as a textual heterogeneity allow for both ontological and political possibilities and an overcoming of the oppressive modernist notion of the natural body, even of its male and female gendered forms, for these too become surfaces on which we can inscribe new versions of our embodied selves. Haraway's argument leads her to propose the basis for a more democratic techno-science and society, through, not despite, science.

Many have argued that Haraway's optimistic account of the cyborg is unsatisfactory, for it renders the physicality of the body simply as text and script rather than as a deeper lived experience (see e.g. Caddick 2001; Ebert 1996) and ignores the way the digital world it occupies is much less open to the heterogeneity she believes and advocates is possible (see e.g. Slevin 2000; Jordan 1999). From our own perspective, we acknowledge the need to recognize the plasticity of the body as it is opened up to, and made more mutable by, new technologies, and especially those we find in the domain of medicine, such as telemedicine and reproductive technologies. But we also want to stress how the informaticized (and geneticized) body has become subject to (digital and genetic) codes that, though reconfiguring the body and its lived experience, do not thereby always work towards its 'emancipation'. In the next few chapters we want to ensure that this tension between the opening up and closing down of options and subjectivities is a defining feature of new medical technologies.

This chapter has also suggested how the medical black bag might be sociologically opened, again not merely in terms of exploring the social construction of medicine, but also showing how the locus of medicine has stretched way beyond the site represented by the 'bag' itself. Thus, doctor–patient relationships need to be understood as part of wider socio-technical networks that construct heterogeneous and competing conceptions of NMTs, and their relation to the existing science base, nature and the body. The clinic is increasingly linked into national and international data libraries, DNA gene banks, stem cell repositories, and national information systems that help to compile clinical guidelines founded on so-called evidence-based medicine: all these developments redefine the meaning and management of health care and the body while subjecting clinicians to greater direction by the state.

At the same time, although there is considerable pressure towards new technologies being developed and framed within an already accepted technological 'regime', new sources of health technology and information outwith the conventional orbit of medicine – via the internet, through the market – open up an arena through which NMTs are produced and consumed: the individualization of health care, the emergence of health advocacy groups, the redefinition of aspects of health as lifestyle choices mean that medical technologies are much more explicitly socialized, subject to and shaped by diverse interests that lie beyond the boundaries of the formal health-care system.

In turn, the institutional and organizational context through which people access medicine is much broader, co-evolving with the very technologies that are opening the black bag, notably informatics and diagnostics. The latter, in particular, through the increasing investment in IT systems that enable computer-aided diagnostic tools (giving early indication of illnesses such as dementia, for example), or over-the-counter genetic tests for both single- and multi-gene disorders, weakens the hold of the 'medical gaze' on patients as self- and commercially driven health care gathers pace. Simultaneously, new risks emerge – of falling into a therapeutic limbo where diagnosis is not complemented by treatment; of dismantling professional and state management of health while opening the medical arena to new types and sources of (lay and competitive commercial) knowledge that may both empower yet confuse; of creating a distribution of risk allocations and costly medical insurance that increases social inequalities, and that stigmatizes and targets groups said to be susceptible to different disease and disabilities; and, finally, of creating a much wider vocabulary and language of health that cuts across and occupies cultural arenas and everyday practices – work, leisure, lifestyle, food, sexuality, the environment, and so on – to a degree not seen before.

Our metaphor of the doctor's black bag begins to look less successful in concealing the complexities and indeterminacies of clinical technology. Not only does work in STS open the bag, its characterization of the contemporary changes wrought by NMTs suggests that the bag looks rather battered as a symbol and site of medical knowledge and practice. One simple reason for this is that the deconstruction of the significance of the bag parallels the deconstruction of the patient as a site for medical intervention. As Morgan (2001) has suggested, we see the disappearance of the patient 'as a generic, stand all patient' (p. 23). In our next chapters we will examine how STS, and related work in the sociology of health and of the body, describes and explains the changing terrain of medical diagnosis, practice and care as shaped by current NMTs. We begin with reproductive technologies, the first 'stage' in another metaphor – the lifecourse – that we have used as an organizing device to tell our story.

3

Reproducing Medical Technology

Introduction

In this, our first substantive discussion of new medical technologies, we start our journey across our metaphorical figure of the 'lifecourse'. We ask how technologies are influencing two forms of reproduction: the reproduction of human bodies in the context of assisted pregnancy, and the reproduction of bodies for *others*, especially the field of bioscience as a domain of knowledge. Hence our chapter title, 'reproducing medical technology', chosen to suggest these linked but discrete activities made possible through the reproducing capacities of NMTs.

Lest this suggest that the power of medicine is all encompassing, it is crucial to recall our observation at the end of Chapter 2 that medical technologies are as likely to deconstruct as to reconfirm the biomedical model and its control of both the meaning of health and medicine and the site of their 'delivery'. That is to say, medical technologies act in a multivalent way *at the same time*: advanced techniques used to gain a more sophisticated understanding of the body (or mind) can, simultaneously, open up new and quite different questions (and answers), not only for medicine, but also for other social actors – such as lay people, bioethicists, non-medical sciences, regulators, insurance companies, forensic workers – who will voice their opinion on just what it is that needs to be understood. Our examination here of 'reproducing medical technology' illustrates how new developments, such as cloning, go beyond the conventional confines of the midwife, gynaecologist and maternity clinic – even beyond the conventional sense of a 'mother'.

This process of the opening up of medical science to the influence of multiple interests with differing priorities can be found in many areas. Indeed in the one field that has as its primary role the setting of health priorities we can see it at work: 'health technology assessment' (HTA) is an important tool that state agencies use in many countries to determine the clinical efficacy and effectiveness of NMTs. Despite its attempts to assess technologies through the deployment of evidence-based review and a close commitment to the primary tool of medical evaluation, the randomized controlled trial, HTA finds it is having to embrace much more provisional and socially diverse criteria for judging the merits of a new device, drug or therapy (Berg et al. 2004). This is not simply a genuflection towards the inclusion of more 'voices' but a recognition that the very questions being posed by technologies today cannot be answered by the standard terms of reference set by a purely biomedical model. This is especially true in the context of reproduction, especially the maternity clinic, where the assessment of new techniques – such as ultrasound or computer-aided support tools – for antenatal intervention is undertaken. A purely biomedical approach may lead to clinical interventions that the prospective parents regard as inappropriate or that produce findings of uncertain significance.

The reproduction of bodies

Medicine has been inextricably involved in altering what we count as the commencement of 'human life' and thereby the initiation of the lifecourse, and so is also involved in controversies over which entities should be understood as the bearers of ethical rights. This has, of course, been a very long-term trend whose roots can be traced far back through industrial modernization. The new institutional formations of hospitals, schools, sanatoria, and so on have all been instrumental in an increasing segmentation of life into distinct periods such as childhood, adolescence, adulthood and old age, each carrying distinctive rights, duties and obligations.

Before the nineteenth century, for instance, there was little difference seen between the now separate states of adulthood and childhood status and experience. The gradual pathologization of childhood as a special site for medical investigation and the rise of specializations such as neonatology and paediatrics were to shift the boundaries of human political subjectivity, resulting in the production of the child as something quite distinct from the adult. This fragmentation has continued apace, with new specialisms increasingly pushing and pulling at the boundaries of the lifecourse.

In regard to the beginning of a human life, in the nineteenth century there was little distinction made between occasions of death at birth and miscarriages and abortions in early pregnancy. As Armstrong notes, all were simply taken to be 'non-live' births (2000, 248). The *pre*-born were yet to become the object of medical activity and the concerted political scrutiny evident in today's frenzied disputes over cloning, embryological research and foetal surgery. In the UK, it was not until as late as the 1926 Births and Deaths Registration Act that stillborn mortality was legally defined as occurring after twenty-eight weeks (ibid.). This segmentation of the early part of life not only established a detailed temporal trajectory, but also transformed the traditional beginning of life.

Since then, new technologies of reproduction (especially imaging), more so than legal shifts, have transformed things further: technology, and not merely the legal system, plays a greater role in the segmentation of life. Increasingly, boundary disputes have pursued the lifecourse into the womb and into ever-earlier phases of gestation, fertilization and pre-fertilization. Numerous spheres of technical activity and innovation here have been important in two ways: in providing a range of techniques that 'assist' the reproductive process (such as *in vitro* fertilization and ovary-stimulating drugs); and in pushing the *temporal* horizons of 'humanness' further and further back, with the attendant politicization of the embryo and contests over its legal and moral significance (Petchesky 1987).

In recent years, the field of 'new reproductive technologies' (NRT) has been a key focus for debate about these developments, especially as they have affected women. Research in the social sciences examines the dynamic relationship between clinical innovation and the changing experience of reproduction. An excellent example of this work is the feminist critique *The New Reproductive Technologies*, edited by McNeil, Varcoe and Yearley (1990). Much of the focus of that book challenged the gendered culture and inequalities of science and offered an exploration of the medico-technical environment of the time, particularly the then rapid introduction of IVF and its attendant political wrangling over the status of embryos, eggs and sperm. Contributors to the volume overwhelmingly addressed a specific focus of reproductive technology – infertility.

Over a decade later, infertility treatment through IVF is still a major issue for many women, and increasingly so as a result of lifestyle changes leading to delayed pregnancy into the mid-thirties and beyond:

freezing eggs (taken from a woman when younger) may improve the chance of a later pregnancy for someone who seeks to develop her career before maternity. This personal control over reproductive labour may help to overcome the gendered disadvantage of female life chances in the occupational labour market. At the same time, delayed pregnancy via IVF still places the burden of reproduction on the woman rather than the man, even though some 30 to 40 per cent of infertility among couples has been linked to *men*. Moreover, although gradual improvements in efficacy have been made, not only do these inequities in the burden of reproduction remain, IVF is still relatively poor in ensuring successful pregnancy. It is also not free from risk itself, but, as Beck (1996) might observe, generates new risks in its attempt to deal with the problem of infertility: in a small minority of cases IVF babies may be smaller, and some may have birth defects (including heart problems, Down's syndrome, club foot and cleft lips and palates; see Hansen et al. 2002); and there has been concern expressed that, in the longer term, the risk of ovarian cancer for those women aged over fifty might increase following their exposure to drugs promoting super ovulation for harvesting of eggs (Ness et al. 2002).

IVF also continues to pose questions about ownership of the embryo, which can become especially contentious where, for example, partners who produced the embryos separate and do not agree on their subsequent use. Questions are also raised today whether those donating eggs, embryos or sperm should be guaranteed anonymity (as was the original legal position in the UK following the Warnock Report of 1990), preventing those children born through surrogacy tracing their biological parents.

While developments in regard to infertility are still not only highly gendered but also legally and politically contestable, other technical changes have extended the domain of reproduction in new and often unexpected ways. There has been a rapid expansion in genetic diagnostic applications and methods for their delivery through new service arrangements and consumption points. These developments rebound back on IVF: one reason for the UK considering removal of donor anonymity in regard to eggs, embryos and sperm is because of the opinion that those born through donation may want to trace their genetic inheritance. This is because of the view that genetic diagnostic techniques have greater precision and so value in providing information about susceptibilities to genetic disease. This health-related reason for tracing parenthood would of course reveal the gap between the social and biological parenthood of the inquirer: no doubt, in part it was precisely to avoid this, to ensure that the idealized model of unified social and biological parenting remained intact, that the original Warnock inquiry favoured anonymity. Of course this model is deeply engrained in Western culture and is precisely why so many seek IVF treatment. As Becker (2000) observes in her recent report on infertility,

> Women and men in this study expressed the need to persevere with infertility treatment because they felt entitled to fulfil the norm of biological parenthood. People place the struggle to conceive within Western conceptions of culture and biology. (2000, x)

The potential for the uncoupling of the biologies and conventional social relations of reproduction from each other has led feminists to discuss more diverse forms of socio-biological relation, including same-sex parents, adoptive and donor parents, and so on (see e.g. Shanley 2002). Few, if any, could have anticipated such developments without the arrival of these new technologies. Just as significantly, the intervening years have seen accelerated innovation in gene sequencing and functional understanding of the role of genes and proteins, all of which now again change the basis through which reproduction is lived and experienced. The heavily orchestrated announcement of a first draft of the human genome attests to the degree of novelty and change experienced in the decade leading up to the new millennium.

Compared to the situation discussed by McNeil (and similar contributions by Spallone 1989; Bartels et al. 1990; Birke et al. 1990; and McNeil and Franklin 1993), these technical developments have extended and redefined the boundaries of what we mean by NRT. And it is precisely because of this that the legislative and bioethical apparatus that is responsible for the area has groaned under the weight of new cases, possibilities and rights claims. A whole raft of declarations by national bodies across Europe and North America especially has appeared that seek to define the boundaries of what is and what is not acceptable: typically, regulatory agencies proscribe the buying and selling of embryos, germ line genetic alteration, cloning human embryos, or (in some cases) the creation of embryos for research purposes only.

That these and other proscriptions can be commonly found indicates that the regulatory agencies of the state are concerned to ensure some degree of control and governance over the impact of the new biotechnologies shaping NRT. The effect of these technologies is to enable the conventional boundaries between the social and the natural to break down. The possibilities this throws up – such as so-called designer babies – or the rapid extension of ex-vivo reproductive research using supernumerary embryos, requires social ordering, as Crook (1999) has argued, where the state has to determine in conjunction with a multiplicity of competing interests the best way to manage both the benefits and the risks linked to these technical developments. This simply serves to emphasize that the new technologies cannot be understood as being vehicles through which there is a *restoration* of the 'natural' biological process of reproduction: while it is true that reproduction is made possible where it might not otherwise have been so, the new technologies also dramatically *change* the way its socio-natural dimensions (physical, temporal and political) are to be understood. Farquhar (1996) points to this tension when she says of reproductive technologies:

> The contradictory liminal space they occupy is a multiple and shifting location – one sliding somewhere between recuperating *and* revolutionising reproduction and kinship, between reanchoring fissured 'core' identities *and* completely destabilising conventional representations and expectations. (1996, 6)

The state and the wider public sphere have to build new forms of discourse, as Strydom (1999) argues, to manage the social dislocations – and the new 'mode of reproduction' – that the biotechnologies of reproduction have brought. Some of the more significant of these dislocations and areas where we find heightened regulatory activity include:

- oversight of the body as a natural laboratory for research by both public and private organizations
- oversight of reproductive choice increasingly defined as a matter of consumption and 'procreative possibility' that also attracts major commercial interest
- the regulation of the cloning of human embryos and the creation of embryos for research purposes
- regulation of the transfer of embryos between humans and other species
- the prohibition of the creation of animal–human hybrids.

The role of the state and professional expertise in managing these issues and their associated risks, many of which relate to boundary identities, may not always work in a direction that might be regarded as equitable to competing human rights. For example, some feminists point to the role of the diagnostic technique amniocentesis as a means of determining the female sex of embryos in poorer countries such as India. Although it was originally developed to detect chromosomal abnormalities in foetuses, it is widely (though illegally) used in India for female 'feoticide' (Baria 1999). This, of course, not only raises (again) the political (and gendered) rights of the pre-born, but also points to the wider domain of *contraceptive* technologies associated with managing reproduction at both an individual and a population level. Just as genetics has been used to redefine reproduction, so immunological science has sought to develop immuno-contraceptives, also known as 'anti-fertility vaccines', to prevent conception (primarily via the woman) in the first place. And again this is used in the highly politicized context of WHO programmes of birth control (Richter 1996). Here we see quite starkly how reproductive technologies may serve some 'rights' rather than others. And this is why there is considerable debate between the role of these technologies as enhancers of choice and as a vehicle for a new eugenics, or, as Rapp (2000) puts it, the 'simultaneously liberating and eugenic aspects of this technology' (p. 3).

The politicization of reproduction via NRTs is evident elsewhere. Petcheski (1987) and Overall (1987) have shown how, for instance, new and emerging visualization techniques such as ultrasound produced the embryo as a visually and politically potent symbol of early human life. Consequently, the 'full public view' of the embryo introduces it into spheres of social action in new and unexpected ways. The inclusion of a scan image in the family album attests to the rise of a relatively unprecedented form of prebirth familial biography (Mitchell and Georges 1998). Similarly, the visually available embryo enters controversial political terrain in disputes about termination and whether or not, and at what stage, the embryo can be credited with sentience. Feature-length camera footage of the embryo's development, in natural history genre, now routinely figures in the campaigns of anti-abortion organizations for the very reason that they offer a visual reference for life that otherwise remains unseen. The pictorial representation of the embryo has, perhaps as much as specific debates over the rights of the unborn, been crucial in providing a vehicle through which a range of discourses and practices has emerged.

The visualization of the embryo is important in the field of preimplantation genetic diagnostics (PGD). This is the first technique that combines IVF and genetic diagnostics, but, as ever, the embryo upon which it focuses also combines those elements of political, cultural and economic resonance beyond the clinic. As Franklin and Roberts (2002) say, drawing our attention to their 'visually iconic' status,

> [Embryos in PGD] are highly contested political objects, highly regulated legal objects, and increasingly are highly valuable commercial objects as well. Embryos are arguably increasingly important as visually iconic objects, and they are undoubtedly seen as highly sacred objects, in particular by the Catholic church. (2002, 2)

And once – given the pre-eminence and privileging today of a visual culture (Petchesky 1987; Urry 2000; Beaulieu 2002) – the embryo occupies a place in not only reproduction but *representation*, it is a much more mobile and plastic object, found in a variety of contexts. Again, as Franklin and Roberts observe,

> The embryo is beginning to make appearances within the mass media in brand images, in advertisements, in news programmes, and in various other contexts. As well as images of fertilised eggs and human embryos, images of embryo manipulation in the form of microinjection imagery have become more visible: a clubwear t-shirt, the front page of a national newspaper, in hospital promotional literature. In sum, the embryo has become a more central figure – legally, visually, and culturally – in what might be called the public reproductive imagination. (2002, 3)

Moreover, as Epstein (1995) has pointed out, one effect of this process is that the meaning of the embryo is increasingly shaped by those who control these images, rather than the woman who produces the embryo: 'As internal imaging techniques became more available and accepted, women's own testimony began to lose credence' (p. 233).

The contested cultural, political and social dimensions of NRT are also evident when the question of rights is framed in terms of rights to choose, that is, to have some control (as a woman, as parents, as the unborn itself) over reproductive outcomes. It is this point to which we turn now in a discussion of reproductive agency.

Mythologies of reproductive agency

Notions of choice, rational autonomy and the production of the contemporary individual as a 'consumer' have been at the heart of sociological accounts of geneticized reproduction. Indeed, the extension of genetic technology has itself been in part dependent on the production of both individual and institutionalized liberal democratic rights discourse with which the person has been invested.

Of course, notions of the 'right to choice' have served as strong legitimations for access to and control over the use of new reproductive technologies, particularly for women's movements. Latterly, however, feminist critique, as McNeil notes, has become much less sanguine about the conditions under which reproductive choice is exercised and the assumptions of individualism on which it is based: 'There is potentially something asocial about the focus on "a woman's right to choose". It begs the question of who has the right to such choices, thereby ignoring how race, class and sexual orientation influence the possibility of choice' (McNeil et al. 1990, 10).

The extraordinarily powerful values invested in notions about reproductive choice are suspect for the very reason that they tend to obscure the many other forms of agency through which technologies are constituted. Medical innovation takes place in the context of a highly complex interaction between patronage networks, financial services, industrial and public research networks, and health-care providers and regulators. The selection of products and services, often squeezed between powerful market pressures, defines the kinds of 'choices' that characterize contemporary reproductive life. Such products include a range of techniques for the 'infertility market' as couples seek reproductive advice and diagnoses. Both large and small firms offer fertility enhancement, contraceptive technologies, and diagnostic techniques and kits to a global market, and the pressure from the health insurance sector placed on couples grows as diagnostic techniques foster a greater demand for more information about prospective genetic or related disorders. Commercial interests also favour direct-to-consumer sales, avoiding the filter of regulatory or professional oversight of products, stressing the value of a quick, client-centred service. But, as has been seen for over a decade now (see Milunsky 1993), these tests can create high levels of anxiety among patients, who then have to seek medical advice from health service practitioners. As Rapp (2000) has noted: 'When corporate labs advertise speedier results, they do not necessarily report whether their test kits are as accurate as more traditional cytogenetic methods' (p. 219).

The desire and seduction of technical promise itself often limits and constrains agency and so 'choice', especially in a social climate that attaches tremendous value to parenting and to reproduction as *the* defining feature of adulthood. For example, the potential 'success' of IVF is sufficiently possible while being elusive enough for people to endure long and often fruitless fertility treatments (Franklin 1998; Overall 1987) that can for many women be extremely discomforting and painful: egg extraction, for example, might lead to haemorrhage or pelvic inflammatory disease. Yet ways of avoiding becoming a hostage to fortune are often extremely limited, especially in the context of technologies which are themselves offered as the 'only hope' (Brown 1997). And behind much of this is the extraordinarily powerful notion that women should 'naturally' desire to have children.

In reproduction, the paradigmatic example of this is the confluence of expert and popular discourse around the notion of the 'biological clock'. That is, the biologically deterministic assumption that nature itself structures desire, irrespective of the many other reasons one might hold *not* to reproduce. There are few better examples of the overwhelming authority attached to 'biology' than the apparent 'natural' inevitability of the desire to reproduce. In addition, as McNeil notes, the fact that the word 'biology' denotes both the epistemological discipline (biological reasoning) and the ontological object (our biology) attests to the difficulties faced in trying to reclaim bodily experience from expert disciplinary discourse (McNeil et al. 1990, 14). These kinds of pressures easily combine with the clinic's innovative capacity to deploy technical measures to relieve those conditions that it has itself been instrumental in defining.

So choice is not an innocent term. Indeed, it is even instrumental in the production of new forms of reproductive culpability and blame. Choice in the context of reproduction has been critiqued before (Katz Rothman 1986) but has now taken on a new relevance as reproduction is ever more shaped in relation to genetic technical innovation where, at different levels, one can be held accountable for the genetic constitution of one's progeny.

Genetic counselling now emerges as the locus within which many of these dynamics now converge. Packed into the modern genetic counselling process is the assumption of 'informed' individuals exercising their 'choice' under non-directive neutral advice from an impartial specialist. Rapp (1988, 2000) has shown, however, that the exercise of choice and the cultural capital on which it often depends is highly unevenly distributed among women, reflecting their ethnic, cultural and socio-economic diversity. Genetic counselling in the US, for example, is very uneven in its availability to different socio-economic groups, especially for low-income and minority populations outside of large metropolitan areas (Cunningham 1998). Even where genetic counsellors themselves have come to regard non-directive counselling as untenable, it remains a formally required feature of genetic reproductive services (Petersen 1998). Of course, while some of the misgivings about genetic counselling might have increased over the years, the practice itself is not necessarily new. Of the highly sensitive postwar period for human genetics, Turney and Balmer observe that:

> what was on offer was not treatment, but 'counselling.' And it was based on a notion, usually tacit, of 'responsible' behaviour which often reduced to understanding risk estimates in the same way as the presiding physician and acting accordingly. (2000, 406)

But, as Turney and Balmer go on to note, the important difference between today and the period in which genetic counselling first took shape (*c*.1940s) is that counselling now takes place in reference to an actual diagnostic test rather than the reading of a family tree. Petersen (1998) similarly notes that, until recently, counselling 'was limited to offering families information, sympathy, and the option to avoid child bearing. For the most part, geneticists assumed that "rational" families would want to prevent recurrences of births of children with genetic disorders or disabilities' (p. 256).

The arrival of new diagnostic technologies alters the balance of 'who decides' and on the basis of what kind of evidence. The locus of the decision-making is often framed within the terms that seem to be set by the artefact of the test itself, with all the power and persuasiveness that pervades scientific-diagnostic instrumentation. Despite this, as those working in science and technology studies (such as Prior 2001) and medical sociology (such as Hallowell et al. 1997) have shown, genetic tests are much less likely to be foolproof positive markers of susceptibility towards a genetic disorder. Indeed, where the uncertainty of diagnostic tests has been acknowledged by clinicians in clinical cases, there is some evidence to suggest that it is this that is much more likely to *enhance* rather than undermine or compromise reproductive choice. As Franklin and Roberts (2002) have shown in their ethnographic study of pre-implantation genetic diagnostics (PGD), uncertainty can have value if it means that prospective parents can determine how to manage and interpret the information provided by clinicians rather than have decisions imposed upon them. However, they point to the complex relationship that parents have towards the embryo inasmuch as their evidence suggests that prospective parents deploy discrete notions of 'care' to warrant a range of choices they make about their treatment. There is not, in other words, a singular notion of 'choice' that we should seek in the clinic that works to support one consistent set of decisions. Instead, 'care' towards an embryo might be expressed not simply in terms of an attachment to it as a potential child, but also as a research object that can be given to benefit other couples.

> Patients also frequently described the opportunity to donate their embryos for scientific research as means by which they could repay a sense of indebtedness for the opportunity to have a highly technologically advanced and complex treatment such as PGD. (Franklin and Roberts 2002, 4)

Testing times

The discussion of PGD raises for consideration the wider issue of testing in NRT. PGD is one of four tests typically used. The other three are 'carrier screening' of prospective parents to determine whether they carry a genetic mutation that might be passed on to their offspring (as in Tay–Sachs' syndrome or cystic fibrosis); prenatal testing (such as amniocentesis); and newborn screening of babies for disorders (such as phenylketonuria) that can be treated: in the US, for example, four million newborn are screened each year and on average over 3000 identified as carrying serious disorders. The tests or screens need not be genetics-based (i.e. molecular). Other techniques, such as blood, chromosomal or biochemical tests (Burke 2002), are used as well. In regard to genetic tests alone, there are almost 800 tests that can be performed to determine genetic disorders of one form or another; however, many of these are unlikely to be found in clinical use, and more in the research laboratory. Most clinically based tests focus on single-gene disorders at the level of the individual (such as Duchenne's muscular dystrophy), and a recent Canadian study suggested that less than 10 per cent of tests have a role in wider public health.

The first tests used extensively were prenatal tests, which became available in the 1960s, based on amniocentesis and chromosomal tests rather than genetic testing, and were for Down's, Klinefelter's and Turner's syndromes (Turney and Balmer 2000, 408). While only a rudimentary application of molecular genetic biology as such, this laid some of the organizational and technical-cultural ground rules for what would later become a more widespread regime of prenatal *genetic* screening. Affected women would be offered a termination, and this helped to establish the precedence whereby tests can be offered even when the range for remedial action is no wider than abortion.

This would later become a much more highly politicized regime, with the rise of the disability movement largely opposed to the removal of otherwise socially valuable populations.

This wide range of tests may seem to be simply a reflection of the evolving sophistication of clinical intervention, searching for reproductive anomalies as in the past. However, we want to argue here that there are a number of significant differences in testing today: increasing technical sophistication has led to earlier, but more contested, uncertain and highly politicized testing regimes. We discuss some of these aspects here.

The case of Huntington's disease (HD) and genetic testing illustrates much that is *new* about reproduction technologies. Huntington's disease is somewhat typical of the way contemporary testing has pushed further and further back into ever-earlier stages of the lifecourse, as we noted in Chapter 2 through reference to the work on genetics by Prior and his colleagues (2002). Adult presymptomatic tests for HD were developed in the late 1980s following the identification of a linked marker for the disease (Cox and McKellin 2000; Wexler 1995). The subsequent identification of an HD-associated mutation in 1993 led to the production of a more targeted test. Initially available as an adult presymptomatic diagnostic, testing was subsequently developed for prenatal applications and is now also available as a pre-implantation diagnostic. So our first point of difference relates to the sense in which developments in the technology of testing have continually redefined the notion of a reproductive 'anomaly' further up the biological chain not only before *in vivo* reproduction but also to a degree where the criteria for determining reproductive anomaly become less clear.

Second, the increasing availability of tests – genetic or otherwise – does not mean that they are universally welcomed by all. In some cases, the emergence of more, and more targeted, tests has been seen as valuable, especially by patient advocacy groups, which have been shown to have been particularly important in promoting the tests (as in Hagendijk and Nelis's (2002) study of patient groups in the UK, US and Netherlands). At a more individual and family level, however, and again with reference to sociological research on HD, we find that many people do not wish to know whether they have a risk of the disease (Downing 2002). In part this is because of the impact such information will have on themselves, potential offspring and wider kin members who may be at risk. In terms of a measure of reluctance to take a test for HD, Burke (2002) reports that '[a] 10-year experience in the United Kingdom suggests that only about

20 per cent of those at risk for Huntington's disease pursue such testing' (p. 1870). This points to a second feature of testing today that we suggest marks it out from the past: this is the sense in which clinical tests are much more public, contestable, and collectively shaped entities than in the past. As we shall see below, this is illustrated by the role of insurance companies in demanding individuals take 'genetic responsibility' for their health risks.

A third feature of genetic tests that is particularly pronounced today is that the clinical uncertainties surrounding the meaning of tests are both paralleled and complicated by the cultural contest between lay and expert versions of heredity. Biological notions of inheritance based on genetic links and traced through dominant and recessive genes do not necessarily map onto people's own perceptions of biosocial heredity (Richards 1996). The latter are based on kinship and in fact are more likely to determine how people actually perceive biological inheritance itself. Thus, where people are close in social or familial terms because of affective ties, these will be translated into their concept of blood or biological linkage. As Richards (1996, 220) exemplifies this, 'from this we would expect people to see their genetic connections to their parents and children as closer than their genetic connections to their siblings.' It appears from the evidence that genetic counselling has very limited impact on these perceptions of closeness/distance.

A fourth feature, as we noted towards the close of Chapter 2, of contemporary genetics research is that it heralds a move towards a regime that is both more predictive yet less therapeutic and that, thereby, there is a disparity between diagnosis and the availability of workable treatment regimes. As Burke (2002, 1870) explains, with regard to Huntingdon's disease:

> The identification of risk does not necessarily lead to treatment options. . . . If the mutation is present, the person's risk of Huntington's disease is virtually 100 percent, given a normal life span. Yet, no effective intervention or preventive treatment is currently available. The choice to be tested is thus highly personal, and test results have the potential to be stigmatizing or psychologically harmful.

This disparity between diagnosis and treatment has led to some interesting responses from within medicine itself. One has been to declare that 'society' and patients have created a situation described as the 'premature medicalization' of the field of genetics. As Melzer and Zimmern (2002) say,

Genetic tests for markers that may not result in symptoms for half a century or more could be new examples of a process of premature medicalisation – of attaching the 'disease' label before it has been established that prevention or treatment is clearly beneficial. Treating the presence of a genetic marker as though it were the clinical disease can be very unhelpful. (2002, 863)

This comment is aimed mainly at the onset of susceptibility tests now available, but clearly, in the case of HD, the genetic marker (a faulty gene in chromosome–4) and the disease do converge and symptoms may not appear for many years. Yet no treatment is available there, so is the HD case one of 'premature medicalization' too? What is perhaps 'unhelpful' is the way the diagnosis/absence of therapy characterizing much contemporary genetics threatens to create not only anxiety among patients or the 'worried well' but also resentment against the medical profession itself. The diagnostic/therapeutic gap may be especially linked to late onset genetic disorders but seems to be creating early onset of *social* disorders.

Finally, we should note that the *socialization* of genetic tests – in the sense that tests have a social and not merely a clinical currency and meaning – has meant that, both in and outside the orbit of medicine, different social actors have sought to mobilize genetics for their social purposes. The intentional application of positive eugenics to produce embryos specially selected for certain 'desirable' attributes, whatever they may be, is an obvious illustration of this. Here not only does reproduction go beyond the notion of restitutive intervention for a 'normal' pregnancy, it moves towards what is stigmatized as a 'designer' pregnancy. Put bluntly, it asks: What is to count as a body worthy of reproduction?

Some argue that there is little new in this 'positive' or 'new' eugenics (Kerr and Shakespeare 2002) to distinguish it from earlier forms of selection on political or economic grounds. For numerous commentators, strong and enduring continuities link the eugenics of the past to current interventions in reproduction through genetic counselling, screening, and other forms of diagnostics. It is, no doubt, naïve to distinguish between the harms of the past and the benefits of the present according to whether one is coerced (the past?) or free to make a choice (the present?). While no doubt less coercive, the micro-politics of the newly geneticized reproductive ethos is powerfully persuasive, especially in those cases where termination of the foetus remains the only course of action for women presented with a positive result to a genetic test.

Even so, it would be misplaced to make crude accusations of selection and discrimination against prospective parents making reproductive 'choices'. The issues are complex and fraught with risks that are both political and personal. Sometimes these two come together in very explicit ways: we can see this in the UK in the application made in 2002 by the Hasmi family to seek regulatory approval (from the HFEA) to use PGD to screen Shahana Hashmi's embryos for one that could, when born, be a potential cord-blood donor for their other son, who has beta-thalassaemia. Initial approval was subject to appeal by the pro-life group Comment on Reproductive Ethics. The application was subsequently refused in the High Court, where it was decided that the HFEA had gone beyond its legal remit (see *The Independent* 2002).

While such cases illustrate the contested politics of genetics, the socialization of genetics is also said to occur through what Koch and Stemerding (1994) have called the *entrenchment* of genetics in society, where 'we' all become subject to or consumers of genetic technologies at different points in the lifecourse, whether ill or otherwise. The growing availability of genetic tests over the web and 'over the counter' is a process that not only gives further momentum to this entrenchment but also creates major policy and regulatory problems for the state.

A key problem is where to draw the line between those tests that might be met through public health resources (whether in socialized health-care systems as in the UK or mixed private/public systems as in the Netherlands, Sweden or the US) and the private market. In most countries, criteria are in place that determine the terms on which someone can seek a genetic test through a publicly funded practitioner or clinic. If a prospective parent believes that they should secure access to a test but fails to meet these criteria, there are private-sector agencies that can provide it. Moreover, the private sector, keen to build its market for genetic tests, targets (through advertising – especially on the web) particular ethnic minority groups that have a history of specific genetic disorders, such as sickle cell anaemia or Gaucher's disease. Regulatory and professional constituencies have been quick to challenge the value of this commercial activity: as a recent review (Gollust et al. 2002) in the US claims:

> [Commercial] advertisements may provide misinformation about genetics, exaggerate consumers' risks, endorse a deterministic relationship between genes and disease, and reinforce associations between diseases and ethnic groups. (p. 1764)

In the UK, similar concerns led, in 2002, to a national consultative exercise being mounted by the Human Genetics Commission (HGC

2002). The HGC is a government body established in 1999 following an overview of UK regulation of biotechnology, with its primary role that of providing information and advice on issues that are likely to have an impact on the health service. The HGC proposes to develop new guidelines on the relative place, legal status, and role of privately provided genetic test services. While this illustrates the specific issue of regulatory concern over tests, more generally it points to the ways in which, as Lindsay (2002) has argued, regulatory agencies have had to broaden their remit from a primary focus on scientific issues to much wider concerns: 'policymakers are now obliged to deal with increasingly diverse discourses within the policy arena and conflicts over what is the most appropriate, correct or legitimate way of discussing the technology' (p. 1).

The entrenchment of genetic testing will, of course, as noted above, be heavily dependent on the position taken by the private insurance sector. There is a tension here between insuring genetic risk at a broad, collective level, based on a form of solidarity (through the shared burden of public health insurance, for example) and risk covered via 'mutuality' through insurance taken out by clients to cover specific risks. What is at present of most interest to companies are late onset disorders – such as HD or hereditary breast cancer. What is of most concern to individuals is that, if they decide to take a test, they might find their premiums increase dramatically or that they become uninsurable, even if unaffected. Reproductive genetic tests will similarly grow in importance, but, as we noted earlier, predictive genetic tests are not always good predictors of the likely onset of disease in children; however, insurance underwriters would not necessarily see this as the basis for ignoring such tests. On the contrary, insurance works on the basis of calculating the chance of marginal and perhaps small unknown risk: the greater the knowledge of something happening the lower the unknown risk and the less rationale for providing insurance. Hence, there are actuarial drivers in the commercial sector that will mean that, unless the state proscribes this, companies will seek genetic information via reproductive tests when they regard the results as predictive and when they deem this economically in their interests to do so.

Differences prevail, however, in how insurance is organized in different countries. Merkx (2002), in her study of the Dutch and British insurance systems' response to genetic tests, describes how both countries' regulatory agencies expect firms to act in a socially accountable way. We can note the critical observation in this regard reported by the UK House of Commons Select Committee:

> The insurance industry has failed to give clear and straightforward information about its policy on the use of genetic test results to the public, and appears to be uncertain itself about what exactly its policy is. We call on all insurance companies to publish a clear statement detailing exactly which genetic tests results they will consider (both positive and negative), for which conditions and under which circumstances, as soon as possible. (HoC 2001, 1)

Yet what accountability means in practice can vary. As Merkx points out, for example, where there are cases of a family history of genetic disorder, in the UK insurers seek a negative test result from a related new client, whereas the Dutch accept this client's right 'not to know'. She stresses how such differences reflect distinct 'social positioning' of the industry in the two countries, distinct social configurations between the multiplicity of actors found with an interest in genetic tests. Thus, in the UK, a decision in October 2002 by the regulatory agency the Genetics and Insurance Committee (see GAIC 2002) that those with a family history of HD could be asked by firms to take a test reflects the view of the UK regulator that the tests for HD are accurate, such that a negative result would mean a new client would not have to pay any additional health premium. This investment in the warrant of test accuracy has not been adopted in the Netherlands.

So far in this chapter we have been exploring some of the main ways in which NRTs have redefined the reproduction of bodies through new imaging techniques, IVF, genetic screening, diagnosis and tests. We have argued that these technologies have had a major impact on the way in which embodied reproduction is organized, defined and regulated. We have also suggested that there are a number of key features to this process that mark it off from the social ordering of reproduction in the past, especially through the ubiquity and entrenchment of testing and the increasing ambiguities of the meaning of reproductive choice. In our concluding section we will return to this issue of how novel NRTs are today. One element of our later argument will be in regard to the way contemporary NRTs are affecting the relationship between the reproductive body and medicine itself. It is to this issue that we now turn.

Reproducing the body for others

A chapter title of a book by Robertson (1996) is called 'Farming the uterus: non-reproductive uses of reproductive capacity'. This notion of 'farming' nicely captures the sense in which the reproductive body is a site through which biological material and information is harvested for scientific, medical and commercial purposes. In this section we want to explore this issue more fully by discussing the role of IVF, stem cells, cloning and the creation of 'artificial life'. These developments also appear elsewhere in the book. Here we focus just on their relationship to reproductive science and emerging concepts of the body.

IVF and stem cells

One of the significant shifts in IVF is the scale of embryo numbers stored in cryo-preservation, many hundreds of thousands. While many of these will be used by patients who deposit them in case there is a need for further infertility treatment, many patients have assigned the legal rights of supernumery embryos to medical science for scientific purposes.

In the UK, for example, the Medical Research Council has (in 2003) set up a national embryonic stem (ES) cell bank. Banks are also being established elsewhere, though not in the US, where only those ES lines that were in existence before August 2001 are available for use. People in the UK who have had IVF treatment and have embryos that they no longer wish to use will be asked to donate them for research. However, more importantly, embryos are produced not only by *in vitro* fertilization but also by a process called 'cell nuclear replacement', where the nucleus of an egg is removed and replaced with the nucleus of the patient – from, for example, a skin cell – and then subject to an electric charge such that it replicates in the same way as an 'ordinary' embryo would. This is known as 'therapeutic cloning'. Here embryos are being created expressly for use in research projects rather than in regard to the reproductive hopes of the patient. The newly constructed embryos would be (as with normal embryos) destroyed after fourteen days: any attempt to reimplant this embryo into a uterus would be a criminal offence, since it would involve 'reproductive cloning'. The current UK policy here derives from the Donaldson Report (2000), which justifies this research on the basis that 'Such embryos can be seen as being created simply as a means to an end for use as a product source' (DoH 2000, 319, p. 8).

A key shift here is, as Shachar (2001) observes, that 'female reproductive capacities are used by these physicians as *laboratories*' (emphasis added); while debates over infertility and women's control over their bodies are still of major importance, they have been broadened to become debates over the very site and meaning of reproduction. Reproduction has, then, moved far beyond the specific question of 'reproductive choices' made in clinical settings, and in doing so makes the feminist critique of NRT more difficult to define primarily in terms of ethical and political choices and rights of women. Wider questions about the impact of therapeutic cloning on the direction, regulation and boundaries of scientific medicine itself also need to be asked.

The ethical aspects of cloning have also been given greater sharpness in Australia, where it has been proposed to use tissue from aborted foetuses to culture new cells (Robotham and Smith 2002). As we noted above, ethical concerns are highly politicized, and, at a European level, the European Parliament in 2003 moved towards a ban on embryonic stem cell research (especially after concerns expressed by both Germany and Italy). However, as in the US, regulatory agencies have allowed embryonic stem cells to be used for research *where they had already been collected as such* before the introduction of the ban. Inevitably, this raises the question of whether the identity of the pre-existing embryos is different from that of those existing after the legislative proscriptions, a point that many human (foetal) rights lobbies have used to seek legal injunction against ongoing research.

Stem cells, those cells that form very early in an embryo's development and from which 'stem' our different organs and tissues, have become a major research area for biochemistry, biomedicine and molecular biology. The clinical value of stem cells is that it might be possible to use them to treat diseases such as Alzheimer's or Parkinson's (through the reintroduction of nerve cells), but the (bio)scientific value beyond this clinical aspiration is evident in the establishing of national and international research networks around broad molecular biological interests. Moreover, stem cells also have potentially high commercial value, and there are currently corporations in the US and Australia that make them available on the global (research) market.

Stem cells are an important route through which the promise of the human genome is said to be likely to be delivered through their providing a better understanding of the relationship between genes and larger molecular structures, especially the distinct proteins that give cells their specific functionality. Work on stem cells is also of relevance to those working in immunology and transplantation inasmuch as the question of rejection of donor organs or tissue has been a long-standing problem for research scientists. This is an issue to which we return in Chapter 5 in our detailed discussion of xenotransplantation, prosthetics and stem cells as a means through which the body might be provided with alternative or 'substituted' forms of embodiment, especially there with the deployment of stem cells derived from adults rather than embryos.

The more general observation we want to make about stem cells is that they are clearly reproductive in a biological sense of depending on cell division, but how they reproduce and for what purpose is far removed from the specific arena of the reproduction of children. Derived from embryos, stem cell repositories that are currently being established across advanced research groups in the US, Australia, Japan and Europe are much more about dealing with disease and pathologies or about the creation through cloning (see below) of sources of tissue or organ. The laboratory takes precedence over the maternity clinic.

Reproductive cloning

The second main field that we want to consider where reproductive technology looks beyond the immediate medical domain of application is that of cloning. Reproductive cloning clearly does have medical claims made on its behalf: for example, it has been advocated – by some – as an answer to the problem of an infertile couple who are unwilling to accept donor sperm or surrogacy. However, beyond this, it has to be seen as part of a wider research regime not least because, at present, human reproductive cloning is illegal. There have been claims made by clinical researchers (such as Antinori 2002) and by marginal groups (such as the Raelian sect in December 2002) that, contrary to the prevailing law, they had cloned a human baby, though this was discounted as unlikely by orthodox research science. Animal cloning is not, however, illegal, and here work on the basic science of cloning provides a much broader context within which primary research is being pursued. Issues raised here have implications for human cloning were this to be approved in the future.

Possibly the most recent episode in reproductive science that we might say represents a break from the past began in 1997 with the claim by researchers at the Roslin Institute in the UK that they had produced a 'viable offspring derived from foetal and adult mammalian cells' (*Nature*, 385, 881). This, of course, was Dolly the sheep. The production of Dolly, and the frenzied media interest that surrounded her, was not only seen to challenge conventional notions of parent–progeny relations and the 'naturalness' of farm-reared livestock. It also disturbed core social notions that anchor the idea of identity within a biological individuality. If Dolly was biologically cloned, how could she have a separate identity (even if her popularization in the media meant that, for a time, she was something of a woolly celebrity)?

The cloning of Dolly has had a number of remarkable dimensions to it, much of which has been documented at great length in social, scientific, legal and popular commentary. But, with respect to our discussion here, there are a number of points that merit particular mention.

The debate that rose up around Dolly has its unmistakable roots in the phenomenon of the geneticization (see Lippman 1992) of self and identity. In fact, the ferociousness of the controversy about cloning is a direct measure of how successful the culture of geneticization and genetic reductionism have been. The heart of the problem lies in the assumption that seeking to produce a 'genetic' copy of an individual represents a contravention of the right to a unique identity. The application of cloning in human reproduction has then been uniformly taken as potentially burdening a person with the knowledge of having been created to substitute for, replace or mimic another. It has therefore become clear that much of the opposition to cloning is made possible by a shared and pervasive sense of equivalence between a person and a purely biological concept of genetics. Corea and Petchesky (1994) make much the same point with regard to older debates about embryological research and the troublesome notion of conception. They argue that the belief of individuality commencing at conception is a direct reflection of biologically deterministic outlook of contemporary reproductive culture.

However, contemporary genomics is also directly implicated in several important counter-discourses. The first of these recognizes the highly complex and multifactoral interaction between genes, environments and events. Where genetic research once focused overwhelmingly on relatively rare single-gene defects, research capacity associated with the Human Genome Project is now increasingly coming to bear on the multifactoral causes of disease and development. Much of the outcome of this recognizes that selves have an entirely unique and unreproducible relationship to their environment, times and events, in relationship to genetic factors. Therefore, the assumption that cloning will lead to exact copies of individuals is, in many ways, based on an unmerited notion of the role played by genetics in identity and distinctiveness. The cloning controversy, then, has become a catalyst for more nuanced understandings that may ironically come to undermine the assumptions on which it was based.

But cloning can also be seen as part of a wider move towards the redefinition of 'life' and its meaning. Paul Rabinow (1992) argues that, in late modern society, 'Nature will be known and remade through technique and will finally become artificial' (pp. 241–2). The artifice of cloning in creating new life without conception or fertilization certainly suggests a 'remaking' of nature. The biological is not only mutable but can be imagined in new ways. This has gained increased momentum through the emergence of so-called Artificial life or ALife research, which depends on linking the power of informatics and computing to the genetics of DNA. As Helmreich (2000) says, 'When biology becomes an information science, when DNA is downloaded into virtual reality, new ways of imagining "life" become possible' (p. 2). He goes on to argue that

> Twentieth century biology has, under the spell of understanding DNA as a code-script, conflated vitality and textuality – in the process assigning the realm of the digital to the really real, the 'secret of life,' genes, and the analog [*sic*] to the epiphenomenal world of the organism . . . [such that] 'artificial' life can be every bit as 'real' as 'natural' life. The 'reality' of life does not hinge on its organic origin. Artificial life contrasts not with real life but with natural life. (2000, 2–3)

This should remind us of Donna Haraway's cyborg commentary on and prescriptions for more 'leaky distinctions' (1991, 152) between animals, machines and human life (see also Hayles 1999). However, we should not presume that novel 'life forms' in ALife embrace the cyborgian freedom from dominant ideologies sought by Haraway: as Helmreich has shown, the genetic algorithms of ALife typically reproduce dominant cultural assumptions within them based on white, middle-class heterosexuality (see Helmreich 1998). One of the most powerful notions – that is the creator of a highly profitable industry in cosmetic medicine – is that ageing is unwelcome in Western culture. Some of the claims made on behalf of cloning and stem cells relate to this aspiration to 'eternal youth'. For example, it has been suggested that progenitor stem cells – so-called telomere cells – could be cloned and introduced into the human body to ensure our organs and tissue remain young – indeed, even that we could 'grow progressively younger' (Kurzweil 2001). Here, the lifecourse loses all sense of unilinearity.

At the same time, cloning and artificial life are subject to another common dominant assumption and practice in late modern society – that they can enter the circuit of consumption and assume exchange value. Here the re-productive power of these technologies is also a productive power for private capital. The commercialization of bio-informatics – via patenting, for example – is long established yet has been highly contentious, especially in regard to debates over the patenting of 'life' or 'human beings'. The University of Missouri in the US has, for example, been granted a patent on its technique for cloning 'mammals' that does not expressly *exclude* reference to humans within its scope.

For some, developments such as the Missouri patent reflect the degree to which human life is being commodified, and not surprisingly they have sought to challenge the body–property link. But the degree to which this is likely to be successful is limited, since patent authorities have tended to accept patent claims where they are seen to contribute towards national competitive interests.

In regard to this question of the commodification of life, Franklin (1998) has argued that Dolly the sheep is not only a cultural product but one that creates a novel form of property, a form of genetic capital that she describes as 'breedwealth'. This refers to the property claims made in patenting the technique whereby the patent rights to cloning Dolly confer ownership not only on the animal *per se* but on the technique that is to be used for future breeding too. This of course is not new, inasmuch as patents have always been designed to control process rather than the specific product where and when they can, and where and when patent authorities have allowed this. This strengthens a patent claim and ensures licence income (from those who seek to develop similar products) is much higher. However, Franklin is right to stress that the 'value' generated by Dolly resides not only in securing rights to a breeding line (as a 'template' for other clones) but also in its promise to offer an improvement in the genetic stock in a much shorter period of time than is typical – a compression of time taken to add (economic and biological value) to sheep. Of course, stem cell cloning might in theory replace the need for livestock itself – one of the 'visions' breeders have is of the production simply of meat as tissue, rather than as animal. Here reproduction moves towards the removal of any sentient being (a sheep, cow, etc.) and, as such, heralds a move towards the *de-ethicalization* of genetics. The furore surrounding the patenting of life would no longer be deemed to be relevant. This 'vision' might for some, of course, be a nightmare, and presumably the end of abattoirs!

Conclusion: reproductive boundaries and temporality

The two parts to this chapter have discussed ways in which new reproductive technologies related to genetics, imaging, IVF, stem cells

Table 3.1   Reproductive technologies and social change

Continuities	Discontinuities
Assisted/restorative reproduction of children	Break in the socio-biological boundary – increasing diversity of reproductive relations
Consolidation of the biomedical model of conception/reproduction	Locus, control and role of NRTs extend beyond the boundaries of the clinic and pregnancy
Temporal horizon of the 'pre-born' pushed back	Temporal horizons of reproductive entities multiply and in different directions
Choice and agency present but compromised at the point of the clinic	Huge expansion of political and economic actors shaping public definitions of 'choice'
Reproduced bodies (babies)	Reproductive tissue/organs (clones, stem cells)
Reproductive rights	Deconstructed rights and the de-ethicalization of reproduction
Risks and unintended consequences of modernist science	Regularization and standardization of bio-informatic reproduction

and cloning are shaping the meaning of both the reproduction of the human body and the reproduction of medicine. There are both continuities and discontinuities to these processes. We have tried to capture the main points of both in the summary of contrasting points in table 3.1. In broad terms these suggest a change both in the boundaries of what we understand reproduction to be and in the temporal properties that it has.

Table 3.1 indicates where the material and technical dynamics of contemporary NMTs are both fracturing and creating anew the social ordering of reproduction and its place in the onset of the lifecourse. We believe that these contrasts indicate how far reproduction has to be seen as practices, forms of knowledge, and diverse bio-entities that occupy a diverse range of cultural arenas. There are many aspects of these technologies that appear to echo the findings of earlier work, especially by feminists and medical sociologists. One of the more important of these is the continuing ambivalence that NRTs create for female patients, whose choices over diagnoses and interventions are fraught with anxiety, pain and loss of control. However, our closer analysis of the intermediation of society and technologies suggests that there are new processes at work that point to the need for further research in the field of science and technology studies, especially in searching the genetic and informatic framing of reproduction.

One point too is clear, that is that the medical black bag – our metaphor for professional, disciplinary and cultural privileging of all that is clinical – while still a key repository holding the reproductive process, no longer captures or contains the wider socio-economic shaping of reproduction. Property relations, social relations, political relations, ethical relations – all are subject to non-medical claims and agencies. It is unlikely that these shifts would have occurred had it not been for the combined effects of informatics and genetics, so closely linked (as we saw in our discussion of ALife). So interdependent have these sciences become that one might be tempted to coin a combinatorial term, such as 'inforgenics', to capture this convergence.

The term 'geneticization' has, however, some value in emphasizing the importance of genetics science on reproduction. As Lippman suggests, geneticization refers to the practice whereby 'differences between individuals are reduced to their DNA' (1992, 1470). In one way the 'geneticization' of reproduction can be seen as an extension of earlier moves towards redefining the beginning of life, where life's boundaries are pushed back and new political entities distinguished (such as we mentioned with regard to the status of the 'pre-born' in the 1920s). But the specific attributes of geneticization, its meanings and implications are entirely different from the preceding fields of neonatology, paediatrics and other disciplinary ways of defining the onset of life.

The contemporary period has then seen the production of the genetically pathological human, whose source of disease is inherent and internal, as opposed to being born of external diseases, pathogens, risks and hazards. Where once disease susceptibility might be seen to have commenced at birth, with exposure to a universe dominated by the rubrics of germ theory, genetic pathologization is distinct in that it both precedes and supersedes the individual. The individual – as embryo and beyond – is today constituted as pathological or non-pathological, normal or abnormal, according to quite distinct logics of genetic characterization, long before it even comes into being and continuing long after.

Of key significance here is the shift, with the contemporary emergence of molecular genetics, towards the understanding of genes as data, information, bytes and letters. Our fetishization of the gene has had the effect of shifting agency away from bodies and towards genes, replacing the body as a whole with 'a set of readouts from within the cell, dissolving into information' (Lippman 1992, 401). The mapping and sequencing of the human genome has extended the complex networks of human life and those of other species further and further away from the body as a bounded object and the person as a relatively bounded subject. The world's gene sequencing enterprises, together with the establishment of highly sophisticated DNA libraries, have had the effect of 'turning the body inside out' (Turney and Balmer 2000, 411). The notions of kinship and familial cross-generational heredity are no longer applicable in the way that they once were. The body and its ties to kinship have in many ways been scattered and reordered into data and information in libraries and biobanks and combined into new tests for future diseases of which one could once have been happily ignorant.

This sense of the reproduction of the body as the reproduction and programming of different forms of information suggests a (bio)-scientific management and standardization of the gene. Reproduction is now a highly complex and heterogeneously distributed activity. It cannot, we have argued, be defined simply in terms of the generation of new bodies, nor is it simply the generation of a body of medical knowledge. The arena within which reproduction takes place is no longer that of kinship and biomedicine alone but the wider domains of industrialization, information innovation, product development and the political machines (Barry 2001) that endeavour to order it. It is constituted, knowingly or not, in the wrangling over gene patenting, the use of patient records by the pharmaceutical industry, the operations of the insurance sector, the values attached to disability, and much else. All of these factors have produced what we might tentatively call a 'new mode of reproduction', the new forces of which, in terms of tools and materials, are essentially bioinformatics-based. Such forces take the form of genetic characterizations, tests and recombinations into novel life forms whose essential properties can often be known in advance. In the next chapter, we explore how these technologies are deployed in the move from the reproduction to the *maintaining* of the body.

4

Maintaining the Body

Introduction

In the previous chapter we explored how the reproduction or commencement of the body is being reshaped according to the emergence of new technologies. In particular, we charted a complex trajectory in which the scope and range of medical technology has extended further and further into the earliest stages of life and before. These successive shifts – from birthing to conception and into preconception – have been instrumental in the production of entirely novel life forms and political subjectivities. Such entities are quite literally the primary resources – in terms of flesh and meaning – underpinning the contemporary innovation of reproduction. The commencement of life is now a site for the mutual reconfiguration of both social and natural processes, or what Rabinow has called 'biosociality' (1992). This has depended to a greater or lesser extent on methods by which nature, and the human body in particular, is made available or 'made ready' for innovative intervention.

In this chapter we shift from the *reproduction* of the body to the *maintenance* of the body. We will be examining novel technological methods for maintaining the body's functions and capacities as it moves through processes of ageing and decay. Increasingly, care of the body has come to depend on relatively new developments arising in information-based fields such as telecare and telemedicine, bioinformatics and biobanks. Today, maintaining the body is a problem of technological apprehension or capture requiring the production of new systems for codification, storage, accessibility and distribution. The object of maintenance and care then is no longer simply the individual body, but representations or traces of the body in globalized systems of information and data management.

Maintaining the body is indeed now a matter of maintaining vast informational architectures, requiring continual innovation in order to render the body available to modern medical research and practice. Here we will be looking, in turn, at the production of the medicalized body within three such informational systems.

In the first place, the emergence of telemedicine suggests a relatively new conduit for the delivery of health-care services. But, more importantly, it defines systems of technical apparatus for abstracting bodies from context, lifting or expropriating them from the specificities of time and place. This is the case not only for patients but for clinicians too, who increasingly have to maintain bodies at a distance, frequently using hi-tech visual and diagnostic techniques. Such bodies are mobilized through newly sophisticated intermediaries, pointing to quite different experiences of the clinical encounter for both lay and expert participants.

Second, the electronic patient record (EPR) is another development in which the body is maintained both as an individual physical entity and as an abstract informational artefact. Here, the writing and maintaining of the body as a record of pathological biography shifts from predominantly paper-based formats increasingly to digital and interactive formats. So, how traditional forms of record keeping and newer electronic versions compare remains open to question.

Third, we will turn to some of the related developments in bioinformatics and pharmacogenomics, new systems of data gathering and processing that have greatly influenced the way in which drugs and diagnostics are being reshaped. Here, in quite unparalleled terms, the body is simultaneously being globalized through DNA sequencing and functional genomics, and yet being localized, particularly in terms of the concept of 'individually tailored' diagnostics and drug regimes.

Before going into more detail on these three areas, it is important to elaborate on the broader tensions that we think are being articulated here. On the one hand, the focus of medical maintenance has shifted outwards, away from the body itself, rendering it mobile across vast networks of data, information, biobanks and other archival systems. Maintenance has become a question of stabilizing the order of the body across distributed systems. This is a dual process in which the minutiae of the body are being explored in ever-greater micro-detail and then scattered macro-globally. So, on the other hand, the globalized distribution of data is accompanied by additional processes of individualization, oriented to the personal specification of the individual.

Methods of body maintenance, clinically and therapeutically, are therefore based less and less on notions of the 'generic' body. Where once a 'one size fits all' regime governed the clinical gaze, the logic of medical technology is increasingly directed at separating out individuals from collectivities. While processes of individualization become less generic and more focused on the person, the conditions for individualization require collective characterizations through population data, information, mass tissue-sampling and so on.

In one respect then we can observe a process of cosmopolitan expropriation in which the body is rendered available to the knowledge needs of research communities and innovation industries. This gives rise to new methods for acting back on the body, thereby *in/corp/orating* globalized networks of medical technique into the individual body. As Rabinow observes, glossing Foucault, the symbiosis of expropriation and incorporation has been a foundational element in the sustained logics of biopower:

> Historically, practices and discourses of biopower have clustered around two distinct poles: the 'anatomopolitics of the human body', the anchor point and target of disciplinary technologies on the one hand, and a regulatory pole centred on population, with a panoply of strategies concentrating on knowledge, control and welfare, on the other. (Rabinow 1992, 236)

Focusing more closely on the concepts of individualization, a whole cluster of relatively new considerations comes into play. The body physical is defined through a collective characterization of the body that increasingly prizes the clinical standardization of embodiment. The specific characterization of the body as isolated and distinct from other bodies is part of the process through which benchmarks of collective comparability are built. We might even say that the technical tools of individualization are necessary conditions for the practical execution of standardization.

Very often, a more traditional analytical tendency has been to view these relations on collectivization and individualization as inherently subjugatory. That is, the technical apparatus being developed to maintain the body is just another twist in the whole story of medical-industrial domination. And yet we are far from passive in our consumption of novel and innovatory techniques for body maintenance (Novas and Rose 2000). Numerous accounts of technology and consumption point to the way people are actively involved in interpreting and recoding technology, often in entirely unexpected and unintended ways. In general terms, this is as true of technological consumption *per se* (McLaughlin et al. 1998; Grint and Woolgar 1997) as it is of medical technology in particular (Berg and Mol 1998; Casper and Berg 1995).

In short, maintenance is an emerging technical regime that combines the polarizing tendencies of individualization on the one hand and collectivization on the other. These tensions are important formative aspects of the contemporary body for both individuals and communities of knowledge and innovation.

Body maintenance as a *physical* process of maintaining health depends on the *social* process of maintaining categories of health and illness that are sustained culturally. These categories are used to read our bodies and to decide whether the problems we experience are acute, chronic, serious or everyday. To a greater or lesser extent, we draw on a medical discourse to set the standards of normality, and to tell us how we should behave to meet these standards and so maintain the body in health. This becomes collectively experienced, for example, through public health programmes that, in preserving standards of 'public' health, presume thereby to secure private (individual) health – through vaccination, sanitation, nutritional standards, health education, and so on. The technologies that make this private and public maintenance possible are under constant development through bioscience and clinical and public health research, which offer more and more sophisticated techniques for measuring, managing and delivering health. The stethoscope, while still an important instrument in providing a general diagnosis of a patient's health, only 'works' so far, and is often followed by more sophisticated devices that peer beneath the corporeal surface. This changes the focus of the diagnosis to examine increasingly narrower regions and sites within the body, whose pathologies can only be treated by more specific and carefully selected drugs, by micro-surgery, by precision laser techniques, and so on. While traditional markers such as blood, urine and faecal tests are still crucial to diagnoses, today they are often only the beginning of a journey patients face as they move down one rather than another clinical route. Indeed, patients may move down multiple routes as the different specialists they consult provide their – often competing – diagnoses.

The new technologies and the forms of knowledge and expertise on which they depend are deployed through organizational agencies – such as national health delivery systems. These organizational structures, of a clinical (public or private), research-based or regulatory nature, can be seen as social devices that orchestrate and express our understanding of the body. We can draw here on a concept suggested by Vaughan (1999) that he uses to describe the role of large-scale organizational systems: he calls them 'contemporary machineries of knowing'. Health agencies can be seen to function in this way too. That is, they work to produce and mobilize a variety of forms of *know-ledge* about our bodies, their pathologies and their treatment. This is then deployed such that we might also, continuing this notion, see them as contemporary machineries of *care*, providing relief or release from illness and disease, though unfortunately they can also be the cause of pathology and disease, through iatrogenic illness, as we go on to discuss in Chapter 6.

When we think of body maintenance here, we can therefore consider this process as one that involves important organizational dimensions that maintain two senses of the body physical and the body collective. What one is maintaining here, therefore, is a set of social and material relationships as much as human health. As such, they depend massively on the institutionalized forms of trust that are vested in them: for example, national blood services depend on a broad social trust invested in both the physical and collective bodies that make them up.

Maintenance of bodies is also shaped by commercial interests, for whom the securing of popular trust is more problematic. The social relationships that relate to knowing, caring and rationing are disturbed and need to be put on a new footing. This has created major political and ethical difficulties for government, determined on the one hand to promote private-sector innovation, yet on the other hand to do so within a regulatory regime that can be seen to be legitimate. Maintaining the body becomes a subject of concern over who controls information about bodies. These tensions are most apparent in countries that have had long-standing provision of socialized health care. The 'provident state' (Beck 1996) presumes a collective body that needs to be maintained according to some agreed standards of basic care. This depends on trust, whereas, the more health provision is provided via the private sector, the more this depends on a contractual relationship. Risks and benefits of health care become defined in terms of the relations between the provider of a health technology and the consumer of that technology. As a result, accountability increasingly, it seems, resides in the contractual relationship between the providers and users of technologies rather than via a wider social accountability that makes requirements of the provider of technology *before* offering that technology to society.

Often, of course, there is an ongoing tension between the provident state and the private sector, and hybrid agencies are often developed to try to resolve difficulties that arise. For example, health commissions are set up to oversee the development of public–private initiatives, such as genetic databanks or data management systems. Putting matters relating to knowing, caring and rationing on a new social basis is likely to be highly problematic.

It is possible to argue that the way we have described the physical and collective levels and agencies through which the body is maintained have been with us for many years, if not centuries (Foucault 1976). What we have called here the 'machineries' of health act at the individual and wider social levels. Public health programmes, epidemiology, national health records of one form or another, and so on, stretch back into the past and do so precisely because they are driven by the social disciplining and regulation of health that occurs in advanced industrial cultures. Might it not be argued that what we are seeing today is merely an extension of these earlier processes? Is there something distinct about new medical technologies: are NMTs now acting in qualitative different ways in their maintenance of the body-physical and body-collective? And we might ask if this is to do with the play of the technologies themselves, or whether they are coupled with wider changes in the pattern of health seeking and delivery. It is to these key questions that we now turn, initially through a consideration of telemedicine, the electronic patient record (EPR), bio-informatics and pharmacogenomics.

Telemedicine

The tensions between the physical body and the collectivization of embodiment are being played out through the deployment of new technically mediated health service arrangements. Telemedicine represents a developing field in which information and communication technologies (ICTs) are becoming increasingly instrumental in the delivery of health care, often on the basis that they are intended better to suit the individual needs of patients. If expectations are to be believed, as patients we need no longer travel enormous distances in order to enter into a consultation with our practitioner. Instead of having to endure long-stay institutional care, we can be better monitored and our health maintained in the privacy of our own homes, albeit alongside a somewhat reinvented notion of 'privacy'. In general telemedicine is said to offer enhanced access to specialized expertise (particularly in rural locations and for people with limited mobility), a reduction in travel times for both doctors and patients, and the possibility of new and perhaps more productive doctor–patient interactions (e.g. as in telepsychiatry). In other words, telemedicine has often been associated with higher standards of care, lower costs, shorter waiting times and a greater transparency in the quality and provision of health care. These are just some of the desires and aspirations embedded in the notion of 'virtual care'.

Telemedicine does indeed represent new methods for ordering the temporal and spatial arrangements of the bodily encounter with the clinic, but it is far from straightforward whether this benefits patients and health-care regimes equally. The institutionally legitimized discourse of telemedicine as 'delivery' implies a directional logic, that the clinic is being taken out of its built walls and now delivered to the doorsteps of its spatially distributed clientele. This sense of ICTs transporting the clinic to patients has long figured in the fantasies and ambitions of medical technology. As early as 1936, Sir Crispin English confidently predicted in the *British Medical Journal* that, within twenty years, 'telephones with television will be in regular and practical use . . . the doctor will see on the television screen the tongues and tonsils of his [*sic*] patients.' English went as far as to suggest that, even in urban Britain, 'it will be common practice for you to visit patients by aeroplane' (in Porter 2001, 35).

While times have moved on since the days of Sir Crispin, the rhetoric of telemediated delivery, of the clinic transported out to the patient, has remained largely intact. The statement is expressive of the sustained promises associated with telemedicine by many national health-care providers:

> Telemedicine offers the potential to deliver integrated, collaborative care with improved equity of access, quality and efficiency. It will allow specialist care to be brought closer to the patient. Services can be delivered locally offering reductions in travelling costs and time. (UK NHS Executive statement, 1999)

And yet this individualized logic conceals the collective standardization of embodied maintenance. That is, ICTs facilitate the availability of the body to highly centralized regimes of clinical organization. Viewed in this way, the directionality of maintenance is reversed. As Cartwright points out, 'The techniques of the field are central components of a spatial social ordering of subjects into populations within a newly converged global health network . . . telemedicine is not simply a new approach to delivering health care better, it is a method of tailoring health-care communities to match the demands of a global health economy' (Cartwright 2000, 347).

Telemedicine represents not just a reordering of the clinic but rather a reordering of the way bodies are literally expropriated into the clinical regime itself. Most of the technical applications we associate with telemedicine actually have their origins in quite different sectors, in business, retail, financial services and entertainment. Their technical attributes are not necessarily new therefore. While their integration into the clinical worlds of specialist health service delivery do indeed demand changes in working practices and alterations to governance arrangements, the major implications have to be in relation to the newly radical availability of the body to clinical observation. Or, rather, 'the techniques and practices that make up telemedicine do not so much discipline bodies as they offer new and relatively benign ways to organize, assess, compare, and rank bodies in the form of client pools, catchment regions, or populations' (Cartwright 2000).

The increasing utilization of powerful databases together with monitoring regimes for segmenting and characterizing bodies is fundamentally 'actuary' (Cartwright 2000) in the traditional sense of the word, referring to the compilation of statistical tables by insurance clerks. On the basis of this, a whole panoply of new possibilities for accessing and collating bodies becomes possible. Centralized rationing judgements can be made about the allocation of resources across health-care organizations under finite conditions of scarcity. New and innovative comparisons can be made about the efficacy of treatment protocols. The performance of various institutional capacities can then be audited by decision-making structures and health-care management.

An actuarial spatialization of medicine therefore represents an additional contemporary turn in the developing 'gaze' or 'le regard' of the clinic (Foucault 1976):

> It is as if for the first time for thousands of years, doctors, free at last of theories and chimeras, agreed to approach the object of their experience with the purity of an unprejudiced gaze. But the analysis must be turned around; it is forms of visibility that have changed. (Ibid., 195)

The visibility of the body is manifest in the constitution of professions, techniques and institutions and is then more properly understood as the *disciplinary* gaze. The gaze depends upon methods of viewing and arranging bodies spatially. The linking of skills and technology together in 'technique' is the basis of the organization of disciplines, their means of establishing themselves as a source of knowledge and expanding their networks of relations over time. There is an implicit theory of technology here, evident also in Cartwright's account of telemedicine, which views the technology as a benign or plastic material capacity for meeting disciplinary needs and demands.

These new communicative arrangements are therefore highly flexible and are worked out in quite different and unpredictable ways according to variations in context and who uses them. Given the broad range of technologies in telemedicine, it might be useful to illustrate this discussion through a particular example. Dermatology (specializing in skin disorders) has become increasingly drawn into telemedicine as a means with which to engage with patients. To health-care management and policy-makers, it seems logical to view dermatology as predominantly a 'visual discipline', whereby skin disorders are diagnosed by being compared alongside textbook illustrations, or what is known as a 'dermatological atlas'. A common assumption then is that clinicians might just as easily diagnose a skin condition by looking at an image of the body as looking at the body itself, *in situ*, as it were.

By contrast, dermatologists dismiss this characterization of their field as a 'wallpaper matching' oversimplification of the diagnostic process (Mort et al. 2003). Substituting visual representations for face-to-face patient consultations suddenly brings into focus features of conventional diagnosis that were not previously obvious (Brown 2000). Touch, for example, is not possible in a telemediated consultation but is seen as essential by many practitioners. The discussion and dialogue between patients and dermatologists too is severely restricted in technically mediated conditions. Teledermatology raises additional difficulties in terms of the sheer variety of the localities in which a body is photographed. Colour, magnification, lighting all vary according to differing times and places.

So, then, these attempts to render bodies mobile across information networks are grounded in the practicalities of day-to-day practice. Clinicians often resist threats to 'hands-on' patient contact and the substitution of autonomous expert judgement by ICT-mediated diagnostic automation (Treichler et al. 1998; May et al. 2001). Such shifts can be interpreted as a challenge to the cultural status of medical work, a deprofessionalization of expertise and a threat to clinical autonomy and judgement (Kember 1995). As Mort, May and Williams (2003) say, 'The production of a clinical narrative about the patient, which . . . is central to the constitution of a medical identity, finds its counterpart in the digitisation of the lesion itself. Against this reduction of the patient to image, we should note that medicine itself is reduced. The dermatologist's role is confined to diagnostic reasoning against an image on the screen of a personal computer' (p. 278).

Clinical specialists are, then, having to embrace at least some of the new opportunities related to arrangements of convenience and, quite possibly though not necessarily, greater efficacy. Telemedicine has the effect of displacing the traditional role of the medic as primary observer and instead projects the observer into a complex world of technical and resource dependence. So, ironically, we see clinicians becoming objects of surveillance technologies that open up their own mundane/tacit practices to scrutiny as either compatible or not with the emerging visual culture.

Examples like this one are also a cautionary note to sometimes overzealous interpretations by scholars of 'cyber culture'. It is quite clearly the case that the body is not indispensable, nor is it vanishing or disappearing from social life and the medical encounter, as some scholars have suggested (Kroker and Kroker 1987). Fantasies of virtual substitution – replacement of 'wet bodies' by 'dry silicon' – have then largely been debunked and described as the 'wet dream of the dry platform'!

Nevertheless ICTs represent more efficient capabilities for maintaining the body within a changing nexus of disciplinary practice. That is, new technical mediations of the clinic imply important shifts in the clinical gaze, the most significant of which is the decline of the physical architecture of the panoptic hospital and the rise of 'surveillance medicine', a more effective and dispersed spatialization of medical knowledge no longer tied necessarily to a building but embedded intersubjectively (Armstrong 1998). The new spatialization 'sees' medical knowledge devolved to the family (Donzelot 1977), the community (Smith and Horden 1998), the carer (Heaton et al. 2003), but now increasingly mediated by new technologies for monitoring and observing at a distance and ever more so via broadband digital media.

Importantly, the maintenance of the body within the clinical regime has been mobilized through various forms of inscription, a form of corporal textualization whereby the body is 'fixed' and maintained as a textual, though increasingly binary, documentary object. Clearly, the scripting of the body covers a great many aspects of disciplinary formation that have together constituted the historical corpus of medical-disciplinary formation. However, what we would like to turn to now is one particular feature of the changing documentary maintenance of the body, the electronic patient record (EPR).

Maintaining electronic biographies

The apprehension of objects in nature is fundamentally premised on script-making of all kinds. In clinical practice, this process is now mutating from a paper narrative to a digital multimedia medium. Changes such as these necessarily imply a spatial and temporal reconfiguration. Inscription collapses time and space by making immediately available what was once unavailable because of temporal and spatial distance. Latour's term 'immutable mobile' (1987) denotes at least two key features of inscription and directs us to a number of salient features of the emerging EPR. Inscriptions have an immutability or obduracy that protects them against degeneration or corruption. Immutable mobiles are therefore able to traverse vast distances while maintaining their own consistency and, crucially, the analytical integrity of their object, in this case the electronic patient. Inscriptions can then be gathered at 'centres of calculation' that now have the capacity to set scripts alongside each other. They can be cross-articulated in hitherto impossible ways. That is, they can be combined to provide fresh opportunities for contrasting things in nature, comparing them, combining them, and so on.

EPR is now a key site for the exercise of the body's maintenance within this new clinical architecture. But in order properly to understand its implications we have to examine the longer continuities from which it emerges as a method for the actuarial compilation of bodies. Over time we can observe that the maintenance of the body within the actuarial nexus has increasingly depended on new methods for abstraction, the extraction of the body from its lived-life context and its representation within mobile scripts.

In order better to understand the operations of EPR we must take account of that which it is intended to replace. As Berg and Harterink (1998) note in their account of early twentieth-century patient records, paper records have a wholly distinctive ordering of the body, spatially and temporally, both in form and in content. For instance, paper records have their own temporal, chronological and even narrative properties. They generally register the patient's course through various treatment episodes, and ideally draw together the diagnoses of different specialisms. These might be successively or sequentially arranged in case notes, corresponding to the biographical lifecourse of the patient. Even the yellowing of paper over time materially corresponds to the ageing of the body and its course through the process of medical textualization (Nygren et al. 1992).

As new disciplinary spaces opened up the body, through the special-ization of medical professional culture, the narrative of recording the body has become increasingly fragmented. Different scripts recording a patient's treatment often exist contemporaneously across different specialisms and services. Paper-based records often exhibit duplica-tion problems and attest to the rivalries between competing scripted accounts of the abstracted body.

Record keeping produces a novel temporal spatialization of embodi-ment, it becomes 'loosened from the workings of the day-to-day life networks that permeated the hospital walls . . . studying the X-rays and other forms, doctors could enter the space of a tumor that grows, or a fracture that heals . . . Similarly, patients encountered different specialists, each focused on their own domain, and each carving out, with their probes, questions and interventions, a separate instantiation of this novel body' (Berg and Harterink 1998). Berg and Harterink ask the question whether or not the emergence of the EPR will repres-ent a reordering of patient subjectivity equal to that produced by the advent of the paper record. Their answer is inconclusive but advo-cates that an understanding of the novelty of EPR can only be glimpsed comparatively against its paper-based alternative.

While recognizing these continuities between past and present actu-ary technique, the newly emergent electronic format for recording care is distinct from its antecedents in a number of key salient respects. Most paper records are ordered chronologically, but EPRs allow a much more dynamic hyper-linked basis on which to access different dimensions of treatment and health-care management. This expands and extends the fragmented character of patient information, a process already begun by disciplinary clinical specialization. The chronolo-gical order of a patient's care progression is reflected in the con-tinuous temporal thread of the paper record. For those practitioners accustomed to paper records, the EPR format represents unfamiliar temporal territory seemingly abstracted from the time series of birth, childhood, adulthood and old age. While it goes too far to suggest that EPRs fail to embody at least some narrative characteristics of time series, they undoubtedly represent a further temporal abstraction of the body from the lived continuities of the lifecourse.

Moreover, scripted into the concept of an EPR is the objective of making data placeless, timeless and contextless. In an electronic for-mat, patient information is likely to be increasingly everywhere and nowhere at once. Logically, the separation of the body's record from place and time is a necessary condition for the further extension of clinical actuarial capability.

EPR also implies quite new regimes of governance, particularly in respect to differentiating between those who should and should not have access to information. That is, the placelessness of electronic information entails new risks and threatens the boundaries that once prevented sensitive data finding its way into the wrong hands. The newly distributed character of patient information across networks raises far-reaching questions about confidentiality and consent, and the need to overcome these concerns through firewalls, passwords and restricted access. In other words, there are important attempts here to introduce 'placeness' and 'timeness' back into the movement of patient information. Nevertheless, the production of these newly established boundaries is a continually negotiated business that is likely to demand ongoing critique and surveillance.

It is also clearly the case that there are huge difficulties in transferring the maintenance of the body from one format to that of another. Indeed, in many respects, the vision surrounding EPR far outstrips the practicalities of implementation. Stabilizing the body electronically and in terms that are functionally satisfactory for clinicians has met with any number of difficulties. These go well beyond questions of insufficient resources and into complex problems of acceptance by both patients and clinical staff. The design of EPR has tended to be based on highly idealized understandings of medical practice that fail to reflect actual conditions in the clinical context (Goorman and Berg 2000).

Paper records and EPRs are situated in quite distinct contexts of meaning, practice and materiality. On the one hand, attempts to implement EPR have become bogged down in the duplication of running both forms of inscription simultaneously. And, understandably, this has been seen to generate a greater workload for practitioners. But differences in form between the two, and their contrasting abilities to render the body available, reflect quite distinct forms of practice that are themselves undergoing change and transition. EPRs will no doubt, as their innovation develops, inherit many of the artefactual traces of paper while also generating quite novel practices and routines into the act of recording the body.

Nevertheless, the shift towards electronic formats raises the potential for new information inequities between patients and providers. Of late, inclusiveness within the treatment rationale has been signalled by increased access to and control over records by the patients themselves. The patient- or 'client'-held record has been an important signifier of patient advocacy, a document that remains physically 'with' the body that it represents, updated and added to as that body moves through various aspects of clinical care. In practical terms, the advent of EPR shifts these boundaries of ownership over records away from patients and back to the clinic again. Potentially, the patient-held record may well belatedly duplicate its more comprehensive digital version, but quite possibly undergoing a process of paring down and translation in the process (Jones et al. 2002). The costs of duplication here are more far-reaching than simple offences against health-care efficiency. Instead, duplication creates new scope for specialization and potentially deeper rifts between expert and lay medical discourse.

> It is important not to simplify the debate and assume simply that the hand-held paper record as it stands is *necessarily* accessible to clients – it depends on the type, content and context in which the client-held paper record is devised and operated. The same questions will apply to EPR. If [paper records] are replaced by EPRs could they *erode* client access to records? If EPRs are to run alongside CHRs then there are implications for duplication of records in a service which already has to ensure record availability in many locations. (Ibid.)

The maintenance of the body, its stability in electronic and telemediated formats, has now become the concerted focus of the medical technological industries and policy-making alike. Both entail new capabilities for marking the individual and specifying its properties as distinct from others, while also exploding the body into previously unattainable levels of global mobility. We now turn to another site within which these processes have been just as evident, but this time more strongly situated within biomedical research communities than, as yet, within clinical practice.

Bioinformatic embodiment

Banking (on) bodies

Clearly, then, the shifts towards the new immediacies of an electronic platform for previously paper-based records extend the capabilities of clinical industrial 'centres of calculation', to adapt Latour's (1987) phrase. Or, rather, the clinic has become a newly relevant key site within what Hevia (1998) has called the 'archive state', the reach of which has been consolidated through relatively unprecedented ICT-mediated relationships between the state, clinic, industry and patients. Nowhere has this been more evident than in recent debates on bioinformatics, biobanks and emerging arrangements to make health-care records and DNA samples more available to public and private research communities (Brown and Rappert 2000; Tutton and Corrigan 2004).

Bioinformatics, defined broadly as the combination of genomics and advanced computing, is increasingly central to research in the new genetics. The sequencing, storage and retrieval of genetic data have all generated new possibilities for understanding the medical significance of genes and proteins. The Human Genome Project, together with numerous other initiatives, has resulted in the production of standardized genetic benchmarks against which individual variations can be compared.

We will return to some of the questions raised by new pharmacological regimes below, but for now we want to remain focused on the relationships between embodied identity and these newly emerging architectures for creating and maintaining vast networks of genetic information, including family medical histories, genealogical data and lifestyle information. In particular, we might ask, in what way do these newer networks relate to more established depositories of patient information and, indeed, cells and tissues?

By way of contrast to the use of ICTs in clinical delivery, bioinformatics raises more acute considerations in respect to intensifying pressures towards the commercial commodification of the geneticized body. Now, clearly, this will vary dramatically according to context, as for instance between the more privately oriented US and more public health-care contexts. Nevertheless, the changing governance of patient information, and the implementation of associated bioinformatic architectures, has far-reaching implications for how people interpret the integration of their bodies within newly forming networks of biomedical calculation.

Bioinformatics is central to numerous controversies surrounding the ownership and control of genetic information, including the patenting of DNA sequences, the reuse of patient records commercially, and the commodification of the cell-lines of indigenous peoples in the Human Genome Diversity Project (Wheale 1998). There are continuing, and ever more acute, tensions relating to access, expertise, funding and intellectual property.

These changes in the relationships between public and private sectors are accompanied by important changes in the way embodiment is conceived and the basis of the relationship between those who manage information and the people from whom that information is taken. That is, we now have to ask to what extent the resulting body is a collective-public or individual-private corporeality.

Samples of tissue and patient records are far more than simply abstract 'bytes' of data. Rather, they are highly corporeal, even visceral, substances loaded with meaning and situated in a nexus of value that can be changeable over time. Indeed, the further one travels in time and space from the original moment in which a sample is taken – and the conditions of consent and explanation of that moment – the greater it seems are the vagaries surrounding its ultimate utility and function. On the one hand we have the local moment of sample-taking, and on the other hand we are now increasingly conscious of those latent globalized times in which derived patient information ultimately becomes usable in ways presently not yet known.

Much of these latent prospective uses have an impact on the relations of meaning, the mutual obligations and reciprocities, that we use to 'think through' whether or not our bodies can or should be 'given' and to whom. Intensification of privatization and commercial utility would of course be less of a problem if it were not for the long-term basis on which patient information and tissues have normally been available to research communities, namely 'voluntary donation' within the putative altruism of the 'gift economy'. Gift is a concept that we raise on a number of occasions throughout this volume in respect to both surplus IVF embryos and transplantable tissues. And, of course, gift and its associated notions of voluntary altruism are now seen to be subject to increasing destabilization (Tutton 2002; Waldby 2002). A series of scandals surrounding the retention of organs without consent, in a number of national contexts, has exacerbated these and related anxieties.

Questions such as these, and the underlying basis of the relationships between subjects and institutions, are crucial to the politics of bioinformatics. Most notably, though by no means uniquely, in 1998 the Icelandic parliament gave exclusive twelve-year rights on its population's patient health-care records to the private bioinformatics company deCODE genetics Inc. (Chadwick 1999; Palsson 2002). The small size and internal homogeneity of the Icelandic population, together with the existence of an exhaustive public health record extending back over many years, made the register a precious asset to product development. The key point about the Icelandic case is that the sheer availability of the information, the fact that it was simply there, was a sufficiently compelling reason to take actions which may otherwise be judged unethical (Sigurdsson 2001). This all takes place within the context of a plethora of presumed future benefits put into circulation to warrant the transgression of patient ownership, in addition to making a case for commercial investment in the Icelandic initiative in particular and genomics generally (Fortun 2001). Clearly in this and numerous other contexts a clear connection between voluntary donation and actions taken was far from evident (Rose 2001).

Justifications for making individual patient records available to commercial exploitation in the Icelandic case were oriented around the future promise and potential of wealth generation for the Icelandic people generally, and individual shareholders specifically. Indeed, legitimizing rhetoric was persuasive enough for many Icelanders to invest heavily in deCODE shares, adding their voluntary financial contributions to the involuntary contribution of their medical records made on their behalf by the state. The subsequent depreciation of deCODE's share value, after the Nasdaq collapse of 2001, adds the loss of financial wealth to that of the biowealth contained in individual patient records and genealogies.

While there can be no mistake that there are specific properties to the Icelandic case, developments elsewhere have seriously called into question its assumed distinctiveness. For example, on 21 December 1999, the UK High Court ruled that the secondary use of anonymized patient data for commercial development did not breach confidentiality. In effect, this opened up two UK databases – the GP Research Database and the UK Primary Care Database – to more relaxed access conditions. Controversially, the ruling asserted that, since the data is non-patient-identifiable, this removes the necessity for consent to be given for secondary use. This is but a small illustration of the newly emerging actuarial complex into which specific patient health-care information is being absorbed under equally novel regimes of ownership, informed consent and privacy (Brown and Rappert 2000).

The moves being made globally to establish similar repositories of patient information in order to improve competitiveness in emerging bioeconomies are key foci for important tensions emerging at the juncture between the individual, the state and corporations. Crucially, these questions depend on new forms of subjectivity and conceptions of embodied identity, especially in respect to the multilayered motivations behind personal participation in globalized forms of genetic research. Take, for instance, the initiative by UK medical agencies to establish 'Biobank', a repository of 500,000 biological samples (together with the health records and lifestyle data) voluntarily donated by a 'representative' sample of the population (Meade 2000). Recruits, the funding agencies believe, will be essentially motivated by the same bonds of community that encourage people to give blood and donate tissues without expectation of payment.

And yet, one must ask whether and to what extent these more traditional notions of community are sustainable in the emerging contexts of what Franklin calls 'biowealth' (S. Franklin 1999). Indeed, as Tutton points out, there are patently obvious differences for people between an 'economy of blood transfusion, in which the blood itself is of immense value and is used to assist someone in emergency medical need', and an 'informational economy of research, in which blood is merely an easy way of getting to the DNA' (2002, 537). Gift might not necessarily therefore remain for long the basis on which people conceive of their relationship with the wider actuary medical complex. Tutton's study of healthy volunteers participating in gene sequencing initiatives demonstrates that motivations for participation in research are quite distinct from notions of altruistic giving. Rather, involvement can stem from the desire people have to endorse various genealogical and racial identities, especially where participation promises to illuminate personal heredity.

What we have so far attended to are these parallel processes of the expropriation of bodies into macro-networks of information and the subsequent incorporation of these networks into the micro-processes of individualization and geneticization. We now want to elaborate on this latter dimension, the production of embodied difference, by exploring the fusion of genetic diagnostics with a new generation of drug therapies.

Pharmacogenomics (PGx)

The maintenance of the body-individual and the maintenance of the body-collective, the vast information repositories that now characterize the actuarial complex, have rarely been more directly linked than in the context of potentially new pharmaceutical medicines. Throughout the 1990s, most of the world's larger pharmaceutical firms became engaged in the process of retooling their approach to pharmaceutical innovation, anticipating the possible utility to drug design of the Human Genome Project and related endeavours. In particular, highly sophisticated screening and database systems for managing and accessing information would allow a more deliberate and directed approach to the production of new compounds. Alongside this has emerged a new lexicon of drug development expressed in the terms of pharmacogenetics and, more recently, pharmacogenomics. The former describes research into the genetic variability of individuals to drugs, based on the different ways in which they are seen to respond in terms of efficacy

and toxicity. Classical pharmacogenetics, then, proceeds on the observation of phenotypes, observable differences in the expression of drugs
from one individual or population group to that of another.

While there is some crossover, pharmacogenomics is now commonly
taken to mean the identification of particular drug response genes,
and depends increasingly on determining the actual operation of certain genes, or gene expression. In a sense, then, this latter dimension
of new drug innovation suggests a shift in attention from individuals
per se to genes. Its emergence also parallels the shift from the huge
sequencing exercise of the Human Genome Project to more detailed
work on functional genomics. The design of drugs will, if theory
works in practice, no longer depend so much on the vagaries of
clinical trials but will be worked out at a much earlier stage in the
laboratory. There is considerable work yet to be done before any of
this is achieved, however, and at present we are more likely to see
pharmacogenetics impacting more directly on the implementation of
clinical trials.

The motivation for huge pharmaceutical investment in the area is
that current drug design is, according to recent industry rhetoric,
inefficient, costly and even dangerous. In the late 1990s, George Poste,
former chief executive officer of the then SmithKline Beecham, began
citing the many statistics that indicated the scale and magnitude of
adverse reactions and mortality associated with taking medicines (Poste
1998; see also Lazarou et al. 1998). Over 100,000 deaths annually
in the US, Poste observed, can be attributed to the adverse responses
to licensed drugs. Many more people either respond poorly to drug
treatment or indeed suffer moderate to severe side effects.

Suddenly, it seems, drug companies have become much more candid
about the former failings and risks of their products and the methods
used to create and regulate them. The motivation for this level of
frankness stems partly from the need to create pressures on public
policy in order to gain better access to patient information, and con-
solidate existing public domain genetic data in addition to privately
held treatment records. Within the emerging actuary complex of pharmaceutical innovation, then, the production of 'personalized medicine'
rests on the parallel access to equally personal genetic information.

We need, however, to be cautious about overplaying these notions
of individualization arising at the juncture between the pharmaceutical industry and health-care consumers. This is in part because, as
many commentators suggest, it would simply be economically unsus-
tainable for the industry to oversegment their market. Indeed many
flatly reject the notional future of personalized pharmaceuticals on

this basis. Rather than attempting to market new drugs to smaller populations, implied within the rhetoric of 'personalized medicine', the industry is much more likely to be searching for larger groups among whom there are fewer genetic variations to drug treatments. 'The knowledge gained by pharmacogenomics', argues Sneddon, is more likely 'to be used to develop extremely effective, broadly tolerated drugs that can be prescribed to the largest possible population' (2000, 161). Segmentation through PGx, if it is to occur at all, is likely to mean a wider number of drugs being made available but to smaller populations of patients, each of whom would be tested as to whether they are going to respond appropriately to the medication.

Nevertheless, the trajectory here illustrates many of the tendencies that have been discussed in this chapter and particularly in terms of these tendencies away from larger populations and towards increasingly more heterogenized groups and towards individuals. No longer, it seems, will pharmaceutical products operate on the rationale that 'one size fits all'.

These processes of segmentation might be experienced differently according to whether or not individuals find themselves included or excluded ('orphaned') from mainstream drug products. Both new knowledge about genetic difference and response rates to drug products imply economic considerations in terms of judgements about health-care provision and reimbursement, for instance, where a product designed for smaller groups may cost more than one directed at broader population markets (Sneddon 2000, 163).

These notions of individualization are likely to be evident in the way pharmacological products merge with genetic diagnostics. The diagnostic will be necessary in determining whether and which pharmacological intervention is likely to prove more effective than another and at what dosage.

Crucially, then, the taking of medicines is to become intricately woven into the taking of tests. Now, clearly, administering drugs and pharmaceuticals has often proceeded on the basis of a clinical examination or assessment of some kind, even including the testing of blood, urine, and so on. And this connects or projects subjective embodiment into the distant worlds of pathology labs and clinical observation. However, as we noted in Chapter 3, unlike many other forms of diagnostics with which people are more routinely familiar, genetic tests are loaded with particular meaning and resonance (Downing 2002; Richards 1996).

Of course, some forms of testing are directed at the detection of the presence of bacterial and viral agents, many of which can be conceptualized as transitory or fleeting. These may be states of sickness from which the body can, though not always, recover through decontamination. Genetic tests, by contrast, are much more fundamentally linked to inherent and hereditable notions of self and familial identity. Such tests are embedded in highly geneticized and essentialistic discourses about the body. These are today core values in respect to our sense of individuality and are therefore a focus for potent anxiety and fascination in equal measure. As such, the prospect of wedding predictive genetic tests to drug prescription raises important questions about likely patterns of acceptance and resistance across both lay and expert groups.

As Sneddon points out, 'as more genes that influence drug response are discovered, there is likely to be not only an increase in the number of tests carried out, but also a difference in the way these tests will be used . . . pharmacogenetics could mean routine screening of generally healthy people' (2000, 151). Widening the 'worried well' population is one of the most important contemporary drives for the pharmaceutical industries. One of the key indicators of this has been a vast explosion in the number of 'lifestyle' and psychopharmacological medicines currently dominating drug markets. Many of these are characterized by relatively loose definitions of pathology, particularly in the case of mood disorders, as in the case of children and now adults medicated on Ritilin to counter 'attention deficit disorder'. Many of these products, particularly in the case of Prozac, have been dogged by conflict over adverse reactions (including suicidal tendencies) and questions over the role of drugs in treating metal health problems. Increasingly, it seems, PGx may play a stronger role in making connections across our states of mind, notions of genetic identity and pharmaceutical medicines (Novas and Rose 2000; Healy 1997).

These shifts potentially place genetic testing on a much more routine basis than it occupies today. Accordingly, similar questions arise here to those of the electronic patient record discussed above. That is, maintaining the stabilities of inclusion and exclusion, access and security, is likely to be a key focus for negotiation in the handling of diagnostic data, both for the individual and for larger actors within clinical innovation and beyond, particularly for insurers and employers.

The same questions raised elsewhere throughout this volume are just as relevant here. The expansion of pharmacologically related genetic tests implies the potentially burdensome production of unwanted diagnostic information, possible new conflicts between the 'right to know' and the 'right not to know', and new routes and scope for discrimination both within and without the health-care sectors.

As with many of the fields of technological development discussed in this volume, the relative novelty of largely future technologies makes it difficult to offer data-driven conclusions to these and other questions. Pilnick suggests that such technologies often operate within sociological blind spots where speculation merges with the very process of symbolic-material innovation itself. Pharmacogenomics and pharmacogenetics are effectively 'untested in a social sense as well as a scientific one. Whether they will come to be accepted as a routine part of health care depends not only on their technical efficacy, but also on how they are perceived and constructed by those who use them and who they are used on' (2002, 115).

Conclusion

In this discussion we have sought to explore various new formations in the way bodies are maintained, both as entities subject to pathology and decay, and as objects of increasingly distributed spatial orderings. We have seen a polarization of the body individually and also collectively. That is, on one level we routinely embody NMTs in order to maintain the integrity of our physicality. These embodiments are a mixture of technologies and expertise, various regimes of materials and symbols.

But, at the same time, these regimes are increasingly emerging from more dynamic global systems of information that are themselves the objects of maintenance. The expropriation of the body from context and its scattering across global networks is inherently volatile, subject to all sorts of potential threats and instabilities. Politically, for instance, the globally distributed body is routinely contested when it is seen to contravene notions of personal ownership and self-determination. This has been evident on those occasions where courts have had to rule on whether patient records should or should not be made available to third parties and for purposes other than direct patient care. We have seen that deCODE and the Icelandic database represents one among any number of cases arising internationally. Technically, too, the maintenance of the spatially distributed body has raised numerous difficulties in respect to standardization, the interoperability of different systems of technology and clinical nomenclature or language.

Several core concepts from the corpus of science studies are useful here in characterizing some of the changes that we have explored in this chapter, particularly in respect to these problems of stabilizing the representation of bodies such that they can become more mobile as the objects of maintenance. Callon's notion of 'intermediaries', for instance, highlights the way in which relationships can be character-ized in terms of the entities that pass between them. An intermediary can be therefore 'anything passing between actors which defines the relationship between them. . . . Actors define one another in inter-action – in the intermediaries that they put into circulation' (1991, 134–5). The benefit of observing or 'following' such intermediaries is that they act to describe the elements of the network that are brought into association with one another. The examples to which Callon refers include *things* such as literary inscriptions, scientific and technical texts, computer software, technical artefacts, instruments, disciplined bodies, contracts and currencies. Intermediaries, then, can be 'texts' such as scientific journal articles and patient records, or 'objects' such as a computer and even a door, or 'skills' such as those of a clinician or knowledge sought by a patient, or 'money' invested by shareholders in companies that promise a profitable return, and so on.

The digital image of a skin condition, for example, once in circula-tion across a telemedical system, simultaneously describes the nodal points in a network of relationships while becoming a point of arti-culation for the identities of clinicians, patients, system designers, policy-makers, in addition to artefacts themselves. We could see that such intermediaries are also highly volatile and deeply unstable. A system designer might struggle long and hard to maintain the visual integrity of the skin, but those other key diagnostic markers, such as touch and talk, may have been lost in the process of constructing the intermediary. The resulting representation subsequently proves un-satisfactory and becomes the basis on which dermatologists are forced to articulate those aspects of diagnosis that cannot be incorporated into the telemedical consultation, those richly tacit aspects of diag-nostic observation and judgement.

Law's notion of 'emissaries', a metaphor derived from his account of the mercantilist expansion of Portuguese imperialism, defines three classes of emissaries – documents, devices and drilled people/docile bodies (Law 1986). Latour's (1987) network constructions too require a mobile agent which will extend the power of a spatially and tem-porally restricted actor. Here, the 'immutable mobile' expresses the compressed reduction of complex material/semiotic networks into inscriptions which are then transportable and which embody a set of prescriptive codes.

As we saw in the teledermatology case, maintaining immutabil-ity over time and space is never a given but something that has to be achieved, running the risk of failure such that the network of

Table 4.1 Maintaining the body

Continuities	Discontinuities
Localized clinic	Distributed clinic
Paper patient records – clinical dossier	EPR – multimedia interfaces
DNA sequencing	Functional genomics – proteomics
'One size fits all' drugs	Genetic population-specific drugs
Prescription based on symptoms	Prescription based on a genetic diagnostic

relationships may subsequently fall apart. The shift from paper-based to electronic patient records is similarly rife with instabilities. Practitioners may be familiar with the temporally sequential biographical account of paper-based records, the yellowing of the paper with age, the order in which pages are bound, etc. A new and unfamiliar temporal reordering must be negotiated and learnt, inheriting some properties of the previous format while shedding others.

The formation of the various national and international tissue banks similarly expresses these tensions between immutability and mutability. To what extent can original conditions of voluntary consent and participation be maintained or rendered immutable as, in the future, new uses emerge on the horizon? Will the immutability of data, tissues, samples, stem cell-lines eventually degrade the further they travel in time and space from the point at which they originally entered the actuary complex? Is it possible, legally and even technically, in the temporally extended future to maintain the present spatial separation between clinical patient information and information circulating in juridical, insurance, and commercial pharmacological sectors?

So parallel to these questions of immutability are issues of change and novelty, continuity and discontinuity. Finally, then, we want to suggest several brief distinctions that can be seen to define key shifts in the maintenance of the body through 'new' medical technologies (see table 4.1). These overwhelmingly converge on the sweeping informatic basis of the way in which the body is apprehended, both personally in terms of identity questions about health and systemically in terms of the bureaucratic provision of health care, together with research and the industrial utility of embodiment.

In the next chapter we discuss the relevance of NMTs to the reshaping of embodiment through new technologies of replacement and substitution. That is, the widening limits of the global actuarial complex discussed in this chapter can also be seen to introduce new materials and tissues into the body, as the body's faculties succumb to the processes of ageing, disease and decay. The following chapter takes as its theme the notion of the body, or its parts, as 'substitutable' through transplantation and prosthesis. So while this chapter has placed its emphasis on the body maintained as a largely *expropriated* object, the following chapter attends more explicitly to the physical incorporation of novel entities *into* the body.

5

Substituting the Body

Introduction

In many ways this book has so far addressed itself to the way in which the body is increasingly being extracted from itself and distributed across vast networks of disciplinary expertise, information and technical innovation. This happens within the local confines of a hospital where, as Mol (2002) has shown, the patient's body is spread across a number of departments to be logged, tested, and treated by quite discrete medical professionals. In the previous chapter we drew attention to the wider sense in which this dispersal might occur through the notion of actuary medicine, where the body is abstracted out of context, expropriated from its subjective state, and newly integrated into complex *global* repositories of data and tissues.

This chapter explores another, equally pervasive, dimension of this process that works in a rather different direction. Just as contemporary biotechnologies mobilize the body across diverse social, economic and regulatory arenas external to its physical form, so these same technologies and their networks act to reshape the *internal* constitution of the body through transplantation and substitution. These two processes lead to a reworking of traditional notions of the interior self and exterior non-self. Globalized medico-technical networks can be understood to be reordering the internal substantive nature of the body such that any sense of the taken-for-granted boundaries separating inside from outside, internal from external, become open to question.

Illustrations of this process within medicine are seemingly endless. As the lifecourse proceeds, and processes of disease and decay advance, we find ourselves increasingly presented with options and possibilities for substituting our ailing body parts with those sourced from elsewhere. Each of the distinct sources or origins of transplantable tissues presents quite different associations and problems. In this chapter we want to elaborate on some of the recent tendencies within transplantation and implantation as a form of substituting the body and its parts. This potentially covers a wide range of developments, including human-to-human transplantation (allotransplantation), transpecies transplantation (xenotransplantation), prosthesis, stem cells, gene therapy and more besides.

And of course, each is accompanied by its own unique set of difficulties. Take for instance the relationship between established forms of transplantation between humans and, potentially, between humans and other species. Questions such as immunological rejection together with subjective responses to the incorporation of another's tissues take on an entirely new resonance as medical innovation looks to animals as a source of tissues and cells. The promise and prospect of xenotransplantation raises questions about the symbolic and material boundaries that lie between recipient humans and source animals (Lundin 1999a, 1999b; Brown and Michael 2001a). Questions surrounding the physical constraints on such transpecies couplings merge with cultural issues relating to the place of non-human animals in a human symbolic repertoire and the moral reorderings this creates (Michael 2001; A. Franklin 1999).

Where xenotransplantation inspires a rethinking of species identity, prosthetics and biomechanical implants raise questions about the relationships between humans and machines, organic and inorganic (Wilson 1995; Ott 2002). Here, the underlying mechanical metaphors that for so long have underpinned the disciplinary relationship of medicine to the body take on new resonance.

With the advent of nanotechnology, the mechanical metaphor moves into even more nuanced terrain. The diminishing dimensions of implantable biomechanics, down to the vanishingly small, further blurs harder distinctions between self and non-self, biology and device. Moreover, the nanotechnological vision of miniaturized robotics adds animate and autonomous agency to tiny implants, making boundary distinctions even more problematic.

STS scholars are interested in changes such as these for the very reason that they provoke such searching questions about both the limits and the seduction of new corporeal and material couplings, together with the way these new amalgamations are constituted in systems of knowledge, expertise and law. Our argument here emphasizes how these combinations reflect an ongoing process of change whereby humans and non-humans are in a constant state of mutual redefinition. We want to explore the way technologies of substitution highlight certain interpretative and substantive distinctions between human and non-human, human and machine, self and non-self.

The chapter addresses three important areas of innovation in the contemporary substitution of the body. The first concerns transplantation and xenotransplantation, opening up questions about the relationships between donors and hosts, usually of the same species but potentially between humans and animals. Second, we explore some of the debates in prosthetics that have been so useful in illuminating human–machine embodiments. Finally, we turn to more recent developments in stem cell technologies and regenerative medicine.

Transplantation and xenotransplantation

While many of the areas of innovation explored in this volume are embedded to greater or lesser degrees in the continuities of the past, the quite novel questions presented by animal transplants emerge from within and yet contrast with long-standing issues in human-to-human transplantation (allotransplantation).

Using the 'spare parts' of one body to replace those of another developed rapidly during the mid- to late twentieth century, accompanied by a vast explosion in the organizational and disciplinary structures on which the technique has now come to depend. It is probably fair to say that transplantation has been almost synonymous with the whole ethos and spectacle of medical technical progress in this period (Porter 1997). This has included important developments in the immunosuppression of the body's innate tendency to reject those tissues identified as non-self. Cross-infection between donors and hosts has also been at the centre of sizeable research and regulatory activity. The sourcing of tissues, or their 'harvesting' from the dead as well as the living, has pushed back and reordered the legal, social and physical definitions of death and life themselves (Timmermans 2002; Lock 2002). As we discuss in the next chapter, allotransplantation is a key reason for the emergence of technical systems such as 'life support' as a means to keep 'brain-dead' patients alive for tissue sourcing.

Now, the focus of these and many other discussions surrounding transplantation converge centrally on the complex cultural and biological distinctions between human self and human non-self. 'Puzzle

people' (Starzl 1992), as one renowned surgeon came to call organ
recipients, are the modern embodiment of the mechanical metaphor
in medicine. In modern biomedicine, component parts are abstracted
from context and treated in relative isolation from their surround-
ings. Organs, tissues and fluids each have a quite distinct place in the
modern disciplinary architecture of medicine. That is, the body is
literally carved up according to contrasting disciplinary specialisms,
each vying for authority over a functional regionalization of the body.
One of the consequences of the mechanical metaphor is that this
fragmentation of the body has become deeply engrained in the professional and organizational structures of medicine, indicating how
metaphors have not merely linguistic but very concrete-material lives
(Lakoff and Johnson 1980).

Starzl's metaphor of the 'puzzle people' both expresses and endorses
this way of viewing the body. It is far from arbitrary that it should have
been coined by a practitioner of a surgical field that is so synonymous
with the mechanical metaphor of the body. One of its effects has
been to encourage clinical disciplines to view organs and tissues as
though they perform the same function regardless of their being part
of a particular or specific body. If a component part executes a particular task in one machine then it should be able to execute the same
task in another. Fragmentation then is an underlying value or conceptual outlook on which a peculiarly modern relationship to the body
has been based and through which transplantation has developed
(Rabinow 1996).

And yet, the field has taken shape in the context of a tension between
a mechanical view of similarity between bodies on the one hand, and
their manifest actual differences on the other. Differences – immunological, physiological, genetic, dietary, fitness and lifestyle – create
major difficulties for the mechanical notion of the body. It is these
questions of variation and difference between bodies that have marked
many of the debates about transplant innovation.

Transplant innovation has therefore been important in shaping and
challenging any number of cultural and natural objects. Importantly,
it has developed both socially and legally in articulation with relatively
flexible cultural commitments about being human, and about what
can and cannot be done with humans. One key example here is the
long-term emphasis placed on 'gift' in structuring the relations between
host and donor bodies (Frow 1997; Siminoff and Chillag 1999;
Murray 1996; Titmuss 1970). What became the 'gift and commodities' literature in anthropology highlights tensions within transplantation specifically and wider capitalism generally. Capitalist commodity

relations, according to Mauss, depend on a firm distinction between 'things' and 'persons' (Mauss [1925] 1990). Human tissues, it seems, should not be bought or sold because that would contravene the moral ethos that distinguishes humans from commodity goods or instrumental resources. Further, the commodification of body parts might encourage impoverished peoples to trade their only absolute asset, their bodies (Scheper-Hughes 2000, 2001).

And yet, gift and the ethos of altruistic donation have themselves become the site of important critique, not least because of the way they give rise to conditions of guilt and blame for those who may prefer not to 'donate' tissues, while nevertheless coming under enormous pressures to do so (Tutton 2002). As Mauss put it, 'to refuse to give, to fail to invite, just as to refuse to accept, is . . . to reject the bonds of alliance and commonality' (Mauss [1925] 1990, 13).

The relationship of self to other has been explored through a rich qualitative literature on the experiences of tissue recipients. As with most gestures of giving, recipient patients are often understandably anxious to know more about the donor, including detailed biographical information about their age, gender and even preferences and lifestyle (Youngner et al. 1996). There is some evidence that people create new senses of self-identity in response to the newly in/corp/orated organ. In some cases, these processes of identity change may even include accounts of new memories, new tastes and routines that are apparently consistent with those of the dead donor (Lock 2002). These experiences are all illustrative of the way in which subjecthood and physical embodiment become the focus of intense contestation as the boundaries of self-identity dissolve to take account of the identities of once remote others. Prospects such as these, of acquiring a new and unfamiliar subjecthood, have also figured in the interpretations surrounding xenotransplantation in addition to human-to-human transplantation (Rosengarten 2001; Lundin 1999b).

Other distinctions are important here too, not least the sometimes conflicting balance between 'experimental' and 'therapeutic' which has often been seen to have defined the recent history of transplantation (Fox and Swazey 1992; Lamb 1996). There is a system of symbol and meaning in medicine whereby 'therapy' structures the relationships between patients and clinicians, while 'experiment' structures the relationships between research animals and scientists. Often it seems that transplantation has been embroiled in controversy because it has operated at the very cusp of the distinctions between humans and animals – or what is and what is not an acceptable relationship between medical technology and the clinical subject. These 'experiments perilous' (Fox 1988), particularly early on, seemed to contravene the very symbolic order of clinical and technological medicine.

Needless to say, rates of success and how success is measured both clinically and in terms of life-quality have varied enormously across transplantation and over time. And yet, the imminence of death because of life-threatening disease has warranted surgical measures in contexts where prognosis has been poor and the levels of trauma unjustifiably high. Transplantation has, some suggest, been driven by a view where death has been deemed unacceptable on any terms. The 'courage to fail' culture of transplantation, it is argued, has often legitimated unwarrantably high-tech and high-risk interventions (Fox 1974; Fox and Swazey 1992).

These and other border disputes serve as the backcloth to many of the debates and questions prompted by transpecies transplantation, and clearly the picture changes somewhat in the context of innovation around the use of animals as a tissue-source instead of humans. Until now we have made little of the way in which medical technology is, and long has been, inextricably bound up with non-human animals and other organisms. Needless to say, animals figure in medical innovativeness in all sorts of ways today, not least as long-standing experimental objects for modelling human physiology, as cultural repertoires for understanding human identity (Haraway 1989; Franklin 1998), as repositories of genes or models for the human genome, and potentially as new sources of tissues and organs for transplantation (Brown and Michael 2001a). At the turn of the new millennium, the prospect of transpecies transplantation has seen huge investment in research, risk regulation, public consultation and bio-ethical commentary.

Nevertheless, while many features of xenotransplantation are clearly novel, the concept itself is less so. Some noteworthy accounts go back to the seventeenth century and the advent of blood transfusion procedures. In 1667, the Parisian court physician, Jean-Baptiste Denys, gave a feverish young man the blood of a 'gentle lamb'. While suffering no evident ill effects, the recipient did complain of feeling a 'very great heat' rising up his arm, now thought to be the probable result of an immunological response. Later the same year, Denys's British competitor, Richard Lower, performed a similar transfusion at the Royal Society in London. Both accounts reflect a culture committed to a belief that the sensibilities of animals could be transferred across species boundaries through a blood transfusion.

Lower's patient was an excitable and 'eccentric scholar' called Arthur Coga who, it was thought, might benefit from the calming effects of lamb's blood. The sedating result of the procedure was judged to have been successful, and Edmund King wryly wrote at the time that the recipient appeared 'very sober and quiet, more than before' (in Fudge 2002, 106). Coga even corresponded with Lower afterwards to ask for further payment, describing himself somewhat abjectly as 'Your Creature (for he was his own man until your experiment transform'd him into another species)' (Lower [1669] 1728).

The importance of these accounts lies in the way, as today, xenotransplantation blurs the boundaries between material and symbolic risk. Questions of therapeutic efficacy together with the threats of rejection and transpecies disease sit alongside complex cultural understandings of the differences and similarities of humans and animals. Even Coga, while willingly submitting himself to the procedure, was afterwards ambivalent about its implications for his sense of self.

On the one hand, it is tempting for contemporary moderns to look upon early accounts like this as curiously eccentric reflections of a bygone age – a culture and environment where, it might seem, the social meanings of blood were 'falsely' entangled with misdirected understandings of the physical functions and properties of the body's fluids. And yet, as Rosengarten (2001) notes in her essay on xenotransplantation, it is hopelessly misleading to attempt to separate out cultural questions of species pollution and contagion from 'real' risk. Species distinctions resonate with an underlying (either implicit or explicit) register of roles, functions, capacities and attributes, for animals and for humans and our bodily tissues and fluids. The usurping of this classification is cause for both fascination and threat. But such contagion here has not only a physical but also a symbolic meaning, such that we must 'traverse the distinction between the symbolic, as in influence (including emotions), and that of physical disease' (Rosengarten 2001, 170).

Today, xenotransplantation is just as symbolically rich as in the seventeenth century. Here, then, we want to offer a few observations about the continuities and discontinuities that connect and distinguish contemporary debates from those surrounding the medico-technical innovations of Lower, Denys and their contemporaries.

In the first place, discussions surrounding xenotransplantation, even in the highly rationalistic context of contemporary debate, remain saturated with the mixed motifs of awe and loathing (Brown 1999). Xenotransplantation hybrids are complex and sometimes contradictory productions which vividly trouble the boundary divisions between humans and other animals, and also between rationality and emotion, expert and lay discourse, science and culture.

Let us elaborate. On the one hand, xenotransplantation brings humans and animals together within a scientific language and system of knowledge. That is, transpecies transplantation depends on animals and humans being biologically *similar* enough for tissues to be transplanted from one species to another. Importantly, this capability for 'similarity-making' across species has been aided by the use of transgenics (from the mid-1980s), gene deletion technologies, and cloning (from the late 1990s). On the other hand, however, our use of animals in this way can often only be justified because we understand them to be morally *different* from us.

So while *similarity* characterizes the scientific register of xenografting, *difference* underscores its moral and cultural register. Disgust and problems of contagion arise because these two registers (*scientific similarity* and *moral difference*) are brought together in the embodied xenotransplant recipient. The hybrid exhibits a tension and it looks like this: 'How can we physically mix (scientific discourse) if we're so different (moral discourse)'? Douglas's notion of dirt, explained as 'matter out of place', is powerful here ([1966] 1994). To express it as she might have in *Purity and Danger*, morally different matter is put into a materially wrong place.

Just as importantly, the challenge of making donor and host species similar enough (for transplantation) has been rocked by the risks of making them *too* similar, thus becoming a vehicle for potentially catastrophic transpecies disease incidents. While the overwhelming focus of research and development has been directed at overcoming immuno-rejection processes, the concerns of virologists from the mid-1990s has shifted the hub of regulation increasingly towards disease. In these terms, then, there are very difficult logical contradictions at the centre of the xenotransplantation concept. Much of the discourse surrounding the innovation is taken up with negotiating a resolution to the risks of 'too little' and 'too much' similarity, both in scientific and in cultural terms.

At one level or another, almost all commentary and discussion of xenotransplantation tends to invoke themes of disgust or what has come to be known as the 'yuk factor'. One compelling visual illustration of this stems from a moment in 1995 when a Massachusetts laboratory released details of an ear-shaped synthetic structure being tested within a mouse model. 'Earmouse' sparked a storm of press coverage that consistently commented on the bizarre miscellany of a bald mouse scurrying around a petri dish with a comparatively enormous human ear glistening through the skin of its back. In an instant, earmouse became an iconic image of xenotransplantation specifically, and our changing biocultural relationships with other species more broadly. To this day, discussions about transpecies transplantation invariably refer back to and recall the earmouse image (Brown 1999; Fudge 2002).

The event was particularly interesting because, even though it became something of an icon for xenotransplantation and trans-genics, the procedure actually has very little technically in common with transgenics or xenotransplantation at all. The ear under the skin of the mouse was a synthetic mesh, and not a human ear. It was being tested for any signs that it might cause some kind of immune response within an animal host, whether that be a human or a mouse host.

Now, the whole public spectacle of the earmouse was interpreted in several ways. The first was to see it as just another way in which the public can become unnecessarily upset about events in medical innovation, especially when they are seen to be technically uninformed about 'the facts'. This roughly corresponds to what has come to be known as the 'deficit model' of public understanding (Irwin and Wynne 1996). Here, science is thought to be mistrusted simply because people are unfamiliar with the technical and scientific details of the events about which they are concerned. This view of technical illiteracy still continues as a way to dismiss the public as simply having little serious to contribute to discussions about scientific innovation at key moments like that of the earmouse.

A second and more nuanced way to look at debates such as these emerged as a critique of the 'deficit model' and recognized that people are often already knowledgeable. They/we already possess a broader knowledge that often makes institutional laboratory-based knowledge look unworkable, abstract and alien. Such knowledges are neces-sarily important in forming legitimate views about images such as the earmouse. So, more information does not equal more trust. Instead, more information usually provides people with more empirical re-sources with which to express their mistrust of science. This was nicely illustrated by a Wellcome Trust public consultation on cloning where participants were 'furnished' with knowledge about the differ-ent methods of cloning, none of which necessarily resulted in more trust (Wellcome Trust 1998). Instead, people simply used their new-found scientific literacy to strengthen their misgivings. Moreover, far from reducing uncertainty, more information also has the effect of making people aware of the complexities of science and that science does not speak with one uniform and necessarily coherent voice. For that matter, neither does 'the public'.

Instead of earmouse and similar events being viewed as the effects of scientific illiteracy, they might better be understood as important ways for people to think through what is materially and symbolically at stake in transgenic medicine. It has become necessary then for critical commentary on transpecies transplantation to be able to make sense of these kinds of discussions even though they might not be articulated in a way easily recognized by scientific institutions and discourse (Brown and Michael 2001b). Nevertheless, such responses are central to understanding the way species boundaries are being redrawn at all levels of society and nature.

Importantly, these processes are embedded in far wider historical and social tendencies. Xenotransplantation, together with other uses for animals in contemporary medical technology, is both constitutive of and constituted within a distinctly contemporary regard for animals. The place of animals in modernity corresponds to familiar patterns of institutionalized specialization and sequestration. In the following chapter we describe how medical technology has been involved in producing a distinctively modern relationship to mortality, particularly the sequestration of death. A similar process has been taking place with respect to animals. In the most general terms, these processes emerged in tandem with highly industrialized forms of urbanization, consumption and production. The pressures of population density, housing and sanitation made close contact with animals much more difficult to sustain than before.

As these processes of separation took hold, the value of animals within consumption changed too. A cultivated sense of distance between society and nature made it possible for moderns to romanticize animals on the one hand while mass producing them for food on the other (A. Franklin 1999; Michael 2001). This enormously contradictory disposition towards animals has manifested itself in a highly disjointed way. The romantic ethos has become expressed in the discourses of welfare and rights and the keeping of companion animals. But, at the same time, this romanticization is made possible through the sequestration of animal experimentation and industrial meat production, a removal from sight resulting in a separation of flesh and the animal from which it is taken (Fudge 2002; A. Franklin 1999).

Many of these highly contradictory ambivalences are just as evident in the moral reasoning that underpins public deliberation on xenotransplantation, transgenics and animals in medical innovation more widely. Here, participants in such debates are clearly trying to locate themselves and the technology within these broader facets of human and non-human relations. And the reason why both the moral and scientific status of donor animals is so highly contested goes back to these parallel tensions between the romanticization and sequestration of animals. Source animals for xenotransplantation tissues are both immediate to us and yet estranged. Like all animals, they are immediate through the pervasive culture and imagination of animal portrayal, represented in advertising, documentary narrative and much else besides. Animals in these closely proximate terms have been invested with powerful attributes of moral and ethical agency, much like humans are. And yet, social and institutional life is also characterized by architectures (legal and built) for distancing ourselves spatially and temporally from their use in medicine and food production.

These patterns of closeness and remoteness, similarity and difference, serve as the basis for making sense of xenotransplantation and other technologies, both to ourselves and to others. Advocates of xenotransplantation will often draw on the register of sequestration in order to calm wider cultural ambivalence. It is routinely argued, for instance, that using transgenic pigs' organs is ethically no different from eating a ham sandwich or that it is better to use animals to 'save lives' than for the pleasures of eating. In other words, if society sanctions the sequestration of animals into the meat industry then it should also sanction their incorporation into technologies of medicine and transplantation in this case. Another familiar line of reasoning is that there is nothing either novel or exotic about technologies such as xenotransplantation, transgenics or even cloning. Instead, such approaches have been part of technical skill for centuries (Plein 1991). Transgenics is often placed in a historical lineage extending back to Babylonian plant hybridization and fermentation techniques, etc.

All these arguments are a way of creating a sense of continuity between something new (transgenic modification) and something old (ancient methods of animal husbandry, hybridization, ham, Babylon, etc.). But these comparisons are hardly likely to be reassuring or convincing. First, as comparisons, they are too simplistic in that certain dimensions of these lineages are highlighted while important discontinuities are silenced (Brown and Michael 2001b). In other words, xenotransplantation and ham are equivalent only to the extent that they represent superficially analogous uses for animals. But there are other distinctive dimensions that these kinds of analogies ignore. Transplanted transgenic pig hearts are not ingested or digested. Neither is a ham sandwich 'live' when eaten in the same way that an organ is live when transplanted. Indeed, the digestive tract through which food passes is sometimes described as the interior surface of the body's outer skin, but arranged cylindrically within the body. While food enters through the intestinal wall and into the body at a molecular level, a transplanted organ enters the body on a much more substantive and macroscopic level. Similarly, the comparison of new recombinant transgenic technologies to ancient methods of hybridization only works if you ignore the much more accelerated process of transgenics and the new capability to combine the genetic attributes of entirely unrelated species (Adam 1998).

How these changes are interpreted varies dramatically according to different people's experience of embodiment, our sense of change over time and of course the threat of not embodying new technical opportunities when they are presented to us at times of illness. Species boundaries are far from being fixed either symbolically or even materially. The newly emerging, though far from clinically effective, capacity to transfer tissues and genes across species divisions is part of a long-term reshaping of the binary categories separating humans from non-humans.

While disgust reflects the rigidities of a moral order, and a sensitivity to risk, this is often offset by various legitimations. Being presented with a life-prolonging (or improving) innovation may well prompt far-reaching reconsiderations of humanness and species integrity.

In her fieldwork with patients who had received pig neural and islet cells (in treating Parkinson's disease and diabetes), Lundin notes a high degree of pragmatism, with 'survival taking precedence over any ethical or existential misgivings' (Lundin 1999b, 126). The object of innovation here is not only the distinction between one species and another, but between life and death too. Medical technology 'deconstructs death' into a whole panoply of causes and cures (Bauman 1992) and, in Lundin's words, 'makes natural death appear unnecessary, almost unnatural, a phenomenon requiring artificial measures to regain its naturalness' (ibid., 132). So the binary system that aligns death with nature and life with culture has weakened. We will of course be addressing this in more detail in the following chapter, but it is important here to recognize the constantly formative role of mortality in reshaping embodied species identity.

While it is clearly the case that xenotransplantation agitates questions about species identity, these are far from fixed. The underlying order of species classification, both in science and culture, is now the concerted focus of innovation. This clearly contrasts markedly with the more static portrayal of classificatory order evident in Douglas's anthropological account. It is true that pollution requires action: the delineation of a border, the naming of transgressors, the ritual of the purge, the subsequent restoration of a boundary. But highly plastic and transformative rituals pervade the play of difference and similarity in xenografting. These rituals tell us more of the impermanence of social ordering and the transience of boundaries.

If xenograft hybrids have an anomalous or monstrous status – 'matter out of place' or 'dirt' – powerful accounts of desperate clinical need re-embed such hybrids back within a recognized moral order. By locating displaced species-specific continuities (the human, the pig) firmly in a threatened continuity (the dying body), matter is literally put back in a morally right place (Brown 1999).

The recombination of species bodies in this way parallels numerous other boundary rearrangements, particularly in expert discourse. For instance, xenotransplantation has taken shape in a way that has seen previously distant disciplines converge on sometimes competing problems. Take immunology and virology. For immunology, the prospect of using animal tissues represented an important area of expansion for the discipline and the resolution of long-standing organ-sourcing problems. But this brought it into conflict with another discipline concerned with the movement of diseases between unrelated species. Over the past few years, the prospect of xenotransplantation has operated as a meeting place in which these two disciplines have been engaged in processes of negotiation and mutual learning over the risks of rejection and disease. Both have been locked into a complex process of redrawing the boundaries between themselves as different bodies of knowledge and also between animals as different species bodies. Disciplines are thus far from being direct reflections of nature and must instead be seen as cultural and organizational formations with sometimes conflicting goals and aspirations.

Xenotransplantation figures in internal changes within disciplines as well as between them. For instance, while transplantation has long been part of the repertoire of renal medicine, it has only recently become a source of interest to other specialisms, particularly neurology. For a discipline focused on the central nervous system, involvement in xenotransplantation has required a significant change in outlook. For instance, neurologists have long assumed that the brain has a certain separateness from the rest of the body. That is, the brain is understood to operate on quite different immunological principles as a result of what has come to be known as the 'blood–brain barrier' (BBB). It has long been assumed that the BBB offers the brain an 'immunological privilege' not enjoyed by the other organs of the body. Of late, new approaches to treating patients with brain disorders by transplanting neural cells (from both human and pig foetuses) have resulted in a questioning of the disciplinary assumptions surrounding the BBB. In xenograft studies, neurologists have observed powerful rejection processes affecting transplanted cells (Barker et al. 1999). Here species boundaries are being redefined in neurology to reflect this encounter with the world of transplantation and xenotransplantation.

Clearly, then, xenotransplantation has operated as an important touchstone so to speak in the changing relationships between humans and other animals. Some of its features are distinctly contemporary, including highly accelerated methods of gene transfer between unrelated species, and also the prospects for increasingly transplanting tissues. In addition we can observe unprecedented innovations taking place between disciplines and, more broadly, between science and culture. Other features of the approach are somewhat more mundane and embedded in long-standing traditions of moral reasoning and material practice. Nevertheless, the technology has become an important site for innovating species boundaries and the numerous systems of meaning, knowledge and materiality in which they are constituted.

But, of course, xenotransplantation is only one site of innovation in the substitution of the body. If transplantation and xenotransplantation have been significant for thinking through the relations between humans and other species, the embodiment of mechanical devices has been just as important for interpreting the frontiers between humans and machines.

Embodying machines

By way of contrast to the areas of transplantation already discussed above, the use of mechanics in embodiment is far more variegated and diverse. It also covers a much broader spectrum of innovativeness, from the mundane and routine through to the entirely unfamiliar and even quite fanciful.

While some of the far-reaching changes associated with the field are concerned with new materials and techniques, others are much more to do with radically innovative social, political and regulatory change. It is therefore a formidable challenge to offer an overview here that does service to the breadth and scope of these changes. Rather we provide a limited discussion of the more significant shifts that have taken place technically and in relation to social change and scholarly critique.

It might be useful to begin by articulating what kinds of innovations have been fashioned at the juncture between medicine, machines and people's bodies. Bodies have long been extended beyond the

boundaries of peripheral skin through connections to external prostheses. Particularly as a result of successive military conflicts, countless
populations have survived the effects of injury to use devices including wheelchairs and artificial limbs. Today, external prostheses range
from the routine (hearing aids, glasses, cosmetic scar covers, etc.) to
life-sustaining technologies such as dialysis machines, respirators and
systems for supporting patients with liver failure, etc.

In addition to sprawling external connections between bodies and
prosthetic devices, we have seen a growing number of prosthetics
operate under the surface of the body. These include inert implantable
devices such as joint replacements (for hip, knee and now ankle),
devices to correct penile dysfunction, skull-bone replacements, breast
implants, and so on. Many implants are far from inert and instead
actively perform animate functions. Pacemakers electronically regulate the rhythms of the heart. Cochlear implants generate tiny oscillat-
ing vibrations to stimulate auditory nerves. Numerous drug delivery
devices, particularly for diabetics, now operate under the surface
of the body, releasing drug dosages automatically when prompted
by diagnostic sensors. Somewhat more futuristic is the prospect of
nanotechnological devices to fulfil a whole range of functions, from
recoating worn joints to repairing blood vessels, etc.

Even at a cursory level it is clear to see that one of the most interesting analytical tensions here lies between these notions of oldness
and newness, the mundane and the exotic. Mechanical prostheses
have a rich heritage, stretching far back into the Middle Ages and
beyond. For instance, the drawings of the military physician Ambrose
Pare during the mid-1500s depict highly sophisticated mechanical
prosthetic hands and legs for the casualties of numerous French conflicts. Today, figures such as Stephen Hawkins and Christopher Reeve
represent more contemporary expressions of the prosthetic self.

It is fair to say that these notions of the mundane and the exotic
signal important divisions in the interpretation of prosthetics and
implants. For example, many historians of 'assistive technologies'
critically observe that disabled people's experience of machines has
been neglected for years largely because it is seen as simply not up-to-
the-minute enough to have attracted concerted scholarly attention.
Indeed, the recent social science and humanities fascination with
cyborgs is, they note, evidence of an academic myopia that too often
privileges accounts of the exotic over those of the mundane and the
everyday.

The story of prosthetics is coextensive with the history of marginal
groups of disabled people, who have often been overlooked by critical accounts of medicine and technology. Prosthetic limbs and other

body parts, as Katherine Ott notes, are markers of marginality (2002). Unlike the more recently romanticized notions of cyborg identity, the use of mundane prosthetics is born of necessity rather than yearning. 'Voluntary bionics can be very desirable. But when the wearer has less of a choice, or when the technology references disability and not glamour, the attraction of engineered beauty fades. Rehabilitation technology is not worshiped in popular culture' (ibid., 21).

More importantly, prosthetic technologies have evolved in relation to various social expectations about the duties of disabled people to wider society. These might be reflected in implicit yet pervasive obligations towards productive citizenry. For example, the development of cochlear implants to correct hearing loss has raised serious objections from deaf people, for whom the technology constitutes a failure of social inclusivity (Blume 1997, 2000a). Subjects have to undergo a highly invasive procedure that is often painful and distressing in order to 'comply' with mainstream communication. Blume, in his historical study of cochlear implant innovation dating back to the late 1970s, notes how researchers would represent deafness as a 'tragic affliction and the deaf individual as excluded and alone' (2000a, 149). Deaf advocacy organizations, however, have fiercely rejected such victim identities and have had a highly fractious relationship with research communities. Here, then, the embodiment of a device is resisted not because of any metaphysical misgivings about human–machine coupling but because of the risks that prosthesis poses to established and valued senses of identity and language.

The cochlear implant is only one among numerous illustrations of the sometimes conflicting interests of medical research and different communities of users. Many of these conflicts centre on the kinds of role that medicine is fulfilling in the relationship between disabled people on the one hand and wider society on the other. The medical devices industry has been seen as a means of excusing wider politics from its responsibilities to inclusiveness. The logic of medicalized disability, it has been argued, is to identify the 'deficient' body as that which needs re-engineering for better integration into the world. Or, as Ott puts it: 'Diagnosis defines bodily difference as pathology. The process of diagnosis, whether formal or informal, places difference within organisational categories of loss and inadequacy. . . . This is inevitable because that is what medical diagnosis and its social counterpart are for: to a person with a hammer, everything looks like a nail' (2002, 8). Similarly, Jain, in her critique of prosthesis as metaphor (for human-technical relations), recognizes their role as 'that which supplies the deficiency' or that which constitutes disability (1999, 33).

Medical technology and the innovation of prosthetic devices might therefore be understood as an important axis in the 'technological contract' between disabled people and society. Devices mirror in arte-factual terms many of the conventional features of the able-bodied world. That is, materially, they reflect not only 'able-bodied' limbs but also architectures, practices, design and communication conventions. And yet the built environment and its relationship to prosthetic technologies has been the focus of concerted change, especially as a consequence of growing disability activism since the 1960s. Discourse around disability rights has produced important shifts in legislation and made 'access' a core consideration in the design of both environments and prosthetics. To this extent, assistive devices and the context of their usage have been shaped within a process of mutual innovation and adaptation.

For instance, wheelchairs have, according to Woods and Watson, undergone a radical transition from being 'cumbersome machines designed principally to transport a "patient" from one place to another (usually within the confines of an institution, be it hospital or residential home) into powerful tools of mobility' (Woods and Watson 2004). Alongside these technical changes have emerged new registers of political advocacy and self-determination. In essence, the wheelchair now facilitates resistance to paternalistic notions of 'patient care', subverting older designs based on the clinician as principal user. Where once these highly standardized 'political machines' (Barry 2001) were designed for the convenience of the caring professions, wheelchairs are now expected to embody the many different demands of disabled people as *consumers* of technology, and not *objects* of technology. Building on the points above, wheelchair innovation has extended deep into environments of use through, for example, the widening of passageways, alterations to angles of ascent and descent between different levels, etc.

Many of these considerations reflect important changes in the techno-cultural landscape through which new relationships between users and technologies emerge. For instance, while legislative changes are reshaping the built environment, distinctly new regulatory cultures are emerging around prosthetics themselves. Some have suggested that these intensifying democratization pressures are now heralding 'a new era' in medical device governance (Kent and Faulkner 2002). That is, new networks of consumer pressure have been instrumental in reordering thresholds of safety and risk. This has resulted in much greater post-implantation device surveillance and new vigilance systems with which to monitor prosthetics.

Kent and Faulkner's study of new governance regimes affecting implantable prosthetic devices also sheds light on the way small incremental changes both in regulatory structures and in materials can entirely reshape the fortunes of implants. In their account, they explore the cases of two implantable devices that were recently withdrawn from the market place – the Trilucent breast implant and the 3M Capital hip prosthesis, both of which underwent small material adaptations in their design. These adaptations arose because the industry needed to maintain competitive distinctiveness within the market for implants and could only really achieve this by introducing relatively novel innovations into otherwise routine technologies. And yet, even these minor changes were sufficient to destabilize their safety and efficacy. The artefacts showed some signs of premature failure, and doubts were raised about the design changes on which their commercial innovativeness had been built. At the same time, the formation and implementation of the European Medical Devices Directive indicated the emergence of a relatively new governance regime. Hitherto, commentators had observed the powerful pressures of industry on regulation. But this has now, Kent and Faulkner argue, begun to be uncoupled as policy-making becomes increasingly oriented to notions of public participation, or what they describe as 'a more user-oriented shaping of regulation' (2002, 189).

The example of Trilucent breast implants and the 3M Capital hip replacement are important here because of the way they illustrate concepts of novelty on the one hand and the routine on the other. In any discussion of new medical technology it is often tempting to overplay the significance of radical revolutionary change. It is therefore sometimes easy to overlook the way routine technologies can express significant alterations in the relationships between relevant stakeholders and the material attributes of design and engineering. Here, even modest adaptations to the technology resulted in consequences that were ultimately disproportionate to the initial design changes. Equally modest realignments in the relationships between political actors have again resulted in somewhat far-reaching implications for the devices themselves and the many thousands of people into whom they were implanted. These hybrid alignments across humans, machines and institutional forms are notoriously volatile, and it can sometimes take very little for them to behave in highly unpredictable ways.

Evidently, then, the mundane and the exotic, new and old, are highly unstable and interlocking. And yet, still, a persistent thread running through recent social science literatures on prosthetics highlights radically technical dreams of cyber-substitution. As Ott puts it, 'since the 1960s, bionics and cybernetic organisms, or cyborgs, have over-taken more conventional prosthetic devices as the popular symbol of human–machine hybrids' (2002, 21). The cultural conception of technical substitution for human capacities is based on a view that increasingly subordinates nature to technology. Or, rather, notions of 'imperfect nature' are grounded in discourses about technology that stress the inability of nature to stand alone. Instead, the technolo-gical prosthesis adds to, enhances, or compensates for the deficiencies of nature. These views frame much of the discussion about 'assistive technologies' in the context of disablement as they do 'assisted con-ception' in the context of reproduction.

Take, for instance, one such 'prosthetic self' alluded to earlier. Stephen Hawking has come to prominence as probably one of the most widely recognizable contemporary figures in science, certainly in physics. As a result of progressively degenerative muscular atrophy, Hawking has been left virtually paralysed. Almost completely im-mobile, his body is encased in a complex electrical and mechanical system that allows him limited mobility and access to various informa-tion resources. A respiratory infection has resulted in the need for a tracheotomy and now the use of a computer synthesizer through which he communicates with the world. In many respects, he has become entirely inseparable from the prosthetic apparatus that we now associ-ate with him. As Stone reflects on watching him deliver a lecture once:

> exactly where, I say to myself is Hawking? ... a serious part of Hawking extends into the box in his lap. In mirror image, a serious part of that silicon and plastic assemblage in his lap extends into him as well ... not to mention the invisible ways, displaced in time and space, in which discourse of medical technology and their physical accretions already permeate him ... no box, no discourse ... with the box his voice is auditory and simultaneously electronic, in a radically different way from that of a person speaking into a microphone. Where does he stop? Where are his edges? (Stone 1995, 5)

Now, for Hawking, all of this references much that we associate with great scientific genius. In the Western Cartesian tradition, mind and body are arranged hierarchically. Thought hovers outside of the material world that it observes. Great minds are somehow detached or disconnected from the earthiness of natural embodiment. For the true Cartesian positivist, the world is viewed from a distance by a detached and abstract intellect. Hawking is exemplary in these terms; he is literally a disembodied mind with, as Mialet puts it, an 'almost invisible body' (1999, 29). The body that remains is further disguised by the very technological gadgetry that somehow extends the cult of genius and scientific brilliance with which he is associated.

Sentiments of prosthetic romanticism go back a long way. Roy Porter's essay on older visions of medicine's futures notes a growing historical antipathy towards the body as something simply out of keeping with civilizing progress. He refers to the early twentieth-century commentator J. D. Bernal, who looked forward to a time when 'Bodies . . . would be left far behind.' 'Normal man', he argued, 'is an evolutionary dead end; mechanical man, apparently a break in organic evolution, is actually more in the true tradition of a further evolution' (in Porter 2001, 40).

Now this is not to reduce Hawking's reputation to this substitution of his body by technology. Simply that there is a complex indivisibility between the disembodiment of his mind and his reputation in physics and the wider public world. The important point here is that a figure such as Hawking allows us to glimpse the subtle undercurrents of cultural longing associated with the substitution of the body by technology.

Human–machine couplings require that one surrenders identification with singular wholeness but at the same time entertains new possibilities beyond the limitations of the body. These extremes of disgust and yearning represent parallel responses to the loss of organic integrity, or what Wilson calls the 'divided consciousness' of prosthetic life (1995, 244). 'My body seems always to be dissolving, failing in one way or another, needing supplements . . . Each prosthetic modification marks the distance I will have travelled from my original condition' (ibid., 239).

There are then important ambivalences running through contemporary prosthetic culture. As Jain (1999) points out, such devices are simultaneously enabling and yet also wounding. Prosthetics 'supply the deficiency' but they also resolve deficiencies. That is, they signal immobility while facilitating mobility. A prosthesis can 'fill a gap, but can also diminish the body and create the need for itself' (ibid.). They are a source of longing and fascination, as evident in the Hawking case, and yet they are a source of fear and apprehension at having to 'give up' one's nature to technology.

While Hawking seems to have come to represent the utopian undercurrents of 'assisted nature', a similarly recognizable figure, Christopher Reeve, invokes contrary associations. The former actor is indissolubly connected to the life-sustaining technologies that surround him. Even the rhythms of his speech are mechanically synchronized with the respirator that regulates his breathing. But, by contrast to Hawking, Reeve signifies the desperateness of a body seeking *escape* from prosthetic identity. While enabled by the technologies that now substitute for his paralysed body, he is widely recognized as suffering at the hands of his technology.

This is not to suggest that Hawking is in a necessarily desirable relationship to prostheses. But there is little in the commentary that surrounds him to suggest that he is as oriented to an escape from technological substitution. Rather, it seems fitting that scientific reasoning should be embodied within such a highly engineered corporality. By contrast, Reeve is represented, and represents himself, as a desperately unwilling participant in the complex life-sustaining technologies in which his failing body is embedded. He has become a potent symbol for disability campaigning and advocacy, particularly in respect to new and innovative biomedical research. Indeed, the Christopher Reeve Paralysis Foundation is principally geared towards sponsoring innovative research into 'treatments and cures' for spinal cord injury.

And, most importantly, Reeve has taken a high-profile position in publicly defending new research into stem cell technologies and cloning. In this way, then, he has come to represent an important axis in the distinctions between mechanical and biological technologies of substitution. Where mechanical prostheses seem cumbersome and limiting, a poor reflection of the organic faculties they are supposed to replace, cellular therapies and regenerative medicine promise to replace like with like. Or, put differently, stem cell approaches go as far as promising the substitution of self with self.

These then are the important distinctions running across innovative medical approaches to the substitution of the body and its parts. While, xenotransplantation depends on replacing human tissues with animal tissues, touching on human–animal boundaries, prosthetics prompt questions about complex human–machine relationships. On the other hand, the questions related to stem cells centre on what we can and cannot do with replacement tissues cultured using the donor's own DNA to create transplantable life. It is to some of these questions that we now turn to look at cloning and regenerative medicine.

Regenerative medicine – substituting self with self

Events in 1997 gave rise to a new episode in the whole story of transplantation technology. In the wake of the Dolly event, innumerable committees, special reports, publications and public consultations were established and attest to the huge ambivalences that inhere within replacement tissues and their various origins.

Probably the most distinctive aspect of the technique used to create Dolly was the claim that the nucleus of an adult mammalian cell had been 'tricked' into behaving like the very first cell of an embryo. Adult body cells, while tissue-specific, nevertheless contain an individual's full complement of DNA. In the Dolly case, the nucleus was inserted into an unfertilized egg (from which the nucleus had been removed) and was coaxed into the processes of cell division. The resulting animal was then an adult replica of an individual that had in fact died six years earlier. In humans, the technique could be used to create tissues immunologically matching the source DNA.

Inducing adult cells to behave like embryonic (pluripotent) stem cells means that an individual's tissues could be cultured and then instructed to differentiate into a required tissue type. The resulting tissues would then be an exact immunological (histocompatible) match when reimplanted into the body from where they were taken. While most other forms of transplantation (whether from other humans or indeed animals) and implantation (of devices) involve varying degrees of rejection, the Dolly event has opened up the prospect of removing rejection risk entirely, by replacing self with self. From blood vessels and neural tissues to larger organ systems, the promises surrounding stem cells have lately seemed boundless. A biotech company recently announced the successful production of heart cells, beating rhythmically in a petri dish, which stands as just one potent symbol of promise to have emerged from the industrial sector.

The cloning debate, possibly like no other, illustrates the incredible ways in which the temporality of life, in any simple sequential sense, is being entirely reordered. It illustrates why, for instance, in a chapter on transplantation and the replacement of the body, it is necessary to evoke the relationship between biomedicine and reproduction, the subject of Chapter 3. Stem cells, are, as Franklin notes, 'good places to look for indicative evidence of changes in how the social is being defined in the context of biomedicine' (2001, 338). They mark the way biological and social innovation are mutually implicated in one another. More specifically, embryonic stem cells inextricably link the substitution of the ageing body and its parts with other potent entities in modern biomedicine, notably the embryo and the very beginnings of life.

These innovations are closely tied into the different sites from which stem cells are collected. While adult stem cells can be obtained from a person's blood, bone marrow and some other tissues, they are seemingly far less pliant to being redirected to perform other roles when called upon. The promise of stem cells then has come to rest on the availability of embryos, usually 'spare' blastocysts left over from IVF treatment. Now the approach taken to produce Dolly drew embryo techno-politics in an entirely unprecedented direction, and rearranged the social and genetic relations in which embryos and replacement tissues are embedded. Here, of course, the embryo's genetic identity emerges not from two complementary sets of DNA, but from a single genetic source, a single parent.

One of the most powerful organizing distinctions in these newly exotic relations is that between the 'reproductive' and 'therapeutic' intentions surrounding cloning by nuclear transfer. The former has been the focus of concerted prohibitive legislation, with a few occasionally newsworthy exceptions of groups attempting to produce cloned infants. The latter by contrast rests on the argument that nuclear transfer is a necessary step in producing a whole range of cell types and techniques that will, some suggest, ultimately become the mainstay to substituting the body's failing parts.

Boundaries such as this are important in distinguishing between different forms of social and biological risk. In this case, 'reproductive cloning' is defined as a moral issue and ruled out by culturally normative regulation. On the other hand, the regulation of 'therapeutic cloning' comes down to technocratic oversight. These divisions between the social and the technical are never absolute but reflect important emphasis in the regulation of biomedicine. Often these boundaries serve to protect traditional technical expert-led governance systems from the mushrooming of wider political interest and advocacy (Salter and Jones 2002).

Moreover, as Franklin has noted, therapeutic cloning technically compounds existing moral difficulties that attend using either aborted or spare embryos from IVF procedures. In nuclear transfer, 'it is difficult to imagine organized political or religious objection to culturing a patient's own liver cells to prevent him or her dying of liver failure' (Franklin 2001, 346). Nevertheless, strong objections persist from those for whom the early embryo remains a focus of strong political and ethical identification. As we noted in Chapter 3, the envelope of moral community surrounding the embryo is inherently plastic, flexing in different directions according to how, in this case, stem cells are created and also the purposes to which they are put in research and treatment.

These notions of community or commonality are complex and, to date for most people, quite unrehearsed. Nuclear transfer poses entirely new connections between the recipients of tissues and the bodies from which they are sourced. It is as yet difficult to judge in what ways recipients will respond to the creation of what is, in principle, a delayed genetic twin from which replacement tissues would be derived. These are important alterations in the generational chronology of the self and one's lifecourse. Or, as Waldby puts it, stem cells will doubtless have 'unpredictable implications for identity and embodiment. What does it mean when the human body can be disaggregated into fragments that are derived from a particular person, but are no longer constitutive of human identity' (Waldby 2002, 308).

Regenerative medicine implies important shifts in the relationships between donors and recipients. Conventional transplantation of whole organs, tissues and blood, at the broadest level, operates in relation to admittedly problematic ideals of altruistic citizenry and community. Stem cells, however, promise the prospect of replacing self with self, sourcing tissues from 'the very margins of (pre-) human life' (Waldby 2002, 313). Where whole organs are usually transplanted and 'given' complete, stem cells have a far more distributed and fractured identification. Or, rather, 'a single cell disaggregated from the embryo might form the basis for an incalculable amount of therapeutic tissue, transplanted into innumerable recipients, for a diversity of conditions, over an unspecified length of time' (ibid.). More importantly, in what ways would recipients engage with the distinctions and differences between the techniques used to source stem cells from either surplus or specially cloned embryos?

In turn, the reshaping of life in order to create replacement tissues extends from the embryo and into derived cells themselves. The capacity to preserve, store and create, in perpetuity, successive generations of cells from one cloned embryo again stretches the temporalities of embodiment. 'Eternal cell-lines' of regenerative medicine undo the conventionally linear notions of birth, life and death. In a slightly more removed way, the infrastructures on which research and treatment will depend establish tendril-like associations between people and the newly forming repositories and banks being created to archive and distribute stem cells.

This, of course, again raises questions about the basis on which people are prepared, or not, to give up their bodies to integration across vast public and private networks of research. The credibility of tissue banks and archives has been tainted by intensifying commodification pressures on the one hand, and a series of scandals about the retention of organs without consent on the other. Communities of relationality, responsibility and reciprocity are in constant states of change and responsiveness to these and other pressures. 'Gift', as we noted above, is far from stable as the basis on which people do or do not partake in tissue economies. The ultimate purposes of stem cells are not exclusively to provide treatments within a gift economy, but are also the focus of profit and investment within economies of selling. These tensions are likely to be crucial to the way regenerative medicine develops for the foreseeable future.

Again, as with all of the innovative techniques discussed above, different kinds of social and material risks coalesce. For example, there are fears that transplanted cells and tissues may be subject to inconsistent rates of ageing, replication and mortality. Tissues may mutate or continue to multiply uncontrollably within the host body. In these terms, then, live replacement tissues may prove to be just as difficult to regulate *in vivo* as in the institutions and governance structures that seek to regulate them socially, politically and legally.

Conclusion

In this chapter we have explored the role of medical technology in changing the relations between humans and a whole host of other culturally and materially volatile entities, notably machines, animals and human embryos. And it is clear that, in each case, quite new considerations and challenges have begun to emerge, requiring probing analytical consideration if we are to make sense of their relative importance to health and embodiment now and in the future. One means of analysis for us has been to explore some of the tensions within which each of the technologies discussed above is embedded.

These strange couplings are the focus of awe and fascination while also being cause for disgust and loathing. They simultaneously wound their bearers while providing for their enablement and even survival. The substitution of the body threatens the fragmentation of the embodied self. But it also provides for a new sense of wholeness founded in the welcome incorporation of the mechanical, human or animal other. Additionally, there are important tensions played out across what we mean by politics on the one hand and science on the other.

We want to conclude this chapter by exploring some analytical thinking that has focused explicitly on tensions such as these, particularly in the work of Douglas, Latour, Haraway and others. Importantly, we want to suggest a more flexible means of understanding the variability and plasticity of the way people make sense of innovation in the replacement of body parts.

Clearly, notions of pollution and disgust underpin many of the debates opened up above. Put simply, dirt is 'matter out of place', a 'by product of a systematic ordering and classification of matter . . . in short, our pollution behaviour is the reaction which condemns any object or idea likely to confuse or contradict cherished classifications' (Douglas [1966] 1994, 37). Matter has been lifted out of one place and relocated to that of another, thus corrupting some form of binary division. A diseased human organ is removed and replaced with the healthy organ of an animal. A bacterial or viral agent is used to transfer a strand of DNA from one species to that of another. Or the borders between life and death themselves become the focus of a pollution problematic when the unwell living are transplanted with the tissues of the well dead. The derivation of stem cells from an embryo cloned using one's own DNA places one's own embodiment outside of its proper place within our normal biography. In Douglas's terms, the concept of dirt is a pervasive anthropological constant serving to combat disorderly behaviour. The mixing of life and death, animal and human, machine and human, generates new forms of 'dirt'.

Dirt is a complex category that cannot be understood as being necessarily either social or material. That is, explanations for the pollution and the ambivalences that it causes cannot be found 'in the matter itself'. Importantly, then, Douglas contests purely materialist or hygienist explanations which do not also acknowledge the role of the cultural and symbolic. Nevertheless, whether in discussions about xenotransplantation or gene therapy, materialist explanations have some weight, and arguably should do too, given the sheer physical threat of disease contagion, tissue rejection, and so on. But the point is that the hygienist repertoire cannot be lifted out or abstracted from the cultural and symbolic world in which it is embedded. Networks in which, say, biotechnology is constituted as 'risk' are simultaneously dependent on technical and moral activities and values.

Innovation is inherently a process whereby boundaries and new elements are continually reinterpreted and combined, often to produce truly novel entities operating in entirely new relational networks. Technologies of replacement are being deployed in a far from motionless or stable symbolic and material order. Instead of being uniformly resisted, body innovations are just as saturated with desire and fascination. So, in analytically understanding technologies of substitution, we need to be able to soften some of the rigidity that tends to foreground the structuralism of the Douglasian perspective.

In addition to these boundaries between disgust and yearning, replacement techniques are tied to organizing distinctions between science and politics. We could see this, for instance, in the separation between reproductive cloning as a *moral* consideration and therapeutic cloning as a *technocratic* consideration. Latour's *We Have Never Been Modern* (1993) sets out to deconstruct just such boundary-making, particularly between 'science' and 'politics' or between the 'natural world' and 'human culture'. This he calls the 'modern constitution', historically reaching back into the Enlightenment, whereby the practice of science and the practice of politics become increasingly divorced from one another. We have since become accustomed to a world in which science speaks for natural objects or objectively knowable nature. On the other hand, politics speaks for human political subjects and deals in the messy business of values, culture and morality.

The division means that science has been able to operate without having to think of itself as a political or value-laden activity. The only requirement of science is to serve as a 'modest witness' to nature, to interpret what nature would say if only it could speak (Shapin and Schaffer 1985). For science, then, research and innovation has tended to be a neutral activity, simply because political questions lie elsewhere, in committee rooms, parliamentary offices and ethical committees.

Like Douglas, Latour has been interested in the practices that reinforce divisions. So when politics enters into science, the guardians of the modern constitution ritually seek to purge the latter of the former, reinforcing science's distinctiveness from questions of moral order. However, unlike Douglas, Latour is much more interested in the way these distinctions are being transformed. Technologies and knowledges are hybrid or networked assemblages; they are irreducible to either social or natural explanations. On the one hand, we continue to switch between scientific and cultural registers in searching for a handle on the world, only to find that this switching causes the proliferation of a whole universe of hybrid entities. We might actually understand these hybrids as, in Douglas's terms, the by-products or 'dirt' of the modern constitution.

For Latour, the modern constitution separating humans from nonhumans is collapsing under the weight of highly potent material–political hybrids such as clones, transgenes or xenotransplants. The hybrid is then a subversive formation expressing the irreducibility of things. So hybrids have a double-sided resonance here. On the one hand, they have positive potential in forcing moderns to recognize the contradictions of the modern constitution. But, on the other hand, hybrids harbour huge risks. For example, xenotransplanted hybrids have the potential to come apart because of immunological rejection processes, or they may become a conduit for the movement of diseases between hitherto distinct species. Given these and other dystopic prospects, Latour calls for a slowing down of the proliferation of hybrids, a deceleration whereby space is created for hybrids to be analytically acknowledged and represented 'officially' (1993, 12). In this sense, then, Latour represents a mid-point between the stasis of a Douglasian anthropological account and some of the more evanescent positions evident in the work of scholars such as Donna Haraway.

In Haraway's writing, a much more utopian version of the hybrid emerges in her account of the cyborg. Far from being a dystopian figure, the cyborg embraces the prospect of strange couplings that ultimately demolish oppressive dichotomies operating across genders, race, species and machines. It is important here to understand the reasoning behind the cyborg as a political identity, which is somewhat distinct from Latour's use of hybrids as an analytical instrument for documenting the complexity of networks. Haraway wants to promote the hybrid as a means of moving political feminist discourse away from reliance on a single-uniform natural identification. The cyborg is a political identity situated in a context of immense possibility: 'By the late twentieth century, our time, a mythic time, we are all chimeras, theorized and fabricated hybrids of machine and organism; in short, we are cyborgs' (Haraway 1991, 150). So the cyborg is a deliberately political figure that reflects a strong sense of being situated within networks that are potentially both liberatory and yet oppressive. Far from being situated in these terms, Latour's analytical point of perspective, the hybrid, is locationless and somewhat divorced from an overtly political agenda (Michael 2000, 31).

This stress on political subjectivity draws attention to the cyborg as a site of embodied desire and aspiration. The substitution of the body's failing parts with those drawn from other species, machines and embryos emerges out of the aspiration to transcend one's self or one's context, even if that ultimately means the contravention of existing moral and natural categories. A physical fusion with machinery can facilitate movement or strengthen weakened limbs, embodying the tissues of another may extend life, and so on. The situatedness and the politicization of Haraway's cyborg moves us away from the reticence and abstractness of Latour's position and still further away from the stasis of Douglas's account of disgust. This emphasis on situatedness makes the important point that the replacement of the body, like many other facets of health technology, emerges from the embodied circumstances in which pain and suffering is experienced.

Table 5.1 Substituting the body

Continuities	Discontinuities
Human to human transplantation (allotransplants)	Non-human to human transplantation (xenotransplants)
Individual risks of rejection	Population-wide risks of interspecies viral infection
Other humans as tissue sources	Somatic cell nuclear transfer: self as tissue source
Disgust	Cultural innovation

In this chapter, then, we have been able to trace the way in which medical technology, innovation and wider cultural repertoires are involved in a mutual process of change. Without placing too much emphasis on novelty, our purpose has been to locate aspects of contemporary distinctiveness that stand out as key markers separating the continuities of the past from those of the present. Table 5.1 identifies the more significant of these.

The substitution of the body, and the way in which it is ordered symbolically and materially, is in a constant state of transformation and becoming. Each of the three aspects of innovative activity discussed here, in addition to others, implies quite distinct problems and possibilities, both for the experience of embodiment and for analytical scrutiny. In the following chapter, we turn from the replacement and substitution of the body to technologies that attend to the dying and dead body.

6

Technologies of Death and Dying

Introduction

A person's death is seen as an inevitable physical event marking the end of the lifecourse. Despite its apparent inevitability and finality, however, a person may 'live on' through the memories and memorials that follow death, especially where these are made 'sacred' through religious rite and belief. Or, indeed, forms of social death may precede physical mortality through the sequestration of the dying body. In this chapter, we discuss the ways in which NMTs have begun not only to deny or at least hold death at bay, but also to redefine and manage the meaning of death itself. Death can no longer be seen as being defined simply in terms of the biological end of a bounded and specific body, for not only might a person's identity (through memory of them) prevail long after death but so also might elements of their biophysical form in the shape of DNA data, tissue repositories, eternal cell-lines, transplants, stored eggs and frozen sperm. In this way NMTs and the complex of research, regulatory and commercial networks through which they function have redefined death and the point at which death is seen to have occurred.

Indeed in one sense death has been a strong driver of medical technologies, its denial dependent on the development of highly innovative technologies. When these techniques of intervention fail, as they eventually must, new causes of death and technologies that might address them have to be found. And so on, *ad infinitum*. Death-denying innovation is especially associated with the world of the intensive care unit. Here the body's functions are kept alive through a vast array of technologies designed as proxy lungs, heart, liver, and so on. One's body yields up to the technology, a process that Selzer describes as

> The martyrdom of the intensive care unit . . . The man in the bed is to be ventilated, dosed, defibrillated, probed, suctioned, and infused. Most of his bodily functions will be taken over. No longer need he swallow, chew, inhale, or exhale, cough, urinate, defecate, clear his throat, maintain acid-base balance, cogitate, remember, sigh, weep, laugh, desire. (in Lock 2002, 55)

The more that medical technologies capture death, the more the meaning of death is reworked, seen to be the result of different diseases and pathologies, now including 'old age' itself, of course. Death is no longer the cut and swathe of the 'Grim Reaper' but the result of the constellation of disease, germs or 'complications' that set in. The deconstruction of death and mortality into an increasingly complex range of processes and forms means that the end of the lifecourse is less easy to define, as is the meaning of a 'dignified death', though this is often seen as an unconscious, painless passing away. Such a death is dignified as much for the relatives and physicians as it is for the deceased, since it allows for a successfully managed death. This is rarely the case when relatives, carers and clinicians are coping with someone who is in a so-called persistent vegetative state, kept alive through artificial means, often perhaps retrieved from death by being brought back to life, by being re-produced.

It is in fact somewhat ironic that this is the last of the chapters through which we look at the relationship between new technologies and the lifecourse, because we could so easily have chosen death as the starting point for this book, since it is an important impetus for innovation in medicine and health. Nevertheless, the chapter stresses one of the important points that we have tried to articulate throughout this book: that living and dying, at all of their different stages, are being radically reshaped and even reordered through a complex mix of techno-social innovation. In this chapter, we explore some of the technologies that have now begun both to redefine and to fragment death across far more numerous socio-technical worlds than ever before. In so doing, our technologies have generated whole new registers through which think about, experience and embody death and dying.

At the same time, of course, we need to remember that medicine has itself been a source of death – we have already made mention of the many thousands who die each year because of adverse drug reactions or other clinical interventions. But first, we want to sketch out some of the main contributions that have been made by those work-ing in the sociology of death.

The sociology of death

Until fairly recently, the topic of death within the field of sociology was often relegated to the work undertaken by demographers or social epidemiologists, where deaths were viewed in terms of patterns of mortality in a population, such as variation by social class or region. Just as it is possible to measure fertility and birth rates, so a mortality rate can be determined for the population as a whole. These patterns are important indicators of social advantage and disadvant-age, of the links between morbidity (ill health) and its outcome in death as experienced by different groups, and as such have provided vital information for those exploring social stratification and inequal-ity. Although the number of deaths in advanced affluent countries has remained roughly stable per year over the past fifty years, falls in the death rate have occurred over this period. So, for example, while approximately 550,000 people die in the UK each year, the death rate fell from 12.1 per cent to 10.1 per cent between 1971 and 2001 (ONS 2002), though it is lower in the US, at 8.7 per cent. The fall in rates indicates increasing longevity across the population as a whole and might reflect improved nutrition, wider changes in the environ-ment and the impact of medicine itself. We must remember, however, that, when we look at death rates for particular sections of a popu-lation, these will vary considerably according to class and minority groups.

Today, cancer, heart disease and strokes are the primary causes of most mortalities in affluent industrial countries. In part this is explained by the impact of drugs and acute heart surgery, which have extended the life of those who may have died, but who eventually die from a chronic heart problem such as congestive heart failure (CHD). In the US, while hospitalization for most conditions has declined, admissions for CHD increased by 62 per cent for those over sixty-five between 1980 and 2001 (NCHS 2003b). Infectious diseases (apart from AIDS in poorer sub-Saharan Africa and elsewhere) have in con-trast declined dramatically in their effect. Cancer is a broad category covering a variety of different diseases related to rapid replication of cells as tumours in the body, though the pace, mortality level and treatment success vary considerably from one form to another. Cancer is very strongly associated with mortality and has been shown to

prompt very dramatic changes in people's lifestyle and personal priorities (Barley et al. 1999). While other illnesses may generate embar-
rassment for those suffering from them when among others, cancer,
because of its link with mortality, creates a sense of personal and
interpersonal 'pollution':

> The sense of pollution is both an internally felt experience of the can-
> cer eating up the inside of the individual but also the stigma that
> marks the individual from others . . . [resulting] in the loss of friend-
> ships and often the erection of barriers between the patient and their
> close family [while] the retreat into the discussion of everything but
> cancer isolates the individual from their social context. (Tritter and
> Calnan 2002, 163)

Whatever the cause of death, national mortality rates are recorded
without any reference to their *meaning as deaths*, as though the deaths
across the period shown were the same *kinds* of events (or measurable units) even if brought about by different diseases or illnesses; as
Prior (1989) observes, 'despite its central concern with death, demo-
graphy did not quite speak of it *per se*. Instead it spoke of "mortality"
and rates of mortality'(p. 7). And, as Bartley and Blane (1997) have
argued, the mortality figures that recount the cause of deaths can
vary considerably: thus, 'standardized mortality rates' (SMR) attribute
major class differences in risk of mortality to variations in heart
disease across unequal social groups, while the measure of 'years of
potential life lost' explains such risk variation by class according to
chances of accidental or violent deaths. These different measures cannot be resolved simply by further statistical refinement, since, as Bartley
and Blane show, they are the product of a complex set of alliances
between professionals in public health, actuaries, government officials,
and so on. Drawing on Latour's (1987) work in STS and the role of
actor networks as composed of competing 'centres of calculation',
they show how the SMR 'developed into its present form rather slowly,
being adapted at each step to shifting constellations of interests, and
contributing, at each step, to a new consensus . . . At various times an
estimate of "true life expectancy" or "true risk of death" is reached
which is good enough for the practical purposes of most of the groups
involved' (Bartley and Blane 1997, 139–47).

Even so, notwithstanding the need to deconstruct apparently hard
measures of mortality, information on the changing pattern of death
can, of course, tell us much about how society in the past must have
been broadly affected by both much *earlier* and *higher* rates of death.

As Jones (1993) has noted, because of the fact that most people died at a relatively early age, 'For nine tenths of human evolution, society was like a village school, with lots of infants, plenty of teenagers and a few – probably harassed – adult survivors' (p. 307).

This past 100 years or so, life expectancy in affluent societies has nearly doubled, and as a result 'for the first time in history most people die old; perhaps as old as biology allows' (Jones 1993, 308), such that the prospects now for any much greater longevity are slim. This growing longevity has had a marked effect on women in particular. For example, in the UK during the nineteenth century women had to cope with a high rate of infant mortality among their children, and could expect their parents to die much younger than today. Death was, for them, a regular and central – almost routine – part of their role in the family and household, more so, given the gender division of labour, than it was for men. Today, not only will their children survive, but so will their parents into old age, as the 'demographic shift' (where an increasing proportion of populations are aged sixty-five and more) kicks in. This means that, for long periods of their lives, women today are less likely to confront the personal and social demands of death; in the Victorian period, death took place in the home, the woman was expected to go into mourning for her partner for an extended period, and would as a widow, it was presumed, dress publicly in the black crêpe clothes of the bereaved. This is hardly ever seen today, though displays of mass public grief, as with the death of Princess Diana in the UK and in New York after '9/11', have become more common, and indeed take an increasingly similar form, fostered not least by their framing by the media. Such mourning is increasingly informal compared with the past, and its collective expression is possibly related to the need to re-create some sort of connection to a symbolic community, an experience that is rare in our highly individualized modernity (Wouters 2002).

This brief observation above about women's changing experience tells us that the changing demographic statistics on mortality rates should be interpreted not only in terms of health, nutrition and improved medicine but also in terms of the implications they have for the *social management* of death and its meaning.

The *meaning* of death(s) was something that, until relatively recently, had been neglected in sociology apart from one or two notable exceptions now regarded as classics. David Sudnow's (1967) study of hospital deaths in the US showed how death is an orchestrated social event managed by hospital staff in a routinized way, while Glaser and Strauss (1971) examined the ways in which death is socially ordered as a *rite de passage*, a movement from the world of the living into the world of the dead; in this they were developing some earlier work of Van Gennep (1960), who had been particularly interested in the transitional role of funeral rites. Funerals perform an important role in allowing the bereaved to return to normal social life and to handle the body in a socially legitimated way, typically in late modern societies through cremation. As Mellor (1993) has shown, funerals, as every other social domain, reflect the different social class and status differences of the dead and those mourning them. They also reflect cultural narratives of a 'good death', a tragic or an unexpected one, and define the boundaries of acceptably respectable deaths – hence the problem dealing with suicides, often regarded as illegitimate deaths, and certainly so by many Christian-based religions.

The technologies of funeria – memorial sculptures, sarcophagi, 'transi tombs', and even the preservation of the dead via formaldehyde for the purposes of a wake – work to reinstate the decaying and decomposing corpse into society, to, as Hallam and Hockey (2001) say, 'fix it as a visible material likeness of self or other in a stabilised' form. Sometimes, such distancing of the deceased from the realities of physical decay is not possible when there is no body to represent in this way. Not surprisingly, especially problematic for relatives are those occasions where death is not accompanied by a dead body – perhaps as a result of a terrible accident, a plane crash, an explosion or other event where bodies may simply never be found. In such circumstances, three social rituals are denied 'those left behind': determining the 'cause' or facts of the death, a sanctioned and proper disposal of the body, and a stabilization of the representation of the body via a funeral monument.

In more general terms, how sociology should handle death raises some interesting questions. For example, sociology quite rightly endeavours to take account of the play of status dimensions, such as class and gender, which shape and inform all social action and interaction. So, just as each of us is, say, gendered equally, since all of us are going to die, should sociology similarly build into its analysis a concern with death as a *chronic feature* of everyday life? Mulkay (1993) argues that we should not, 'because the attribute of mortality is universal, it does not in itself, lead to variations in social conduct; that is we do not behave in any special way when we interact with someone who is going to die at some point in the future which is at present quite *unknown*' (p. 34, emphasis added). This makes sense, especially in regards to those considered 'healthy', but clearly this may not apply to those with terminal illnesses, with whom we *do*

interact in ways that presume the advent of death. And, as we have
seen in earlier chapters, the impact of genetic screening and tests is
producing a new generation of the pre-symptomatically ill whose
anticipated cause of death is known many years in advance. How
they relate to those around them and vice versa may well be shaped
by this apprehension.

Here, NMTs are clearly not only having an effect on the individual
but perhaps pose new questions for sociology that require we consider a wider social anxiety or, as the existentialist Kierkegaard
(1944b) might have said, a 'fear and sickness' towards death, but one
that is paradoxically created by the very much greater diagnostic
power of (genetic) medicine. As a result, among the different 'trajectories' of death that Glaser and Strauss (1968) describe to characterize different degrees of knowledge about impending mortality, that
referring to *uncertain* death at an *unknown* time is likely to become
the common trajectory for many in the twenty-first century.

This is quite distinct from the anxieties that prevailed in the eighteenth and nineteenth centuries over a misdiagnosis of death (and
so the fabrication of an array of devices that could signal, literally,
from the grave that the interred was alive, if not kicking). Rather, the
very much greater complexity of medical diagnosis, coupled with the
biomedical capacity to prolong life (through specialist care regimes),
means that we are uncertain whether we are on the threshold of
death or have many more years of life. Those diagnosed with cancer
experience this ambivalence in the extreme. We are then in a society
where, as Riley (1983, 213) notes, 'death is increasingly postponed',
yet one ironically where the anxiety and apprehension about its ultimate arrival seem to grow. What this tells us is that the relationship
between our deaths and our technologies is continually being redefined, so shaping the social meaning of death in the wider society. It
is to this that we now turn.

The social meaning of death

One of the earliest commentaries on the social meaning of death was
Berger's (1967) work within the sociology of religion, where he argued
that death is a fundamental feature and concern of all societies. Each
society must find a way of coping with it, not least because by definition it spells the end of all individuals and may in some circumstances
– such as plague – threaten the very survival of a whole community
or society. One does not have to refer back to the widespread plagues

of the medieval period here: the current AIDS epidemic in southern and eastern Africa is seen to pose a threat to the very capacity of some of the poorest countries in the world to survive as such. Like Berger, Giddens (1990) argues that death is a fundamental concern for all societies but its character has changed with the onset of late modernity, where its excessive individualization means that contemporary social structure provides no broad, shared context through which meaning can be handled collectively. Death has become, as Mellor and Shilling (1993) have argued, 'sequestered', or hidden from public view, especially through the hospitalization of death, where 'hospitals can be seen as the institutional expression of the modern desire to sequester *corporeal* evidence of sickness and death away from the public gaze' (p. 418). Elias (1987) says much the same thing, pointing to the way in which modern society creates a sense of loneliness among those who are dying: and the more death is sequestered the more our private experience of it becomes heavy with anxiety. Ariès (1981) argues that this sequestering of a 'new type of dying' (p. 560), seen in Western affluent societies, has simply served to make the topic of death ever more a matter of academic, medical and legal debate: 'Shown the door by society, death is coming back in through the window, and it is returning just as quickly as it disappeared' (p. 561).

Mulkay has explored the sequence through which we experience death – one that involves both social and biological markers. He argues that the social death-sequence has had a strongly gendered character, beginning for men when they retire from work, when their social networks and the occupational identity on which they might depend are lost. The future for the retired has been seen to be very different from those actively in work, and, for those closer to their biological death – older people – hardly to exist at all: 'for hospital physicians and other staff the absence of a future for old people is taken utterly for granted in routine interaction' (Mulkay 1993, 35); not surprisingly, the majority of the aged today die in hospital (see table 6.1).

For women, the advent of the social death-sequence has been more closely associated with widowhood, given that, for many, their social lives may have been defined through their spouse. Clearly, Mulkay's arguments may become less tenable given the broad changes in both marital and household patterns and women's and men's position in a more fragmented, less stable and more open detraditionalized labour market. And the 'ageing society' means that an increasing number of men and women are sharing longer periods of retirement.

Table 6.1 United Kingdom data on place of death, 2000

Place of death	All deaths (%)
Hospital	66.5
Hospice	4.3
Other communal establishments	7.8
Home	19.0
Other private houses	2.4

In regard to children, however, the massive reduction over the past century in infant mortality and the ageing of parents has had two effects: first, it has meant that society is much less able to cope with the sudden biological death of a child, where we no longer have available a social death-sequence within which to locate and make sense of this tragic event. Childhood death was handled very differently in nineteenth-century Europe, where all members of the family, even the children themselves, were socialized into the possibility of early death: there was then a much greater intimacy with death. A child's death today is, however, accompanied by shock and disbelief.

Bauman (1992) sees the social meaning of death to have generated a host of survival strategies, ways in which social actors seek to avoid or put off death through lifestyle choices, healthy living, diet, and medication. Where religion once provided a means through which death could be at least trusted as a route through which an after-life was to be secured, the secularization of postmodern society means we are thrown back on our own devices in coping with death. We become locked into a continual self-monitoring of our bodies and our health, losing sight of the inevitability of death itself. Where there is no collectively shared social engagement with death and no religious alternative to its finality, death is individualized, broken up into discrete events or causes or medical conditions – a heart attack, kidney failure, a brain haemorrhage, and so on. So powerful is this framing of death as specific clinical causes that, as Bauman says, 'we do not hear of people dying of mortality' (1992, 5) or of an 'unexplained' death. We seek to handle and humanize mortality as a project that can be managed by both our lifestyle choices and medical knowledge and intervention. The progress of death is not therefore simply biological, but reflects the way social actors determine when and how the dying process has begun: as Strauss (1971) argued, the 'trajectory' of death has varying duration and pattern, such that 'dying trajectories are, then, *perceived courses of dying*, rather than the actual courses themselves' (p. 13, emphasis in original).

The 'denial of death' (as Becker 1997 had described it) and its sequestration are, according to Bendle (2001), linked to the massive changes wrought during the twentieth century, when death in huge numbers through war became commonplace and subsequently sanitized (such as during the Vietnam War, where death was defined as 'collateral damage'); coupled with the rapid medical management of death, these two processes are said by Bendle to lead to the 'industrialization' of death. The militarization and medicalization of death have created a dominant discourse (or 'episteme') of death that can be characterized as the 'administered' death, in the twin senses of to 'manage' and to 'dispense' with death. In these circumstances,

> life and death may be purchased and consumed, valued and depreciated, managed and administered in a fashion entirely consistent with any other commercial or bureaucratic transaction under 'free-market' principles . . . Whatever broader meaning death possesses will increasingly be associated only with *problems* arising from technical, economic and utilitarian considerations. (Bendle 2001, 353)

Indeed these two processes are linked, inasmuch as many of the medical technologies for maintaining death have originated on the battlefield, or in conflict zones more generally. Let us now look more closely at the medicalization of death.

The medicalization of death

In the past, death was dealt with first and foremost in the domestic setting of the family home: today in many, though not all, cases (in countries such as Germany, the Netherlands and the UK, for example, around a third of deaths are unexpected and without medical supervision) death is managed through and by medical practitioners and located primarily in the medical institution of the hospital. Illich (1976) argued that modern medicine has 'brought the epoch of *natural* death to an end' (p. 210). We have, instead, clinically defined death. On the face of it, the clinical definition of death seems unproblematic: as Nuland (1994) describes it, it is 'that short interval after the heart has finally stopped, during which there is no circulation, no breathing, and no evidence of brain function [where] a brief time remains before vital cells lose their viability . . . [of] probably no more than four minutes' (p. 121). We shall see below, however, that there is considerable debate among clinicians about the ways these signs of death are to be read.

At a very basic level, the medicalization of death is expressed simply by virtue of the legal requirement that a doctor issue a medical certificate, an important marker for the formal beginning of the *rite de passage* to the end of life. As a piece of testimony and 'inscription' (Akrich 1992), however, the medical certificate is not unproblematic, for, as Bloor (1991) has shown, physicians may vary considerably in their diagnosis of the cause of the *same* death. Despite this, physicians believe they deploy a consistent, widely shared, expert-based judgement in making such diagnoses: as Bloor observes, 'As with many other medical practices and procedures, colleagues may have a comfortable impression of local uniformity in certifying practices, sustained by the cursory and intermittent nature of collegiate monitoring . . . which fails to reveal the . . . diversity underlying a general consensus' (1991, 284). Even so, as Seale (1998) argues, most of the time certificates function as they are meant to, to provide a medical warrant for death as having occurred according to a particular disease: 'And as medicine contains the promise of intervention into the course of natural disease, so the death certificate is an indirect promise to the living that death can be controlled' (p. 79). Such certificates serve a wider purpose too, for they are the primary material on which the causes and patterns of mortality are determined by demographers: as Prior (1989, 89) notes, 'indeed, the biopolitics of population is founded on these documents.'

Beyond the contingencies of the issuing of a death certificate, medicalization might be said to have three consequences: first, medicalization often means that the process of dying is prolonged simply because of the impact and use of life-extending technologies (such as advanced ventilatory or resuscitation techniques); the second consequence is a sense of a loss of control over death, experienced especially by elderly people, who may be excluded from the decision-making process surrounding the termination of their lives; and finally, a third consequence is the medical administration of death, whereby the dying and the dead need to be accounted for in terms of the economic costs their end-of-life clinical care will incur. The state provides a rationed support for the clinical management of the dying, in the same way that it does for the newly born: how long a person can be expected to be a burden on hospital services – how long, for example, a hospital is prepared to provide a bed for someone in the last few days before the end of their lives has to be calculated and monitored – a sort of terminal audit. There is perhaps a fourth sense of the medicalization of death, which Walter (1994) draws to our attention: inasmuch as it is the corpse that is a key resource for medical anatomy training, then 'not only are dead and dying bodies medicalised, but dead bodies enable the medicalisation of living bodies' (p. 13).

The question of the medical management of death has long been of interest to medical sociology. Diane Crane (1975), in her study of over 3000 physicians, sought their views on when they would maintain or withdraw medical support. She showed how this decision was not merely or crucially dependent on the physical state of the patient but also on whether that patient would be able to re-engage with social life and social functionality if mortality was indeed warded off. The decision on the medical note – 'do not resuscitate' – is informed by both clinical and *social* judgement about the quality of life of the patient. Not surprisingly, Crane's book was called *The Sanctity of Social Life*. While medical technologies enable what Fox (1988) has called 'life-saving' and 'life-prolonging' techniques, these are not always deployed. There are, however, two areas to which we now turn that epitomize both the life-saving and life-prolonging roles of medicine. These are intensive care units and cryonic techniques.

Intensive care technologies

The most evident site where we see the medicalization of death is the hospital intensive care unit (ICU). Indeed, while medicine, as we noted above, is supposed to be able to deliver a dignified death through its provision of painkiller drugs, in the context of the ICU, new medical technologies are often criticized for their creation of a highly 'unnatural' death, where the regime is 'less focussed on human suffering and dignity than on the struggle to maintain vital functions' (Moskovitz and Nelson 1995, 3). Within ICUs there is evidence that the medical regulation of death follows very clear patterns. Harvey (1997) explored the role of ICUs and found staff would deal with patients in ways that were based on informal definitions of a 'standard' death:

> In the withdrawal of active support in ICU, death becomes a subject of far greater scheduling than hitherto, far greater prescription occurs as to how it shall occur and it is highly regulated. . . . There is a procedural attempt to regulate and produce a standard death. (1997, 731)

Intensive care raises questions about the boundary definitions dividing life from death – and questions about the technical imperative – that is the way in which technologies seem to insist on certain courses of action being taken over others (such as the technical facility to be able to extend 'life' beyond or into 'death', however defined). In popular discourse, the technologies of intensive care are profoundly symbolic of what it now means to be near death – for many of us, intensive care has become the practical and physical location in which our deaths take place, surrounded by respirators, life-sign indicators, drips, and so on. This paraphernalia of the ICU can lead us to assume a highly deterministic reading of the power of the ICU to define the experience of death, and, indeed, evidence from those involved in the clinical procedures of the units seems to bear this out. For example, as Lock reports from her US study of ICUs:

> one intensivist describes the numerous printouts, traces, films, and X rays that result from the close monitoring of patients as a kind of 'displacement'. The subjective experience of the patients – their 'personhood' – is unavoidably discounted and replaced by a medical narrative composed of graphs and traces. (Lock 2002, 235)

At the same time, we should be careful how far we push this, since there is clearly a danger of lapsing into a form of technological determinism here. As Seymour (1999) argues, 'it is within the *practice* of clinical work and the *negotiation* of relationships between people involved in that work that the impact of the application of technology is realised' (p. 693, emphasis added). This helps to explain why recent empirical evidence from Seymour, and others (such as Timmermans 1998) working in the sociology of science and medicine, shows how clinical practitioners use ICU technologies to *mimic* the trajectory of 'natural death' through the gradual closing down of various life-extending technologies. As Seymour puts it, we find that there are

> complex strategies employed by medical staff during the withdrawal of medical treatment in intensive care to ensure that alignment is achieved between the potentially divergent trajectories of 'seen' bodily dying, which is recognised on the basis of clinical experience; and the discursive negotiation of 'known' technical dying, which is informed by data from blood results, monitoring equipment, and investigations. (1999, 694)

In short, the highly technical medicalization of death and 'natural death' are not necessarily mutually exclusive as is sometimes argued, not only by analysts, but especially by the popular discourse associated with the right to die movement, who advocate a 'heroic death' (see Seale's 1995 discussion of this). While it is clear that intensive care technologies may well work to 'dehumanize patients', we should note the way such technologies – as Lock herself accepts – are 'buffered' (2002, 63) by doctors, nurses and relatives.

While intensive care is not necessarily new, its technologies and practice have changed considerably over time, and with each change there have been searching reconsiderations of what it means to be dead or alive.

Anthropologists and historians have demonstrated the connection between intensive care change and its implications for the death–life interface over the past thirty or so years (Lock 2002). These accounts show how the concept of 'brain death' emerged to transform what we understand to be the moment of death itself. As Armstrong puts it:

> Death had been a singular event: at one moment the patient was alive then the patient had died, and the clinician could examine the body to determine whether the patient had crossed the threshold. But during the early 1960s death began to be transformed into a temporal 'trajectory of dying.' Closer clinical examination of the moment of dying produced a multiplicity of different deaths . . . From the early 1960s when the flat EEG reading which was held to mark brain death came to dominate analysis of the moment of death, the time of death became a matter for debate. (2000, 249)

The transformation of mortality took place in complex reference to new technical innovations, particularly ventilation and then transplantation. Classically, physical death was registered through the cessation of the movement of the 'vital fluids', principally blood. Since the condition of 'harvested organs' deteriorates from the time of death defined 'classically', a new register has emerged through which to define death separate from the cessation of the heart's rhythms and the body's fluids. This register is the definition of death as death of the 'brain stem'. Without either ventilation or the need for transplant organs, Lock suggests, 'the condition of brain death would never have been marked . . . and could not have been made into either a recognizable diagnosis or a construct for social analysis' (2002, 239). In other words, brain death diagnosis has been key to both enabling and legitimating the removal of organs that are still biologically viable.

Robbins (1996, 190) argues that there are various ways in which the (dead) body is represented for purposes of medical transplantation: as 'machine' (where organs are 'extracted'), as 'ecological resource' (where organs are harvested for the greater good), as 'gift' (where organs are donated), and as 'commodity' (where organs are 'procured'). These different characterizations of the body–organ relation help us see why Lock encourages us to think of the corpse as a highly unstable hybrid (as Latour 1993 might argue) or cyborg (as Haraway would suggest). Corpses are subject to conflicts of definition between contrasting narratives drawn from nature on the one hand and the social on the other. Indeed, sometimes such narratives work to prevent organ retrieval from a dead body, where relatives simply refuse to allow it to take place (which in the UK and US occurs in approximately 30 per cent of cases; see Robbins 1996).

In looking at intensive care and the corpse, Lock asks the question 'why in specific locales certain cyborgs raise little concern, while in others they create havoc' (2002, 237). For example, death of the brain varies legally across different cultures, legislatures and medical systems. While largely not regarded as a source of danger in Western Europe and America, it was only as recently as 1997 that brain death became a legally recognized state in Japan, and even then only where prior permission had been expressly given for organ donation. In the absence of this, the 'dead' are legally still 'alive' (ibid.).

This relationship between the legal status of the body and its role as a provider of organs is made more complex in the case of suspicious deaths from homicide or accidents that require the intervention of the coroner and forensic police. Medical examiners, as Timmermans (2002) has pointed out, are subject to the competing pressures of both their clinical networks and those within the legal establishment: 'the result has become a struggle about access to the corpse that [has over the past decade] pitted the transplant community's promise of "the gift of life" against the medical examiners' mandate to determine the "cause of death" in forensic cases' (p. 551).

Within the medical regime of the ICU, the category of brain death is itself highly malleable. On the one hand, the technologies of artificial respiration are insufficient to sustain a patient indefinitely, and eventually the heart begins to fail and blood pressure falls. On the other hand, brain death merges into 'self-sustaining' life when respiration is withdrawn but where heart function and respiration continue. In such cases, we see the emergence of the new nomenclature of death and life such as in PVS, 'persistent vegetative state'. In turn, this facilitates a new repertoire of technical intervention, especially feeding, and its withdrawal in some cases.

Much of what we have observed thus far relates to adult intensive care therapies and decisions. There are some significant differences that we have to consider when exploring the role of ICUs in the case of neonatal children. Neonatal intensive care has allowed many seriously ill babies who would otherwise have died to be sustained. However, there are major risks that parents and clinicians take, since survival interventions may themselves generate new long-term risks in the form of disability and compromised qualities of living. Life-and-death decisions about the child's physical and social future have to be negotiated and made where detailed and certain knowledge about their future prospects is not fully to hand. Indeed, as Anspach (1987) has shown, there may be considerable differences of opinion about this future among nurses, physicians and junior (trainee) doctors, each of whom draws on quite distinct sources of knowledge, information and experience when considering the prognosis for the neonate. While some put greater emphasis on technological and perceptual cues as to the condition of the neonate, others, notably the nurses, relied on interactive cues to determine the physical condition of the baby, whether, for example, the latter responded to the attentions of the nurse. However, when particular cases are under discussion to determine whether to maintain the life-support systems, Anspach found that most often it was the physicians' technological cues that took precedence and shaped the final outcome. Contrary to what might be expected, physicians who were much more disengaged from the day-to-day care of the baby would demand unequivocal technical evidence that the care should be closed down, while nursing staff, with their closer emotional ties, would often adopt a more pessimistic prognosis.

This distinction in the sense of proximity to the patient expressed by doctors and nurses is found in all ICUs, not only baby units. For example, Melia (2001) observed the way in which doctors and nurses related to patients, and she reports a case where one nurse reflects:

> It was also hard about the day he died you know 9am and he was just falling to bits and bleeding everywhere, his blood pressure was no good and terrible and the consultant on the ward round said no we have to do everything. I said right OK, I am going to be on your back every second of this morning and every second of the day, because I am fed up of every doctor saying that to me. I said you do halfheartedness and then you just walk away and leave him and nobody does anything, so I will be on your back every five seconds about what is happening to this man – 'his BP is still low, his BP is still low, his BP is still low' – because I had got it up to here because it was the same everyday you know, oh well we have just got to keep going but, to me, he was dead. (2001, 716)

Studies such as those of Melia and Anspach are invaluable in showing how both the diagnostic and prognostic deliberations of the intensive care unit reflect quite different professional definitions of 'sustainable life'. In this sense, their work echoes our preceding discussion on ICUs more generally, where we emphasized the way notions of social and physical viability determine how those on life-support systems are categorized and managed; in the case of adults, of course, such deliberations are also framed in regard to the desire to secure viable organs for transplantation. These debates are simply part of much wider fundamental questions about the relationship of a person to his or her body: as Lock puts it,

> Does the person cease to exist when the physical body dies? And perhaps the most fundamental, most obdurate question of all: What exactly *is* death – physical, personal and social? Obviously answers to these questions depend on values articulated in the broader social milieu. They do not involve conflicts in styles of clinical reasoning about the determination of brain death, but they do result in fundamental differences in clinical practice and patient care, and above all in conflicting ideas about the commodification of living cadavers. (2002, 37)

One way in which the commodification of living bodies is expressed is through the use of cryonic technologies to sustain the body beyond – or before – its death. Typically, this can only be made possible by securing the body – or parts of the body, such as male sperm – as private property to be held in (frozen) perpetuity for future re- or (in the case of sperm used for reproduction) initial incarnation. The social regulation of this becomes more complex where deceased body tissue is being used without consent, as was the case in the UK regarding Diane Blood's desire to use her dead husband's frozen sperm to father a child. Initially, the UK regulatory agency (the HFEA) rejected her request on the grounds that his consent for this reproductive act had not been given prior to his death. In these circumstances, if Blood went ahead and conceived a child, though her husband would be the *biological* father he would not be the *legal* one. However, in 2003 the European Court upheld her claim on human rights grounds. Cryonic facilities are principally offered by commercial organizations that will require payment for the cryo-preservation after freezing not only of sperm, eggs or tissue, but more dramatically of a dead body (or head/brain) with a view to its 'reanimation' when the medical technologies of the future are thought to make this possible.

Cryonics and death-style choice

Cryonics is a field within biomedical engineering that involves the freezing of whole organisms at extremely low or 'cryogenic' temperatures (of between −80°C and −196°C), which is designed to prevent the gradual biological collapse of organs and tissue typically associated with bodily decay after death. However, it is recognized that achieving this is extremely risk-laden, and cell/tissue damage is likely, as shown primarily where the technique has been tested on dead animals. Advocates, such as the American Cryonics Society (ACS), believe that the technique will become viable – and indeed its former president, Jerome White, who died of AIDS, is (or, to be precise, his head and brain are) currently in 'suspension'. ACS encourages their members to take out life insurance policies that will meet the costs of 'reanimation', but most medical researchers and engineers are highly sceptical of the claims made on its behalf. No doubt, too, there will be no readily available actuarial statistics that can be used to determine the risks associated with reanimation!

The technique requires the same sort of medical sophistication associated with major life-supporting treatments such as those linked with ICUs, since cardiac and ventilatory systems are needed post-death to allow for the preparation of the rapid cooling systems used to lower the body temperature. In addition, the preservation process requires a series of tasks described as 'extracorporeal circulation' and 'total body washout', followed by packing in ice, placing in a body bag and deposition in a cryogenic chamber. Rather bizarrely, perhaps, fully paid up and insured members of the ACS are informed that they will be able to carry a 'Medic Alert bracelet or necklace and wallet card which has emergency information and our emergency response phone numbers' (ACS 2003): presumably, dying alone is not to be recommended. Death, in fact, is renamed 'de-animation'. Here the reordering of life presents death events as merely temporary states of biological limbo before the return to life: the de-animation event kick-starts a variety of technical and social networks that act to preserve the person for a new life beyond what is currently defined as clinical death.

The extent to which it is the whole body, or 'merely' the head and brain, that are cryo-preserved appears to depend on two matters: whether the deceased has sufficient material resources to pay for a whole body or solely head suspension, and where the boundaries of 'life' itself are perceived to reside, such as in memory and mind. Indeed, some believe that the medical technologies and the research and clinical networks associated with stem cells and cloning of new tissue and organs, discussed earlier in this book, could be the route through which a new body might be provided. Not only does this highlight the faith that may be placed in new technologies (often among those most distant from the complexities and uncertainties of the technologies themselves), it also raises sociological (and social psychological) questions about the construction of a new life and identity, about emergent 'death-style' choices that might be made in the future, and about the prospective social and legal status of a cryonically reanimated person in the distant future: how would they relate to family descendants, would their rights as citizens have changed if major political turmoil had occurred during preservation, and so on? These questions are yet to be answered, since none of the 'preserved' have been reanimated. Moreover, were they to be, it is not clear how regulatory agencies would respond to this. In addition, unlike the arguments considered earlier in the chapter relating to the sequestration of death, or the 'secret of dying', as Schou (1993, 261) puts it, cryonics is a highly visible, public and orchestrated process that seeks to capture and contain death and hold the decomposition and decay of the body at bay. Cryonics is clearly an interesting social site where we find the aspirations of some people who want to hold on to life to be ahead of the capacities of current biomedical engineering. There are others, however, who in contrast seek not to hold on to life, but to terminate it in such a way that it is a pain-free, 'good' death. It is to this that we now turn.

Technologies for a good death: euthanasia and palliative care

Earlier in this chapter we discussed the role of intensive care technologies in managing death and, in certain circumstances, in such a way that a 'good' or 'natural' death might be secured. What is to count as a good death will depend upon the way both the dying and their kin make sense of the passing away of a relative – it might, as Masson (2002) suggests, be more appropriate to see the way this occurs in terms of an acceptance of a 'good enough' death, to point to the way 'that preferred goals do exist but that preferences often have to be negotiated in a context of limitation and contingency' (p. 191). One of the 'contingencies' with which those involved must cope is the pain of death. This takes us here to an examination of the recent debates surrounding euthanasia, pain control and palliative care as mediated by new technologies. Our sense of 'technology' here pays particular attention to the technologies as socio-technical performances and discourses: euthanasia, for example, while not requiring high-tech medicine for its realization, does demand innovation in legal, ethical and regulatory regimes that oversee the predominantly biomedical management of death.

Euthanasia can be defined as the ending of life through 'assisted suicide'. There has been considerable debate over the legal and moral status of euthanasia, with much discussion over the difference between this active intervention in order to help a person die and the simple withdrawal of medical support where it is deemed that the quality of life for a patient is extremely poor or would require constant life support: the latter is legal, whereas in all countries (apart from Switzerland) assisted suicide is not (Doyal and Doyal 2001). It is the case, however, that euthanasia is now *decriminalized* in Belgium, the state of Oregon and the Netherlands. Decriminalization in the Netherlands (in 2001) reflected the general though uneven move towards allowing euthanasia in some, supervised, circumstances: there was growing pressure from the Dutch medical profession and (some) patient groups to regularize and clarify the legal and moral basis for assisted suicide. It is now estimated that about 3000 (of an average 135,000) deaths per annum in the Netherlands are the result of voluntary euthanasia. Australia's Northern Territory actually legalized euthanasia in 1996 (though the federal legislature reversed this in 1997, but only after four people with terminal cancer had ended their lives with medical assistance; see Grey 1999). Much of the wider debate was crystallized during the Diane Pretty case in the UK: Pretty sought euthanasia to hasten her terminal illness to its end (she was a motor neurone disease sufferer) but was refused in both the UK and the European Court (she died in May 2002).

It is something of a paradox that the move towards greater tolerance for euthanasia in some settings comes at a time when medicine has more and more high-tech interventions at its disposal to sustain life. Yet this paradox is resolved when it is recognized that the sophistication of twenty-first-century medicine, as we noted in Chapter 1, is to deal with most *acute* (life-threatening) conditions, only thereby to produce a *chronically* ill but alive patient. Where this is accompanied by chronic pain, patients and their physicians may well seek a 'dignified' death. As Dupuis (2003) observes in a recent review of the Dutch case:

It is to be expected that every society with a very advanced, high-tech medicine will at a certain moment be confronted with the problem of euthanasia – 'the gentle death' – and will start the debate about it. (p. 64)

One of the main issues found in this debate is the way the legal notion of patient autonomy allows for and confirms here the growing individualization of choice surrounding the use of technologies for death. We noted in the concluding remarks of Chapter 2 that one of the effects of this individualizing process is to blur the boundaries between lay and medical management and our understanding of health and illness, and clearly this blurring occurs here too in the case of death, not least when the occasions of assisted suicide are enabled without physicians, but by close relatives. Euthanasia also creates major difficulties for the state (and the medical profession), since it disturbs the boundaries of state control over, and the wider social disciplining of, the end of life. It opens up new space for the non-expert managing of death. This no doubt helps to explain the level of hostility in the majority of late modern societies towards euthanasia: it is also an action that devalues the life-extending and prolonging techniques that medical systems and networks offer today. In fact it is an act that declares for the reuniting of the biological and biographical body and identity under the control of the dying person. Such control is one that displaces the medical language of the *functionality* of the body – Can we sustain its vital organs? – to the existential language of the *being* of the person.

We should, however, be careful how far we take this argument. For, whereas in the Netherlands, Switzerland, and Belgium euthanasia has been decriminalized, we would argue that the legal and regulatory apparatus that allows physician-assisted suicide acts in such a way as to remedicalize what had been in danger of moving off into lay control. Instead, euthanasia is orchestrated through a degree of medical supervision and administration, while the definition of acceptable assisted suicide has become reinvested with notions of functionality and dysfunctionality. Does the pain experienced by the patient pre-empt the possibility of a future quality of life 'worth' living? In short, the decriminalization of euthanasia has been undertaken in such a way as to reconfirm the oversight of the end of life by medicine.

This reference to pain takes us to a brief consideration of the technologies of 'palliative care'. These are typically (though not exclusively) found in the hospice setting and have often been preferred by those who oppose euthanasia, inasmuch as palliative intervention does not equate to any form of assisted suicide (Matthews 1998). The techniques are used almost exclusively worldwide for the relief of pain associated with terminal cancer (for recent overviews of the field see Clark et al. 2001; Hockley and Clark 2002). The hospice as a socio-technical regime lays claim to a 'holistic' approach in managing death and one that is far removed from that often found in hard-pressed hospital wards, where the terminally ill are more likely to be treated via barbiturates and morphine to sedate and kill pain:

> Palliative care is defined as comprehensive, interdisciplinary care of patients and families facing a terminal illness, focusing primarily on comfort and support. Key aspects include meticulous symptom control; psychosocial and spiritual care; a personalised management plan that maximises patient-determined quality of life; family oriented care that extends through the time of bereavement; and delivery of coordinated services, especially in the home but also in hospital, extended care facilities, day care centres, and specialised units. (Billings 2000, 555)

But, even with this more holistic approach of the hospice, palliative care regimes can be seen as being similarly devised to manage the social and biological death sequences over a much longer period of time – through so-called active care planning. It is, as Field (1996) argues, further illustration of the medicalization and standardization of death.

In drawing attention to the medicalization of death through palliative care we do not see the socio-technical dimensions of this form of clinical management as in some way necessarily demeaning of the end of life. Indeed, Gott, Seymour, Bellamy, Clark and Ahmedzai (2003) show that patients express misgivings about dying in their own homes outside of formal medical supervision: concerns are expressed about the burden placed on their families, about the quality of care and the difficulty in handling what are often seen as the embarrassing and unpleasant physical changes of a body in disrepair and the final stages of life. As a result, they report that there is a strong belief 'that suffering and evidence of bodily "unboundedness" should be contained within institutions', in other words, hospices or hospitals (Gott et al. 2003, 15). Anxieties over the progressive physical decay of the body and the social *dis*ordering this brings to familial relations and personal dignity no doubt explain in part the 'sequestration' of death discussed earlier. This is a position adopted by the medical sociologist Lawton (2001), who stresses how the loss of control over body fluids and emissions is the defining feature of the loss of control over the 'self'.

At the same time, there is evidence that suggests that the institutional regimes on offer – principally hospitals and hospices – vary dramatically in their attractiveness to those in the last days of their life. Seale and Addington-Hall (1994) show that the autonomy promoted among patients in hospices is not always welcomed by them, nor is the way hospices typically encourage residents openly to express their fears and anxieties of dying. As a result, some members might come to regard euthanasia as more welcome than the emotionally demanding catharsis often found in the hospice setting.

Technologies for a 'bad' death: clinical iatrogenesis

As we noted earlier, the medicalization of death has its darker side, in the sense that a small proportion of deaths each year are attributed to the adverse effects of *medicine itself*, or 'iatrogenesis' (literally, harm done by the very provider of a solution): in the UK, the Audit Commission recently calculated deaths from 'clinical iatrogenesis' specifically linked to adverse drug reactions to prescribed pharmaceuticals to have increased sixfold over the past decade to an order of about 1200 per annum. A review of such effects in the US (Lazarou et al. 1998) claimed that there were approximately 106,000 fatal adverse drug reactions (ADR) in hospital patients in 1994. Similar claims have been made in regard to the proportion of drug-derived iatrogenic deaths in Canada (Bains and Hunter 1999). More generally, Illich (1976) argued that medical technologies and the socio-cultural power of the medical establishment actually create morbidity, mortality and a (literally) unhealthy over-reliance on medicine by society at large. In a powerful attack on medicine he argued that there are three forms of iatrogenesis: it is

> *clinical*, when pain, sickness, and death result from the provision of medical care; it is *social* when health policies reinforce an industrial organisation which generates dependency and ill health; and it is *structural*, when medically sponsored behaviour and delusions restrict the vital autonomy of people by undermining their competence in growing up, caring for each other and ageing. (1976, 165)

Illich's ideas have been criticized, not only by the medical profession, but by other commentaries in sociology; Navarro (1976), for example, offers a Marxist critique suggesting that the dependency on medicine is to be understood not as the result of the power of the medical establishment (medical science and national/international medical bureaucracies) but as the power of capital to ensure that we become dependent *consumers* of medical products and services. Hirst and Woolley (1982) have also criticized Illich's romanticized solution to the iatrogenic world in his advocacy of the demedicalization of health through a move towards individualized forms of self-care and self-treatment.

However, despite such criticisms, Illich's broad claim that medicine creates its own harmful effects via an 'iatrogenic loop' echoes the work of Beck (1992), who shows how contemporary (medical and other) science generates new risks, in the 'side-effect society'. To this extent, Illich's critique of medical technologies as generators of the very mortality from which they are supposed to defend patients is on solid ground, as the Audit Commission's figures would suggest.

Many drug-related deaths derive from adverse events that are triggered by the toxicity of drugs when applied to whole populations, beyond, that is, the formal controls of clinical trials. Such trials have been criticized for failing to reflect the heterogeneity (in terms of age, gender and ethnicity) of those likely to be prescribed the drugs. As a result, elderly patients, for example, are likely to metabolize drugs less effectively, leading to a toxic build-up of compounds in the body. In general terms, the selection of the recruits to trials is unrepresentative: as Raven (1999) observes,

> The patient selection is also atypical: characteristically patients are excluded by clinicians if they are not experimentally 'clean' i.e. no significant history or co-morbidity, and excluding themselves by refusing consent to participate. Older patients and women are known to be under-represented in clinical trials. Research has suggested that less than 10 per cent of theoretically eligible patients from a target population are enrolled into trials. (1999, 2)

As we noted in Chapter 4, pharmacogenetics (and the broader and more complex field of pharmacogenomics) promises to provide a bioscientific resolution to the growing number of ADRs. The promise being mobilized here is that medical technologies associated with DNA genotyping can help to identify the variation in patient response to existing or future compounds. Here the move towards the individualization of medicine, noted throughout this book, is presented in terms of a discourse of 'personalized medicine'. There are, though, various risks associated with such a move. As we have seen, the resolution of some risks merely creates new ones, as Beck (1992) would have noted. For example, there are commercial risks for large 'pharma': while pharmacogenetics might revolutionize therapeutics by 'targeting' patients, moving from a 'one size fits all' approach to individualized treatment regimes, the commercial impact if this were taken to its logical conclusion would be the production of a very fragmented market for medical drugs. While this post-Fordist tailoring of the production and consumption of drugs might merely reflect the complexity of the wider socio-technical (and economic) system, it is unlikely to be pursued if it were to mean the death of highly profitable strategies based on blockbuster drugs sold in global markets. Mortality of the pharmaceutical industry itself is unlikely to be self-inflicted.

Conclusion

This chapter has sought to explore some of the key dynamics shaping the death of the body in contemporary (principally late modern) society. The medical technologies most closely associated with death are of two forms: those most acutely linked to the preservation of life, whether in ICU or cryonic interventions; and those that seek to manage the distress of a painful death – via euthanasia or palliative care. In both cases, we have argued, death is orchestrated within a complex of medical, cultural and regulatory arenas that work to determine the boundaries of (sustainable) life and death. In doing so, the boundary between life and death is less well defined. This opens the meaning of death and not surprisingly creates a situation where the management of death is a more complex affair than in the past, involving a socio-technical regime made up of physicians, nurses, medical devices, relatives, ethical discourses and broader cultural norms defining what a 'good' death and a 'quality life' mean.

As we saw in our discussion of the ICU, the growing sophistication of life-prolonging technologies creates a situation where the definition of death becomes clinically more complex and thereby more problematic, especially with regard to the different forms of expertise brought to the clinic by physicians and nurses. Moreover, as Lock (2002) observed, the body on life-support machines has varying status as being more or less 'dead' as one moves from one ethical and regulatory national context to another. And, at the more micro level, these contingencies mean that relatives of the dying – as well as those terminally ill – experience quite different clinical death-sequences in these different settings. The social construction of death in this way opens up the area for closer inspection by sociologists of science, since it is apparent that this process requires the parallel creation of a range of protocols, measures and decision-support tools for use by medical staff: these are deployed according to both formal and informal practices that determine the passage from 'life' to 'death'. The controversies over brain-stem death are made more acute by the role that this has played in the harvesting of organs of those on artificial life support.

And, as Blank (2001) has argued, there are important public policy implications that follow from the tendency towards defining death via the brain-stem route. Pressures on beds and related health resources and a growing number of elderly patients requiring care may lead to a wider range of patients being deemed non-supportable. As he says,

> Adding patients in a persistent vegetative state or with end stage Alzheimer's disease to the ranks of the dead raises many difficult questions, for instance, must the NHS or insurers fund continuing care for a legally dead but still breathing patient whose family cannot let go? The implications for disposal of breathing patients who lack brain functions deemed essential to life are substantial. (Blank 2001, 191)

More generally, we have argued that the move towards 'natural (and dignified) deaths', and the associated growing demand for living wills and euthanasia, is part of the move towards the demedicalization of the body. This no doubt reflects wider social moves to recapture authenticity and identity in this period of 'liquid modernity' (as Bauman 1992 calls it). Yet, we have seen too that, while opening a space for new forms of control over the meaning of death, these alternative ways of ordering the end of life have themselves become gradually incorporated into the medical arena.

The various medical/epidemiological inscriptions of death – either in standardized mortality rates or as medical certificates – serve to define and stabilize both a public health and bureaucratic measure of death. We have seen how these are both socially constructed, and we might anticipate that the technologies of death discussed in this chapter could complicate this process: what, for example, do both inscriptions make of cryonic suspension or the more extensive practice of euthanasia? Preceding the inscriptions of death, sociologists have also pointed to the way in which the medicalization of death creates longer-term 'dying roles' for patients – who are informed of their 'terminal illness' much earlier than in the past. Some conditions (as Field 1996 observes), such as cancer, have been accompanied by

Table 6.2   The impact of NMTs on the meaning of death

Continuities	Discontinuities
Mortality as a measurable statistic	Multiple clinical and regulatory definitions of 'death' open up classification regimes
Emphasis on a 'good' and 'natural death'	Natural deaths constructed through clinical technologies in ICU
Medicalization of death and the management of the dying	New spaces opened up by euthanasia/cryonics
The sequestration of death	The public affirmation of death via living wills and euthanasia
Predictable death trajectories	Growing uncertainties of the onset of the death sequence through early but provisional diagnosis

temporal trajectories of the end of life that enable a patient to take on the 'dying role'; however, such roles are less easily available to those suffering from chronic illness, where the outcomes are characterized by much higher degrees of socio-clinical uncertainty.

Throughout the book we have been keen to explore the changes wrought by NMTs on the ordering of life. Death and the dying body prove no exception, in that we can find both continuities and discontinuities characterizing the management of the end of life. We have tried to suggest some of the key contrasts in this regard in table 6.2.

These broad changes and continuities in the meaning of death point to ways in which death itself is being reordered both socially and clinically. Moreover, they suggest that the end of life will not only be personally distressing for those immediately involved, but will become increasingly problematic for health-care systems and public policy agencies charged with the regulation of death.

It is to these wider policy-related issues and how they might be theorized that we turn in our concluding chapter, which broadens the focus again to the various 'stages' of the lifecourse that we have used to organize our text.

7

Conclusion: Reordering Life

In this closing chapter we will draw together the overall argument of the book and focus in particular on the ways in which the 'reordering of life' can be understood. The chapter is divided into three main parts. In the first section, we provide a discussion of recent approaches to innovation as a general process, and the way an STS perspective complements and goes beyond the more recent contributions made by those working in the field of innovation studies. We do this in order to show how innovation studies have themselves drawn attention to the complexity of knowledge-based innovation. We then follow this by drawing out the patterns of continuity and discontinuity that characterize the interplay of technologies, the body and the lifecourse. Our second section goes on to ask how the discontinuities of NMTs are, to put it briefly, managed by society, especially in terms of trying to reduce the uncertainties and destabilization they create. Finally, we discuss how, despite these uncertainties, we see the positioning of NMTs (by scientists, designers, venture capital, government, etc.) as technologies 'of the future', but in doing so distancing ourselves from any linear claims about the prospective 'unfolding' of NMTs from their current instantiation.

Innovation, continuity and discontinuity

Central to the themes raised in this volume are questions of the way in which innovation occurs and its implications for the lived embodiment of change arising in relation to medical technological innovation and expertise.

Necessarily we have drawn on a wide-ranging vocabulary with which to express the sense of change and alteration, emerging against a backcloth of more stable continuities. The whole point of our discussion thus far has been to tease apart or distinguish concentrations of change, what we have called discontinuities from continuities, the exotic from the mundane. As the volume has proceeded, the 'new' of medical technology has been gradually articulated and recounted in reference to various spheres of technical innovation.

In this, the final chapter of the book, we want to elaborate this notion of innovation as a generative process, giving rise to new forms of life. Such life is by no means simply or exclusively organic but is simultaneously institutional, professional, economic, legal and, of course, individually lived by people whose bodies experience the debilitating effects of illness, disease and decay. Innovation may offer not only a mitigation of these effects, but also the redefinition of their meaning within the lifecourse. We have also suggested that the conventional boundaries of the lifecourse are themselves being extended temporally and spatially, at both micro- and macro-levels, the body-physical and the body-collective.

As we have illustrated throughout this book, biomedical science and technology cannot be seen as the sole drivers of innovation: instead, innovation is a mélange of knowledge, technology, organization and wider socio-political activity that operates through complex networks that vary by technology field. Our focus on new medical technologies is on one of the more complex systems, since biomedical innovation involves products, systems and services that are geared to clinical delivery: there are a whole series of professional, ethical, regulatory and wider political actors that mediate, translate and determine the meaning and perceived utility of NMTs. Moreover, conventional innovation analysis focuses attention on discrete sectors: Pavitt (1990), for example, argued that there are four main types of sector, each of which has its own innovation model. These are what he called (i) science-based; (ii) scale intensive; (iii) information intensive; and (iv) specialized supplier dominated. The new medical technologies that we find in health research and delivery systems incorporate all four forms of innovation: for example, the biobanks under development today are heavily science-based in regard to their ensuring quality of the genetic lines donated and curated, are scale intensive to ensure their longer-term utility to both public- and private-sector users, are hugely information intensive in terms of both the platforms they use and the services they provide, yet will be sole suppliers at a national level and set the terms on which access and use will be allowed.

Apart from the very valuable earlier work of Blume (1992, 1997), detailed exploration of the intersections and complexities of medical innovation has been relatively underdeveloped, especially within the wider discipline of *innovation studies* itself. However, some recent research by Gelijns and Rosenberg (1999) that explored the development of magnetic resonance imaging, CT scans and endoscopy illustrates the way in which contemporary innovation studies are moving to embrace the view that innovative design requires considerable translation and articulation work to secure success in a clinical market.

This view has been developed further at a more theoretical level by the contributions from Metcalfe and Coombs (2000; Coombs and Metcalfe 2000; Coombs et al. 1998), who have sought to model and research what they call *distributed* systems of innovation. As economists of innovation, they seek to stress the ways in which innovation is an activity that is distributed across a wide range of (competing) actors: the locus of innovation shifts from the product manufacturer to a wider range of economic actors setting standards and providing services for the market. In arguing so, they critique both linear and diffusion models of technological innovation. As Metcalfe and James (2001) argue in regard to networks of clinical innovation:

> The social and the economic are inseparable and mutually sustaining. These networks and other institutions are defined in relation to a wide range of actors that include patients and patient groups, clinicians and their professional associations and allegiances, firms and technologists/ engineers producing medical devices, instruments and drugs, academic scientists in universities, hospital managers and regulatory authorities. (2001, 43)

Apart from the evident complexity of innovation networks within biomedical innovation, as we noted in Chapter 1, an important technical aspect of contemporary biomedicine is what Stankiewicz and Granberg (2001) have called the 'molecularization' of medical innovation. This encourages the intersection (and some convergent functionality) across fields such as informatics, genetics and biomedical engineering. As technical platforms become more integrated in this way, so they encourage the move towards what is seen in innovation studies as the 'modularization' of design, enabling the building of standardized interfaces between components of larger systems. The notion of actuary medicine – illustrated through the standardizing of EPR, for example – works towards the systemic integration of interfaces (between primary and secondary care, for example) across discrete socio-technical networks, or, as in the field of stem cells, where its research products are deployed in reproductive or substitutive medicine.

Other contributions from within innovation studies have explored the *uncertainties* of contemporary innovation. Blackler (1999) has, for example, provided a useful model that contrasts innovation dynamics found within emerging networks/activities against established networks/activities: in the former we find highest levels of uncertainty about the innovation path(s) that are still to be built. In the knowledge-based economy, the more we control, as Beck (1992) notes, the 'less we *have* control': thus, while knowledge itself must be subject to increasing codification, the greater capacity for innovation and learning this allows simply means that there is greater momentum given to the development of less controllable, tacit knowledge (Lundvall 2002). We will return to this question of uncertainty and its role in the creation of future prospects for NMTs in the third part of this chapter.

Finally, the 'systems of innovation' perspective (Edquist 1997) draws our attention to the way in which knowledge is generated, codified, managed and shared within and between innovation networks, thus seeking to reduce the uncertainties they confront by becoming more 'self-organized'. Such networks are differentiated in terms of their levels of structural complexity and reflexivity. As a result of the development of these networks, the distribution and use of knowledge occurs not through some knowledge market tending towards equilibrium, but through new institutional structures – virtual universities, science parks, R&D consortia, public and private collaborative links, and so on. In short, innovation is seen to occur at the boundaries of sectors where given hierarchical and disciplinary commitments are traversed (Gibbons et al. 1994) and where the adequacy of conventional knowledge-producing institutions (universities, government research laboratories or corporate labs) is called into question. Moreover, these changes mean that the spatial distribution of knowledge also changes by becoming much less firmly rooted within discrete institutional or organizational arenas (David and Foray 1996).

Such accounts, in seeking to point to the changing and dynamic character of the innovation system, do not wish to de-emphasize the role played by organizations and institutions within that system. On the contrary, it is on the basis of this that comparison between countries is typically made, contrasting the 'institutional architecture' (Malerba 1992) each displays. Differences in institutional structures, the role of intermediary institutions, the character of the industrial (production) structure, the investment in human capital formation and training, are all important: as Anderson and Lundvall (1997) observe, 'systems differ in what they do (specialisation) and how they do it (styles or institutions).' The need to understand the *institutional* character of innovation is stressed, again by Metcalfe and James (2001), in their detailed examination of the development of the intraocular lens. They argue there that 'institutions arise in relation to communities of practitioners, regulatory processes, clinician–clinician and clinician–firm networks and market conventions' (p. 43).

These general arguments advanced in recent innovation studies that conjoin the social and economic, that stress institutional networks, that acknowledge the provisionality of knowledge systems and their markets, clearly complement and move towards the perspective in STS informing this volume that sees innovation as always socio-technical. Actors mobilize heterogeneous networks of innovation that include both humans and non-humans as actants. Networks express the alignments between three domains – human actors, natural phenomena and socio-technical production – and the innovation products they engender are *always* hybrids of all three, never simply just human, natural or socio-technical. As Callon notes, such networks are the 'mechanism by which the social and natural worlds progressively *take form*' (Callon 1986b, 224; emphasis added). Or again, as Akrich (1992) argues:

> Neither the purely technical necessities nor the imposition of certain sociopolitical forms can explain the form taken by innovations. Particularly, the innovation process is described by the construction of an association network among heterogeneous entities, human and non-human actors. (1992, 36)

We saw in Chapter 4, for example, how this has characterized the development of telemedicine: neither the apparent technical advance it embodies nor the governmental drive to mobilize it across health systems actually explains its current shape or 'form' in the clinical domain. It occupies quite different positions across distinct national settings, its status as a discrete technology or merely one that is embedded in routine practice varies, and its contribution to clinical outcomes is highly uneven.

So, in broad terms, it is apparent that there is some complementarity between the most recent, more nuanced contributions made within innovation studies and the work on innovation in STS. However, as we have stressed above, unlike the former, STS requires that we reject any clear division between the human, the natural and the social-technical. We have, in this regard, seen how innovation arises through the novel combination of previously discrete elements and entities. These new relationships constitute new objects for analytical inquiry (the xenograft, the ICT-mediated teleconsultation, the stem cell bank), but as objects that are always hybrid in their composition. It is in these processes of novel recombination that new identities and networks take shape. Indeed, STS scholars would argue that newly incorporated elements in a network of innovation are radically transformed, such that they can no longer be said to be comparable to their 'pre-networked' state: Mackenzie (2002), for example, has described this as a process of 'transduction', whereby the meaning of technical objects/subjects is always in a process of becoming, where the identity and meaning of socio-technical systems are radically contingent and not given prior to their instantiation.

Beyond this, we have argued that hybrid NMT networks generate new forms of life that redefine the experience of embodiment at the physical level and create new forms of life beyond the physical body, as well as extending the meaning of life outside of the conventional boundaries of the lifecourse. 'Life' itself is a multiply hybrid entity that occupies different spatio-temporal domains which are produced and reproduced in these three different arenas through the alliances and competition between actors that give them its meaning. It is this that we understand as the reordering of life – a threefold articulation of life in the physical, extra-physical and meta-biographical domains. Life becomes an object of innovation itself, and one highly contested as a result – as we saw in the debates over IVF and reproduction, over stem cells, tissue regeneration and nanotechnology. It is these shifts in the boundaries and reordering of life that we have argued constitute the core discontinuities that we have examined in this book. But we have been as concerned to describe what we believe prevail as continuities in the deployment and meaning of medical technologies. We can, now, summarize these patterns of continuity and discontinuity.

When considering the continuity–discontinuity divide we should emphasize at the outset that the degree to which NMTs disturb existing socio-technical relations is not intrinsic to the technologies 'themselves': we have tried to show how these boundaries are socially generated through the variable positioning of claims to innovation and the networks through which such claims are built. So, as we argued in Chapter 1, rhetorical claims to novelty and technical progress can founder – perhaps on regulatory concerns – and a repositioning of a technology as mundane offers an alternative route to its acceptance. Gene therapy is one case where we have seen this repositioning occur. So how to understand discontinuity?

Given our argument above, we should seek only to *identify discontinuities in terms of the emergence of novel dimensions to the body–medicine–technology relation*, and not simply to locate novelty with regard to some intrinsic material properties of the technology 'itself'. Clearly, new techniques such as the derivation of stem cells from adult or embryonic tissue require the deployment of certain biochemical tools and research skills that make such derivation possible. The socio-technical significance of these laboratory techniques has to be built through the construction of hybrid stem cell domains that combine the scientific, regulatory, ethical and clinical. As such, the answers to the questions What are stem cells and the techniques that derive them?, What is the meaning of the tissue samples on which they depend?, How are these mobilized through experimental and regulatory networks?, and What is the clinical value that they have? are not pre-given. In a similar way, Franklin (2001) points out that we should not speak of *the* embryo, as though it has one singular meaning or identity. As she observes,

> Which embryos are considered to be useful for various purposes depends very much on who is evaluating them and under what conditions. For so-called normal IVF, embryo morphology is paramount. For PGD, it is not morphology but genotype that matters. (2001, 5)

Moreover, we have also observed – in the case of xenotransplantation, for example – that new techniques can *simultaneously* play transformative and conservative roles. Transgenics both opens up and shows the transience of species boundaries yet has also been presented as a reconfirmation of the animal–human divide. This split serves different discourses and interests and provides the ground on which debate and conflict over identities ensues. The science does not 'speak for itself' – again as we have noted on a number of occasions – but is scripted and inscribed by competing authors and readers.

Any search for discontinuities, therefore, should not be driven by hunting for the 'genuinely' novel, in some essentialist sense, but by the coincidence of techniques, practices and networks that build the novelty of innovative NMTs. Before we summarize where we believe such discontinuities can be found, let us say something about how we regard what is similar, mundane or routine about contemporary NMTs. Again, this is not to reduce mundanity to a property of the technology but to its being framed as such in health and medical networks today. We can identify four broad continuities that characterize the positioning of NMTs.

Our first argument is that all of the technologies that we have discussed in this book are subject to existing, and the creators of new, *systems of classification and measurement*, both in regard to their place in the medical knowledge system and their efficacy as or contributions towards therapeutic interventions in the clinic. EPR, for example, extends in digital form the long-standing paper-based regime of medical records, and reproductive IVF technologies are measured in terms of their contribution to success in generating live births. These serve the requirements of what we have called 'actuary medicine', which necessitates standardized and measurable outcomes and registers that are used to inform decisions over risk, resourcing and technology assessment. More importantly, these registers enable the monitoring and ordering of patients as they track through the lifecourse such that they contribute to the wider surveillance and disciplining of medicine, patients and the institutional networks in which they are found. Moreover, as has been the case in the past, this disciplining of NMTs is also framed by the production and use of ethical codes that seek to regulate clinical research and practice.

Second, the technologies *deepen the medicalization of the lifecourse* and wider society, for they work to confirm the power of the biomedical model and more general biomedical research. As Pickstone (2000a) observes, and as we noted in Chapter 1, we live in an era of 'technomedicine' and one that is increasingly marked by large-scale, globalized markets as well as by niche markets for new medical technologies. The state continues to play a crucial role, as it has in the past century, in the establishing of national medical research and training bases and national health markets, and in confirming the power of the biomedical model through the support it has given to NMTs and their infrastructure (such as the new breed of biobanks). The lifecourse as a physical process is medicalized throughout its journey from the commencement of life to its final ending.

As an extension of the preceding point, we can see that NMTs are found in both specialist and routine clinical centres, such as genetics and IVF clinics or primary care practices, respectively. Here the clinical site acts to diagnose and provide a remedy for a problem defined principally as a health-related disorder. The *immediacy of the clinical encounter is the medium through which the technology is experienced*, whether as a one-off or a multiple series of interactive events. Most importantly, the meaning of the technology in this setting reflects the sort of discursive and practice-based interests and priorities of those immediately involved. This will shape, as we saw in our discussion of ICUs in Chapter 6, the sort of primacy given to a technical rather than what we might call an 'affective' diagnosis of the patient. In the clinical setting, it is also the case that primacy will be given to the physical (rather than the wider 'extra-physical' or meta-biographical) condition of the patient measured against a set of clinical protocols, which not only incorporate and give expression to a variety of technologies, but embody specific expectations about the patient's health based on their age, gender, ethnicity and family history: such lifecourse norms inform both clinical diagnosis and prognosis.

Finally, NMTs are often characterized by biomedics, patients, patient groups and the state as *developments that will enhance individual choice over health care* and the management of illness and disease. This has been a long-standing claim made on behalf of new devices, drugs and therapies. Palliative care enables a terminally ill patient to choose a setting that provides a 'good and natural' death, while euthanasia ensures one that is highly individualized in terms of its manner and moment, even if it is assisted in its delivery. IVF and related technologies (such as PGD) are presented as enhancing choice over reproductive decision-making in the broader context of restoring fertility, coping with potential genetic disorder or, beyond the clinical domain, managing the implications of lifecourse choices relating to occupation and career. These claims about improved choice and empowering patients, are, of course, open to challenge on a number of fronts, as we noted in Chapter 3, including an oversimplified notion of what 'choice' means, whether it is actually available, and the basis on which it is said to be warranted. For example, Franklin (2001) points out that prenatal screening may appear to provide the basis for better reproductive choices, but only if we discount the uncertainties surrounding the prognosis of future disease: as she says,

> Much genetic information is ambiguous: even the presence of an entire extra chromosome may have no effect, while minor, almost undetectable changes such as translocations, can be severely debilitating. This means that the task of translating the molecular language of genetic variation into a meaningful estimation of genetic risk can be extremely precise and still not very accurate. (2001, 1)

Despite such caveats, we can see how NMTs act to reproduce and reconfirm the clinical, professional and broader political status quo that orders and regulates the body–medicine–technology relation. However, we have argued that certain types of configuration lead to

NMTs acting to destabilize the status quo, to generate change in the lifecourse and the boundaries thereof. It is here that we turn to consider the discontinuities that mark NMTs, and in regard to these there are five that we can identify.

First, we have seen in various places in earlier chapters how *NMTs open up and so increase the diversity of existing socio-biological boundaries*, a process that (as with Metcalfe's notion of distributed innovation) *distributes* 'life' across a more complex range of networks. The physicality of a person is dispersed via digital and biogenetic databases and depositories, and through telehealthcare systems. The patient *qua* the embodied person is made absent, and indeed the body itself begins to lose its value as a site of medical investigation. As Frank et al. (1996) argued, in regard to telemedicine,

> we find multiple images and codings in which the body is doubled and redoubled . . . For diagnostic work and even treatment purposes, the image on the screen becomes the 'true' patient, of which the bedridden body is an imperfect replicant, less worthy of attention. In the screens' simulations our initial certainty of the real (body) becomes lost in hyper-real images that are better than the real body. (1996, 83)

In the case of biobanks, a donor may have no control over the use of their tissue for subsequent research. How the 'life' of this tissue is framed and related to its origin is a biopolitical matter to be resolved, not one that is given by virtue of a biological link.

In addition, it is clear that NMTs are mobilized in hybrid networks that work to *extend the spatio-temporal* boundaries of life and the entities that 'have' life, both organically and culturally, and carry thereby more or fewer rights and more or less status as moral entities. The lifecourse becomes a resource beyond any particular (physical) real time and (cultural) social time attached to an individual, a cultural site for social contestation and mobilization (by private and public actors). The resolution of these contests creates artificially defined spatio-temporal boundaries – such as the fourteen days allowed for research on embryos or the five-year 'shelf-life' embryos are allowed before they are 'culled' – that have to be constructed through the negotiation of competing actors (Mulkay 1997; Franklin 2001).

Moreover, the articulation of NMTs through new experimental and applied research leads to what we have called (in Chapter 5) *strange couplings*, a significant discontinuity related to the transgenic modification of species, or the prosthetic reworking of the self via body–machine hybridization. These couplings remake both the natural and the social, indeed redefine the boundaries of each. Cloning is a distinct form of coupling – a form of self-duplication via the self – that challenges the whole basis of the reproductive origin of life itself and, as Rabinow observes, enables the artificial production of nature itself – nature will 'finally become artificial' (1992, 242).

NMTs can also be seen to be *mobilized through non-clinical networks* as sites through which health is produced and consumed. This is heavily dependent on the informaticization (Webster 2002) of medicine and the onset of an 'e-scape' for and from medicine (Nettleton 2004). Here we also see an important route through which the *demedicalization* of health as rooted in tacit clinical expertise occurs, working to deconstruct the locus of this expertise of the clinic. Internet medicine allows the search for non-clinical health therapies, for access to drugs otherwise banned in one's own country, for advice and information via patient groups and user groups that challenge mainstream medical knowledge. This enables the mobilization of much more pluralistic notions not only of health and disease, and their remedy (via alternative medicine), but also of competing definitions of life.

Finally, NMTs have been especially linked to the move towards a *repositioning of choice and consent* beyond the conventional level of the individual, as patient or kin, to the institutional, collective level. Biobanks that deploy the discourse of gift-giving are a case in point, yet, in breaking the link to individual need and risk/benefit resulting from a clinical intervention and replacing this with a wider economic and science-based utilitarianism, biobanks run the risk of creating wider forms of mistrust and critique. While a new biological resource, biobanks are simultaneously sites where regulatory and political innovation has to occur to ensure that they are both legitimated and managed in ways that will carry a broad range of constituencies of interest – including scientists, clinicians, diverse publics, policy-makers and bioethicists. This repositioning of choice depends on innovation in the way such repositories – sourced from individual living entities – are held collectively on behalf of those from whom they are derived.

In general, therefore, we see discontinuities as innovations that traverse customary distinctions between the social and the natural, the cultural and the technological and that work towards the reordering of life: nature-making is simultaneously a process of social-making, or 'biosociality', as Rabinow (1992) expresses it. Regulation and governance in the political sphere and the production of novel biological entities can be seen to be involved in a mutually constitutive process of innovation – reconfiguring each other.

The translation of techniques, objects, entities across networks proliferates hybrids (Latour 1993) such that some of our most defining distinctions become increasingly unstable. The emergence of hybrids presupposes that a novel event has taken place – that discontinuity has 'punctured', as it were, the continuities of the now. Hybrids, as with all chimeras and monsters, suggest that formerly distinct categories of actors, at some particular moment in time and space, have been innovatively fused – presenting new challenges to their assimilation within law, knowledge, personal subjectivity and much else besides. The exotic and unfamiliar pose huge risks and new burdens that need to be managed: indeed, Latour (1993) regards this burden as increasingly acute – requiring the need for new mechanisms to police the proliferation of hybrids. Such mechanisms form the subject of the second main part of this chapter, to which we now turn.

Managing reordered life

How and where, in which spheres of action, do we find these new entities and innovations being 'managed'? And how, in turn, does their management feed back into the process of innovation itself (as, for example, when regulatory networks can be seen to add new momentum to the very innovative risks they are supposed to police)? We describe here three areas that are especially rich sites where we can see actors engaged in strategies for the management of reordered life: these are those of the development of new forms of evaluation on which to base resources for NMTs, the emergence of new regulatory agencies that seek to manage the risk of NMTs, and lastly the identity work they demand at the level of subjective and material embodiment (see figure 7.1). Our intention here is not to provide a detailed, comprehensive review of each of these issues, but to flag up how they act to manage NMTs: in each case we provide a brief example based on one of the NMTs discussed in the book.

Bauman (1993) has suggested that the social condition most characteristic of 'liquid modernity' is 'ambivalence'. By this he means our sense of uncertainty in the face of a range of competing options or choices for action. Such ambivalence and heterogeneity need not lead to a social disordering but rather to one that is based on a mutual sociality and social ethic that acknowledges the uncertainty and fragility of social life (Bauman 1998). But, at the level of the state and its bureaucratic institutions, we are most likely to see a modernist response that prompts the development of a range of techniques

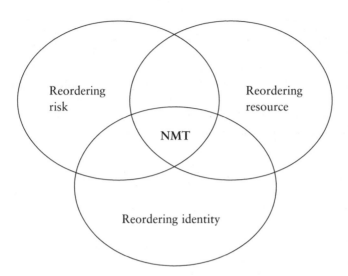

Figure 7.1 Managing reordered life – risk, resource and identity

of surveillance, audit and control, and, crucially, *measurement* and *evaluation*.

In the context of health technologies, one of the most significant developments over the past decade or so has been the arrival of health technology assessment and evidence-based medicine. Health technology assessment (HTA) is found throughout Europe and elsewhere and might be regarded as one of a number of 'political machines' (Barry 2001) that seek to regulate technology and, at the same time, its socio-political positioning (Webster 2004). That is, HTA plays a role as evaluator of the efficacy and resource implications of health technologies while doing so in such a way as to build consensus and so political legitimacy around a series of priorities and investment decisions. It is itself an emerging regulatory science and technology (Faulkner 1997) that can also be seen as part of the wider move towards what Lynch (2000) has called a 'systemic reflexivity', whereby in late modern society 'reflexive monitoring takes the predominant form of cost-benefit and risk-benefit analysis' (p. 31).

Methodologies of assessment are deployed that rely heavily (though not exclusively) on randomized controlled trials (RCTs) and quantitative analysis of the existing or emerging medical technique or therapy. This draws on standardized models for evaluation and comparison based on 'systematic reviews' of existing studies held in international libraries, notably the Cochrane Collaboration. Standardized measures of new technologies can be drawn on to provide directly comparable studies of alternative technologies and so form the basis for investment decisions on resourcing and enable thereby the regulation and control over future resources for health research and delivery. However, the modernist assumptions on which this depends begins to fall apart as the hybridized networks of innovation we have discussed in this volume build NMTs in new directions that create new discontinuities and ambivalences. As Barry (2001) notes:

> standardisation is both expected to reduce blockages and restrictions in the circulation of technology . . . [while at the same time] the development of technology continually destabilises existing standards . . . [and may create] political conflict. (2001, 63)

The technologies of measurement, assessment and surveillance that are used to harness ambivalence merely create a greater capacity for innovation and regulatory learning that fosters more innovatory momentum and discontinuities. Moreover, the ambition of HTA to displace the 'political' from the purely 'technical' – to separate technology *appraisal* from technology *assessment* – often founders on the rocks of competing priorities across the organizational structures and professional demands found in complex medical systems (Harrison 1996). The ordering and reordering of resource is never fully stabilized.

The move towards evidence-based medicine (EBM) has sought to offer some ballast and is now a key feature of health practice and review (Sackett et al. 1997). It parallels and feeds into the HTA arena of activity, as well as being generated as a product from it. Most importantly, EBM transforms clinical evidence from a *discursive* form of knowledge to an *informational* one (Nettleton 2004; Lash 2002). New medical technologies such as telemedicine, new specialist ICU techniques, screening programmes for genetic disorders, new drug compounds or the circumstances in which existing drugs might be used derive their value through their being subject to and approved by review of evidence-based information. Clinicians at the point of treatment are expected to access large, digital sources of information through electronic libraries and databases, but doing this in real time can be highly problematic (Strauss 2002). Not surprisingly, perhaps, the most recent models of EBM seek to restore clinical discretion to the interpretation and use of this evidence (Haynes et al. 2002).

We can illustrate the vagaries of HTA and EBM by a brief consideration of recent work undertaken by Williams et al. (2003) on tele-healthcare. They point out that, 'despite high levels of investment in demonstration projects and systems development, there is little solid evidence about the utility and efficacy of telehealthcare systems that stands up to normative criteria applied elsewhere in health services research' (p. 6). They describe how those directly involved in mobilizing telehealth networks and working towards their incorporation in clinical use have sought to produce criteria for evaluating the technology that are based more on its *promise* as a clinical resource than its current deployment. These criteria have developed in response to criticisms of telemedicine and the relative lack of RCTs in the area. They seek to defend an emerging technology and to construct 'facts' about its utility in ways that meet the demands of an HTA audience. These 'facts' depend more on prescriptive than on descriptive accounts of the value of the technology, seeking thereby to secure at least interim support for this NMT. Here we see a classic example of a reordering of methodological evaluation to seek to secure a reordering of economic and political resource. Inevitably this generates conflict between competing networks. As Williams et al. (2003) put it:

> Importantly, these processes are marked by significant contests and disagreements not only of the kinds of evidence that are persuasive of effectiveness, but also territorial disputes about whose knowledge is authoritative. (p. 15)

As we argued in Chapter 4, telemedicine involves a reordering of the way bodies are incorporated into the clinic. As such, it challenges not only a spatial territory on which conventional clinical practice is undertaken but also a prevailing disciplinary territory and the evaluative regime that oversees it. In doing so, it poses new risks for regulation, as do all NMTs, and it is to this issue that we now turn.

It is fair to say that we are currently witnessing a relatively radical reshaping of regulatory regimes through which risk is defined, monitored, managed and anticipated. This is of course happening on any number of levels and directly reflects the reshaping and formulation of novel entities, hybrids and life forms. Innovation is a way of expressing that various things have been combined in fairly new or novel ways, the risk management of which is likely to be equally innovative. One example that we dealt with at length in Chapter 5 is xenotransplantation, which, like other transgenic technologies, relies on innovating the relationships between humans and other species. Xenotransplantation entails certain risks (rejection, transpecies disease, etc.) in producing hybrid entities that traverse conventional boundaries and borders, in this case, between humans and non-humans. But these species differences also map onto institutional differences between various regulatory capacities, 'different regulatory animals', so to speak. In the UK this could be seen in the novel formulation of a hybrid regulatory body, the United Kingdom Xenotransplantation Interim Regulatory Authority (UKXIRA).

UKXIRA operates at the intersection of a huge number of regulatory capacities under the Department of Health (responsible for procedures involving humans) but also the Home Office (responsible for scientific procedures involving experimental animals, through the Animals Procedures Committee). Michael and Brown's study of risk regulation (2000–03) shows how such innovative regulatory hybrids harbour huge tensions, largely because of the complete novelty of having institutionally to confront novel natures. One of their respondents sat on both the Department of Health's UKXIRA and the Home Office's APC. When the Home Office was presented with a licence application for preclinical research in xenotransplantation, the respondent was legally prevented from disclosing this to the DoH committee responsible for regulating xenotransplantation. There is then a legal firewall in the governance of humans and animals, reflected in the structure of government departments, which is a potential source of weakness in the risk management of innovations such as this that cut across institutional agendas or capacities.

As we have seen, such regulatory innovations and their varied capability to respond flexibly to developments in NMTs are evident in the regulatory shaping of embryos (Mulkay 1997), prosthetics (Kent and Faulkner 2002), pharmaceuticals (Abraham 1997) and much else. And, of course, interestingly the innovation of life and regulation go hand in hand with a reordering of how risk is defined and by whom. Regulatory governance is, in different ways, now subject to an increasing permeability in the boundaries between 'authoritative' expertise and cultural–political apprehension. Notions of 'scientific citizenship' attest to the increasing pressures on regulation towards the heterogeneous, the inclusive and the plural. Where once risk governance was characterized in terms of a close relationship between industry and regulation (Abraham and Lewis 1999), new fissures in this special relationship have seen greater emphasis on public involvement and 'stakeholder inclusion' (Kent and Faulkner 2002).

These pressures on the plasticity of regulation also apply temporally. In some respects, risk governance has been seen to trail far behind developments at the very margins of life (Wheale and McNally 1998). And yet, in other ways institutional innovation to anticipate the introduction of NMTs can often outstrip the pace of innovation in NMTs themselves. So while large-scale regulatory architectures are sometimes hurriedly put in place, those same capacities can lie dormant for lengthy periods because a new innovation has proved to be somewhat more futuristic than expected. UKXIRA, mentioned above, is one such example of this occurring, where policy-making can sometimes be driven by overoptimistic expectations emanating from research sectors. The precautionary principle, and its very many varied versions, again illustrates temporal innovation occurring as a response to the new need to manage the speed and pace of innovation itself.

Our final theme relates to the arena of identity and the ways in which NMTs are embodied. We have seen throughout this book different ways in which NMTs are 'taken into' the body – as PGD, xenotransplants, implants and prosthetics, and the technologies of life extension. Here we want to focus on the diverse ways in which the geneticization (Lippman 1992) of medicine and the body is responded to and 'taken in' by the individual. Much of the literature on the 'impact' of genetics on our understanding of disease tended to regard this as hugely transformative, in regard not only to knowledge of the cause of disease, but also to how it might be treated (see e.g. Kevles and Hood 1992). Many early contributions in the sociology of science and feminist science developed powerful critiques of the potential implications of the new genetics, especially in regard to the reductionist and determinist language it fosters (e.g. Kenen 1994; Nelkin and Tancredi 1994; Lippman 1994; Hallowell et al. 1997). These arguments have since been subject to revision, greater nuance (Petersen 1998) and critique (Hedgecoe 1999), acknowledging the greater ambiguity and uncertainty surrounding both the field of health genetics and its meaning for the practitioner and patient (Hallowell and Lawton 2002). In part this reflects the much greater caution that prevails within the professional research domain of genetics itself (Nelis 2000). The meaning of genetic risk is subject to negotiation between the different actors involved in a clinical encounter, and, as we saw in Chapter 2 in our discussion of Prior's research on the genetic risks of breast cancer, the determination of the diagnosis of risk depends on the play of a wide variety of inscriptions, laboratory and clinical repertoires, and highly tacit 'rules of thumb'.

But we can also see that, for patients, the carrying of genetic risk and the way it is embodied, experienced, or used to frame future life strategies is highly variable. We do not see a homogeneous or uniform response to the clinical determination of risk. Recent work in STS offers strongly contrasting senses of what the embodiment of genetic risk calculation might mean. Rapp (2000) argues that those who are subject to genetic tests or diagnoses find that they are compelled to interpret and manage their disorder in terms of the statistical likelihood of its appearance, displacing wider culturally anchored strategies commonly used to manage illness. As she says:

> the powerful language of risk attached to age, ethnic background, or family genetic history requires family members to focus their thinking through the sieve of statistics, muffling other positions and social interpretations from which they might respond to disease. (2000, 73)

In contrast, Bharadwaj (2002) has shown how, in his examination of the genetically derived blood disorder haemochromatosis (an iron overload), those identified through screening as carriers of the genetic disorder can deploy other 'social interpretations' to make sense of their situation. Clinicians have yet to build a statistical risk profile for the disease, and this uncertainty, coupled with the feeling of not actually being 'ill', has meant that individuals are able to distance themselves from the burden of being at risk or being a 'patient'. Instead, 'the lived experience of the condition [becomes] almost invisible' (2002, 14).

This suggests that genetic risk and susceptibility measures linked to different disease and testing protocols render quite distinct senses in which the technologies of calculation are understood, translated and made sense of by the individual. In some cases, genetic calculation can be incorporated, embodied, and so create a life-changing burden that reorders not only the life of an individual but the lives of their wider kin as well. Elsewhere, as in the case of haemochromatosis, this does not occur. In these different situations, we find contrasting effects on personal (and wider family) identity. The deployment of genetic counselling in both circumstances is not merely about ways of coping with the diagnosis but also about ways of coping with a reordered identity.

From presents to futures

Much of the foregoing discussion has sought to extrapolate key concentrations of novelty, innovation and newness in the reordering of life. To do this we have also identified corresponding continuities or past stabilities against which 'the new' can be recognized. In this sense we have been attempting, throughout this book, to characterize the *distinctiveness* of the contemporary body in relation to NMTs. The discontinuities today open up the black bag of conventional bio-medicine and disturb the modernist claims of the biomedical model of expertise on which it is based. Bauman has spoken of the way in which we experience the (postmodern) world today as 'unequilibrated', by which he means our social condition is best understood as 'composed of elements with a degree of autonomy large enough to justify the view of totality as a kaleidoscopic – momentary and contingent – outcome of interaction. The orderly, structured nature of totality cannot be taken for granted' (1991, 36). Just as Bauman argues that this postmodern condition does *not* displace but rather accompanies a modernist order, so we can see that NMTs similarly express both the reproduction of the body–medicine–technology relationship and also its deconstruction, which may be highly *dis*-orderly and contingent. Indeed, this is how many patients will experience NMTs – both offering the modernist promise of cure and treatment yet simultaneously creating new risks and uncertainties.

But we must also recognize, as analysts of novelty, that much of what we have explored is still being built. Xenotransplantation, stem cell therapies, telemedicine, pharmacogenomics and all their associated heterogeneous assemblages, to greater or lesser extents, remain nascent *potentialities* rather than present *actualities*. Despite gigantic investments in R&D, governance structures and cultural deliberation, many of the promises and expectations associated with these fields could still yet take unanticipated detours from the futures foreseen for them by their promoters.

As we have seen, there is a conspicuous difference between, on the one hand, conception or design and, on the other, the workability of innovation in practice. Indeed, there is nothing to suggest that many of these areas will, or indeed should, ultimately fulfil present-day expectations held of them.

NMTs are populated with innovation concepts whose associated promise has shifted in emphasis over time, often between extreme revolutionary potential on the one hand and despairing disappointment on the other. NMTs commonly exhibit intense and competing discussions about their future potential. And yet the circulation of often flamboyant expectations is an important organizing dynamic, providing motivation, accelerating change and sustaining investment, largely because so many fields are yet to see products through to actual clinical use. When examined over time rather than at any single moment, this 'topology of the future' becomes even more complex. As new activities and 'cutting edge' industries surge forward, just as many seem to fall away from view, as initial investments dwindle, unforeseen problems emerge and an inevitable amount of inertia sets in.

So while expectations appear to be essential to mobilizing activity, early hopes are rarely proportionate to actual future results. Indeed, any number of successive disappointments in fields as diverse as those addressed above have sometimes resulted in lasting damage to the credibility of industry, professional groups and investment markets, especially for those whose hopes have been focused on novel treatments.

So we would like to take this opportunity here at the end of *Reordering Life* to reflect critically on the question of expectations, recognizing that much of the commentary and debate on NMTs, in all the contexts we have discussed, is inherently tied to the manufacture and circulation of hopes and promises. More importantly, we want to offer a reflexive account that forces us to understand our expectations as products of particular times and particular places. That is, expectations always represent certain interests and are always formulated in the context of limited information about the 'real' and future value of innovation (Brown and Michael 2003).

And yet, while it is possible to be critical of the assumptions we hold about the future, it is often far from possible to isolate or insulate our critique from the dynamics of expectations. It is simply not feasible to place ourselves objectively outside the dynamics of hope and expectation as if we were disinterested observers. We may, however, on occasions be deeply critical of the hopes invested in NMTs and cautiously reticent about them; we have to acknowledge that today's contests and disputes are foundational to constructing the future. Futures are not inevitable but, rather, they are 'fought for', resisted, embraced (Brown et al. 2000). Indeed, as Franklin points out in respect to the contested expectations built up around stem cells, 'it is a mistake to think that we can somehow factor out the hype, the media or the work of the imagination to exaggerate either the promises or the risks of new technology. This is not going to be possible, now or in the future, because it is precisely the importance of imagining a future yet-to-be that fundamentally defines the whole issue of the new genetics and society' (2001, 349).

In essence expectations must be understood as fundamentally *constitutive* or 'performative' (Michael 2000). They are introduced and circulated with defining implications for the way in which the future is ordered and reordered in the present. This is what van Lente (1993, 2000) refers to as the 'dialectics of promise' whereby future expectations always embody relations of obligation and reciprocity, the future duty to fulfil a present pledge.

This is as much a material and substantive practice as it is a rhetorical and linguistic one. Of course it is more usually the rhetoric that is most obviously evident in discourse and commentary about innovative medicine. NMTs are saturated with talk of breakthroughs, advances, future visions, progress and great leaps forward. Now this sometimes encourages us mistakenly to think of expectations as principally cognitive or rhetorical, mentalistic projections. And yet, as we have been able to see throughout this volume, future abstractions become materially embodied at many levels, not least the three spheres defined above – risk, resource and identity.

The purpose of articulating a future rhetorically – for xenotransplantation, stem cells, pharmacogenomics, etc. – is that the expectations should transfer from being a speech act to a material act. Or, rather, expectations will become rhetorically 'silent' or 'mute' but materially 'vociferous', so to speak. Immortal stem cell-lines, replicating DNA and biocomputational processes, penetrate the future as substantive bearers of the past's desires and imaginings. The articulation of futures and the rivalry between competing versions of the future have been seen as key to reordering life in genomics and biotechnology (Fortun 2001; Plein 1991), reproductive governance (Mulkay 1993; S. Franklin 1999), telemedicine (Rappert and Brown 2000) and pharmacogenomics (Hedgecoe and Martin 2003).

This brings us to another important point that we would like to stress about the socio-technologies explored in these pages. Expectations are fundamentally *situated* or *located* in real-time current conditions or settings. That is, futures, like pasts, emerge from the pressing needs of the now. As Adam contends, 'the locus of reality is the present . . . the past and the future . . . are constantly created and recreated in the present. The real past, just like the real future, is unobtainable for us, but through mind is open to us in the present' (1990, 24). So, the futures that we attach to NMTs will reflect our present. They reflect our situatedness in terms of knowledge, access to information, uncertainty, and the degree of familiarity we have with innovations that may be relatively novel and whose uncertainties may yet be unknown.

Importantly, expectations are usually much more optimistic for those who are somewhat distant from the complexities and uncertainties of innovation and knowledge-making (Brown and Michael 2003). The historian of technology Donald MacKenzie has argued that scepticism or doubt about an innovation will be far more acute for those closely involved in knowledge production (researchers, etc.) than it will be for the 'users' of that knowledge (future patients, policy-makers, etc.) (1990). One of the things we should add here is that people closely involved in scientific work more usually offer quite contradictory expectations about their field. When wearing a public entrepreneurial hat, they might make strident claims about the promise of their research. But when among research peers, they will be much more cautious. We have two simultaneous roles in play here: researcher and entrepreneur – shifting between acute uncertainty and unalloyed optimism according to different audiences.

This unequal distribution of knowledge – what we might call 'the knowledge economy of expectations' – prompts far-reaching questions about responsibility and accountability for raising hopes far beyond what can be reasonably expected of NMTs in terms of future benefits. To some extent this can be a consequence of the way investment markets are generated around NMTs. For example, research communities sometimes stand to benefit enormously from early share-value growth, while the burden of longer-term failure usually falls on other kinds of community (investors, patients, public-policy makers). Over time, as expectations around early or emerging technologies become more modest and stock values diminish, entrepreneurial communities move into new speculative innovations. As can be seen with fields such as gene therapy in the late 1980s and early 1990s, the scientific investment system seems to have few limiting constraints on the hyperbolic expectations seeded by entrepreneurial innovators.

Our emphasis on the situated nature of expectations is as much a temporal question as it is a spatial one. For instance, where technologies are highly novel there is the evident need to galvanize newly forming relationships, to encourage new interest and raise share value, etc. The more acute these uncertainties, the greater will be the need to draw on the motifs of revolutions, breakthroughs and radical change. So radical discourses about the future are often indicative of the early emergence of an NMT. And, of course, the greater will be the likelihood that things will turn out far differently in the end. And, to some extent, many of the constituencies who look upon these expectations – publics, patients, clinicians, and indeed we ourselves – are intuitively aware that expectations will often be successively raised and thwarted time and time again.

With this final point still hanging in the air, so to speak, we want to bring our story about the reordering of life to a close. Uncertainties abound in the many disparate globalized worlds of medical innovation, and this book has been just as concerned to articulate what we don't know about the future of NMTs as what we do know.

It is fitting therefore that we finish with another caveat, but this time one not of our own making. It is taken from the concluding paragraph to a press release, issued by Celera, the genetic sequencing and functional genomics company. It is a standard formula now used in one version or another by any number of research communities when issuing public statements about their work and its potential value to health. In formal terms, it provides some insulation or 'safe harbour' from the possibilities of litigation by frustrated investors when promises go unfulfilled, as they so often do. And yet, the caveat can just as easily be seen as a poignant expression of the future's uncertainties harboured within today's *Reordering Life*:

> Certain statements in this press release are forward-looking. These may be identified by the use of forward-looking words or phrases such as 'believe,' 'expect,' 'anticipate,' 'should,' 'planned,' 'estimated,' and 'potential,' among others. These forward-looking statements are based on PE Corporation's current expectations. The Private Securities Litigation Reform Act of 1995 provides a 'safe harbor' for such forward-looking statements. In order to comply with the terms of the safe harbor, PE Corporation notes that a variety of factors could cause actual results and experience to differ materially from the anticipated results or other expectations expressed in such forward-looking statements. The risks and uncertainties that may affect the operations, performance, development, and results of Celera Genomics' businesses include but are not limited to (1) early stage of operations and uncertainty of operating results; (2) no precedent for Celera Genomics' business plan; (3) uncertainty of value of polymorphism data; (4) initial reliance on pharmaceutical industry; (5) high dependence on key employees; (6) uncertain protection of intellectual property and proprietary rights; (7) highly competitive business; (8) need to manage rapid growth; and (9) other factors that might be described from time to time in PE Corporation's filings with the Securities and Exchange Commission. (PE-Corporation, 20 January 2000; <http://www.celeradiscoverysystem.com>)

Technical Glossary

Allotransplantation: the transplantation of tissues or organs between bodies within the same species

Assistive technologies: devices or prostheses which 'assist' people who have some 'impairment' or limited mobility

Bioinformatics: the use of computational science in biology – including robotic automation, analysing samples, visualization techniques, comparing data, etc.

Cloning by nuclear transfer: the replacement of the nucleus of an ovarian egg with a nucleus taken from an adult; where successful the procedure leads to fertilization and cell division into a developing embryo

Cryonics: the preservation of tissues or whole bodies, usually in cold suspension

Cytology: the study of cells

Geneticization: a term used to refer to the way in which genetically based understandings of the body and disease have become embedded in wider society and culture

Haemochromatosis: a genetic disorder causing the body to absorb an excessive amount of iron from the diet, leading to damage to the liver primarily, but other organs and joints also

Huntingdon's disease: an inherited degenerative neuropsychiatric disorder leading to memory loss and other problems, generally commencing between the ages of thirty-five and fifty

Iatrogenic illness: disorders which are either caused or aggravated by the clinical intervention of physicians

IVF (*in vitro* fertilization): the fertilization of the ovarian egg outside of the (*in vivo*) woman's body

Nanotechnology: the development of objects and devices that have an individual size of only a few nanometers

Parkinson's disease: a late onset progressively neurodegenerative disease leading to the impairment of a person's movement and coordination

Pharmacogenomics: the identification of genes associated with varying responses to drugs

Regenerative medicine: often referring to the use of a person's own cells (often produced through cloning) to repair or regenerate desired tissues or cells for reimplantation back into the body

Sonography (ultrasound): the use of sound waves to create internal images of the body

Stem cells: cells from which specialized and functional cells can develop. Stem cells occur naturally in the adult body (adult stem cells – ASCs), particularly in bone marrow. Stem cells also make up early embryos prior to cell specialization (embryonic stem cells – ESCs)

Telemedicine: the use of information and communication technologies (ICTs) to monitor, diagnose or treat people at a distance from the clinician

Xenotransplantation: the transplantation of tissues which are derived from a donor species different to the species of the recipient

References and Bibliography

Abraham, J. (1997) The science and politics of medicines regulation. In M. A. Elston (ed.) *The Sociology of Medical Science and Technology*. Oxford: Blackwell.

Abraham, J., and Lewis, G. (1999) Harmonising and competing for medicine's regulation: how healthy are the European Union's systems of drug approval. *Social Science and Medicine*, 48, 1655–67.

Abraham, J., and Lewis, G. (2000) *Regulating Medicines in Europe*. London: Routledge.

Abraham, J., and Lawton Smith, H. (2001) *Regulation and the Pharmaceutical Industry*. Basingstoke: Macmillan.

ACS (American Cryogenics Society) (2003) Getting to there from here. <http://pweb.jps.net/~cryonics/gettingthere.htm>, accessed March 2003.

Adam, B. (1990) *Time and Social Theory*. Cambridge: Cambridge University Press.

Adam, B. (1998) *Timescapes of Modernity: The Environment and Invisible Hazards*. London: Routledge.

Akrich, M. (1992) The de-scription of technical objects. In W. Bijker and J. Law (eds) *Shaping Technology/Building Society: Studies in Sociotechnical Change*. Cambridge, MA: MIT Press.

Anderson, S., and Lundvall, B. (1997) National innovation systems and the dynamics of the division of labour. In C. Edquist (ed.) *Systems of Innovation*. London: Pinter.

Anspach, R. (1987) Prognostic conflict in life and death decisions: the organisation as an ecology of knowledge. *Journal of Health and Social Behaviour*, 28, 215–31.

Antinori, S. (2002) *Recent Advances in Reproductive Technologies for the New Millennium*. Rome: International Associated Research Institute for Human Reproduction Infertility Unit.

Ariès, P. (1973) *Centuries of Childhood*. London: Jonathan Cape.

Ariès, P. (1981) *The Hour of Our Death*. London: Allen Lane.

Armstrong, D. (1995) The rise of surveillance medicine. *Sociology of Health and Illness*, 17, 393–404.

Armstrong, D. (1998) Decline of the hospital: reconstructing institutional dangers. *Sociology of Health and Illness*, 20, 445–57.

Armstrong, D. (2000) The temporal body. In R. Cooter and J. Pickstone (eds) *Medicine in the Twentieth Century*. Amsterdam: Harwood Academic, 247–59.

Atkinson, P. (1995) *Medical Talk and Medical Work*. London: Sage.

Bains, N., and Hunter, D. (1999) Adverse reporting on adverse reactions. *Canadian Medical Association Journal*, 160, 350–1.

Baria, F. (1999) May be baby. *India Today*, 24, 20, 72–3.

Barker, R. A., Dunnett, S. B., and Richards, A. (1999) The rejection of neural xenotransplants: a role for antibodies? *Transplantation*, 68, 1091–2.

Barley, V. et al. (1999) *Meeting the Needs of People with Cancer for Support and Self-Management*. Bristol: Bristol Cancer Health Centre.

Barry, A. (2001) *Political Machines: Governing a Technological Society*. London: Athlone Press.

Bartels, D. M., Priester, R., Wawter, D. E., and Caplan, A. L. (eds) (1990) *Beyond Baby M: Ethical Issues in New Reproductive Techniques*. Clifton, NJ: Humana Press.

Bartley, M., and Blane, D. (1997) Vital comparisons: the social construction of mortality measurement. In M. A. Elston (ed.) *The Sociology of Medical Science and Technology*. Oxford: Blackwell.

Bauman, Z. (1991) A sociological theory of postmodernity. *Thesis Eleven*, 29, 33–46.

Bauman, Z. (1992) *Mortality, Immortality and Other Life Strategies*. Cambridge: Polity.

Bauman, Z. (1993) *Modernity and Ambivalence*. Cambridge: Polity.

Bauman, Z. (1998) What prospects of morality in times of uncertainty. *Theory, Culture and Society*, 15, 1, 11–22.

Beaulieu, A. (2002) Images are not the (only) truth: brain mapping, visual knowledge, and iconoclasm. *Science, Technology and Human Values*, 27, 53–86.

Beck, U. (1992) *The Risk Society*. London: Sage.

Beck, U. (1996) Risk society and the provident state. In S. Lash, B. Szerzynski and B. Wynne (eds) *Risk, Environment and Modernity: Toward a New Ecology*. London: Sage, 27–43.

Beck, U., Giddens, A., and Lash, S. (1996) *Reflexive Modernization*. Cambridge: Polity.

Becker, E. (1997) *The Denial of Death*. New York: Free Press.

Becker, G. (2000) *The Elusive Embryo*. Berkeley: University of California Press.

Bendle, M. F. (2001) The contemporary episteme of death. *Cultural Values*, 3, 349–67.

Berg, M. (1992) The construction of medical disposals: medical sociology and medical problem solving in clinical practice. *Sociology of Health and Illness*, 14, 151–81.

Berg, M. (1997) *Rationalising Medical Work: Decision Support Techniques and Medical Practices*. Cambridge, MA: MIT Press.

Berg, M. (1998) Order(s) and disorder(s): of protocols and medical practices. In M. Berg and A. Mol (eds) *Differences in Medicine: Unravelling Practices, Techniques and Bodies*. Durham, NC, and London: Duke University Press, 226–46.

Berg, M., and Goorman, E. (1999) The contextual nature of medical information. *International Journal of Medical Informatics*, 56, 1–3, 51–60.

Berg, M., and Harterink, P. (1998) Embodying the patient: records and bodies in early 20th century US medical practice. In M. Akrich and M. Berg (eds) *Bodies on Trial: Performances and Politics in Medicine and Biology*. Durham, NC, and London: Duke University Press.

Berg, M., and Mol, M. (eds) (1998) *Differences in Medicine: Unravelling Practices, Techniques and Bodies*. Durham, NC, and London: Duke University Press.

Berg, M. et al. (2004) Technology assessment, priority setting and appropriate use in Dutch health care. *International Journal of Technology Assessment in Health Care*, 20.

Berger, P. (1967) *Sacred Canopy*. New York: Anchor.

Bharadwaj, A. (2002) Uncertain risk: genetic screening for susceptibility to haemochromatosis. *Health Risk and Society*, 4, 227–40.

Bijker, W. E., Hughes, T. P., and Pinch, T. J. (eds) (1987) *The Social Construction of Technological Systems*. Cambridge, MA: MIT Press.

Billings, J. (2000) Recent advances: palliative care. *British Medical Journal*, 321, 555–8.

Birke, L., Himmelweit, S., and Vines, G. (1990) *Tomorrow's Child: Reproductive Technologies in the 1990s*. London: Virago.

Blackler, F. (1999) Organising for incompatible priorities. In A. L. Mark and S. Dopson (eds) *Organisational Behaviour in Health Care: The Research Agenda*. Basingstoke: Macmillan.

Blank, R. (2001) Technology and death policy: redefining death. *Mortality*, 6, 191–202.

Bloor, M. (1991) A minor office: the variable and socially constructed character of death certification in a Scottish city. *Journal of Health and Social Behaviour*, 32, 273–87.

Blume, S. (1992) *Insight and Industry: On the Dynamics of Technological Change in Medicine*. Cambridge, MA: MIT Press.

Blume, S. (1997) The rhetoric and counter-rhetoric of a 'bionic' technology. *Science, Technology and Human Values*, 22, 31–56.

Blume, S. (2000a) Land of hope and glory: exploring cochlear implantation in the Netherlands. *Science, Technology and Human Values*, 25, 139–66.

Blume, S. (2000b) Medicine, technology and industry. In R. Cooter and R. Pickstone (eds) *Medicine in the Twentieth Century*. Amsterdam: Harwood Academic.

Briggs, L. (2003) Shifting the focus of advance care planning: using an in-depth interview to build and strengthen relationships. *Innovations in End-of-Life Care*, 5, 2; <www.edc.org/lastacts>.

Brown, N. (1997) *Ordering Hope – Xenotransplantation: An Actant-Actor Network Theory Account*. PhD thesis, Lancaster University.

Brown, N. (1999) Xenotransplantation: normalising disgust. *Science as Culture*, 8, 327–55.

Brown, N. (2000) *Disciplinary Change in Contexts of Telemedical Mediation: What Dermatologists do without their Skins*. Paper presented at the joint conference of the Society for the Social Studies of Science (4S) and the European Association for the Study of Science and Technology (EASST), Vienna, September.

Brown, N., and Michael, M. (2001a) Switching between science and culture in transpecies transplantation. *Science, Technology and Human Values*, 26, 3–22.

Brown, N., and Michael, M. (2001b) Transgenics, uncertainty and public credibility. *Transgenic Research*, 10, 279–83.

Brown, N., and Michael, M. (2002) From authority to authenticity: governance, transparency and biotechnology. *Health, Risk and Society*, 4, 259–72.

Brown, N., and Michael, M. (2003) A sociology of expectations: retrospecting prospects and prospecting retrospects. *Technology Analysis and Strategic Management*, 15, 1, 3–18.

Brown, N., and Rappert, B. (2000) Emerging bioinformatic networks: contesting the public meaning of private and the private meaning of public. *Prometheus*, 18, 437–52.

Brown, N., Rappert, B., and Webster, A. (eds) (2000) *Contested Futures: A Sociology of Prospective Techno-Science*. Aldershot: Ashgate.

Bunton, R., Nettleton S., and Burrows, R. (eds) (1995) *The Sociology of Health Promotion*. London: Routledge.

Burke, W. (2002) Genetic testing. *New England Journal of Medicine*, 347, 1867–75.

Caddick, A. (2001) Feminist and postmodern: Donna Haraway's cyborg. *Arena*, 99/100, 112–28.

Callon, M. (1986a) The sociology of an actor network: the case of the electric vehicle. In M. Callon, J. Law and A. Rip (eds) *Mapping the Dynamics of Science and Technology: Sociology of Science in the Real World*. London: Macmillan, 19–34.

Callon, M. (1986b) Some elements of a sociology of translation: domestication of the scallops and the fisherman of St Brieuc Bay. In J. Law (ed.) *Power, Action and Belief: A New Sociology of Knowledge?* London: Routledge & Kegan Paul, 196–233.

Callon, M. (1991) Techno-economic networks and irreversibility. In J. Law (ed.) *Sociology of Monsters: Essays on Power, Technology and Domination*. London: Routledge.

Callon, M., Law, J., and Rip, A. (eds) (1986) *Mapping the Dynamics of Science and Technology: Sociology of Science in the Real World*. London: Macmillan.

Cambrosio, A., Young, A., and Lock, M. (2000) Introduction. In M. Lock, A. Young and A. Cambrosio (eds) (2000) *Living and Working with New Medical Technologies*. Cambridge: Cambridge University Press, 1–16.

Cartwright, L. (2000) Reach out and heal someone: telemedicine and the globalisation of health care. *Health*, 4, 347–77.

Casper, M. J., and Berg, M. (1995) Constructivist perspectives on medical work: medical practices and science and technology studies. *Science, Technology and Human Values*, 20, 395–407.

Chadwick, R. (1999) The Icelandic database: do modern times need modern sagas. *British Medical Journal*, 319, 441–4.

Charlton, B. (1993) Medicine and postmodernity. *Journal of the Royal Society of Medicine*, 86, 497–9.

Clark, D., Hockley, J., and Ahmedzai, S. (2001) *New Themes in Palliative Care*. Milton Keynes: Open University Press.

Cochrane, A. (1971) Effectiveness and efficiency: random reflections on the National Health Service. London: Nuffield Provincial Hospitals Trust.

Collins, H. (1990) *Artificial Experts: Social Knowledge and Intelligent Machines*. Cambridge, MA: MIT Press.

Constant, E. W. (1999) Reliable knowledge and unreliable stuff. *Technology and Culture*, 40, 324–57.

Coombs, R., and Metcalfe, J. S. (2000) Organising for innovation: coordinating for innovative distributed capabilities. In N. Foss and V. Mahnke (eds) *Competence, Governance and Entrepreneurship*. Oxford: Oxford University Press.

Coombs, R., et al. (1998) *Technological Change and Organization*. London: Edward Elgar.

Cooter, R., and Pickstone, J. (eds) (2000) *Medicine in the Twentieth Century*. Amsterdam: Harwood Academic.

Corea, S., and Petchesky, R. (1994) Reproductive and sexual rights. In G. Sen, A. Germain and L. C. Chen (eds) *Population Policies Reconsidered*. Cambridge, MA: Harvard University Press.

Cox, S., and McKellin, W. (2000) 'There's this thing in our family': predictive testing and the social construction of risk for Huntington disease. *Sociology of Health and Illness*, 21, 622–46.

Crane, D. (1975) *The Sanctity of Social Life: Physicians' Treatment of Critically Ill Patients*. New York: Russell Sage Foundation.

Crook, S. (1999) Ordering risks. In D. Lupton (ed.) *Risk and Socio-Cultural Theory*. Cambridge: Cambridge University Press, 160–82.

Crook, S., Pakulski, J., and Waters, M. (1992) *Postmodernisation: Changes in Advanced Society*. London: Sage.

Cunningham, G. (1998) *An Evaluation of California's Public–Private Material Serum Screening Programme*. Ninth International Conference on Prenatal Diagnosis and Therapy, Los Angeles, CA, 11 June.

Cussins, C. (1998) Ontological choreography: agency for women patients in an infertility clinic. In M. Berg and A. Mol (eds) *Differences in Medicine: Unravelling Practices, Techniques and Bodies*. Durham, NC, and London: Duke University Press.

Daniel, A. (1998) Trust and medical authority. In A. Petersen and C. Waddell (eds) *Health Matters: A Sociology of Illness, Prevention and Care*. Buckingham: Open University Press, 208–22.

David, P., and Foray, D. (1996) Information distribution and the growth of economically valuable knowledge: a rationale for technological infrastructure policies. In M. Teubal et al. (eds) *Technological Infrastructure Policy*. Dordrecht: Kluwer.

David, P., and Foray, D. (2003) Economic fundamentals of the knowledge society. *Policy Futures in Education*, 1, 20–49.

Dawkins, R. (1976) *The Selfish Gene*. Oxford: Oxford University Press.

DoH (Department of Health) (1998) *A First Class Service: Quality in the New NHS*. London: HMSO.

DoH (2000) *Stem Cell Research: Medical Progress with Responsibility*. London: HMSO [Donaldson Report].

Donzelot, J. (1977) *La police des familles*. Paris: Éditions de Minuit.

Douglas, M. (1982) *Essays in the Sociology of Perception*. London: Routledge.

Douglas, M. ([1966] 1994) *Purity and Danger: An Analysis of the Concepts of Pollution and Taboo*. London: Routledge.

Downing, C. (2002) The model of responsibility: social accountability in the age of the new genetics. Paper presented at EASST Annual Conference, University of York, August.

Doyal, L., and Doyal, L. (2001) Why active euthanasia and physician assisted suicide should be legalised. *British Medical Journal*, 323, 1079–80.

Drews, J. (1995) Intent and coincidence in pharmaceutical discovery. *Drugs Made in Germany*, 3, 81–6.

Dugdale, A. (1999) Materiality: juggling sameness and difference. In J. Law and J. Hassard (eds) *Actor Network Theory and After*. Oxford: Blackwell.

Dupuis, H. (2003) Euthanasia in the Netherlands: 25 years of experience. *Legal Medicine*, 5, suppl. 1, 60–4.

Ebert, T. (1996) *Ludic Feminism and After*. Ann Arbor: University of Michigan Press.

Edquist, C. (ed.) (1997) *Systems of Innovation*. London: Pinter.

Edwards, N., and McKee, M. (2002) The future role of hospitals. *Journal of Health Services Research Policy*, 7, 1, 1–2.

Elias, N. (1987) *The Loneliness of Dying*. Oxford: Blackwell.

Elias, N. (1994) *The Civilising Process*. Oxford: Blackwell.

Elliott, B. (ed.) (1988) *Technology and Social Process*. Edinburgh: Edinburgh University Press.

Elston, M. A. (ed.) (1997) *The Sociology of Medical Science and Technology*. Oxford: Blackwell.

Epstein, J. (1995) *Altered Conditions: Disease, Medicine and Storytelling*. New York: Routledge.

ESRC (2001) Innovative Health Technologies Programme, Swindon, UK; see www.york.ac.uk/res/iht.

Ettore, E. (2000) Reproductive genetics, gender and the body: 'Please doctor may I have a normal baby?'. *Sociology*, 34, 403–20.

Farquhar, D. (1996) *The Other Machine: Discourse and Reproductive Technologies*. London: Routledge.

Faulkner, A. (1997) Strange bedfellows in the laboratory of the NHS? An analysis of the new science of health technology assessment in the United Kingdom. In M. A. Elston (ed.) *The Sociology of Medical Science and Technology*. Oxford: Blackwell.

Featherstone, M., Hepworth, M., and Turner, B. S. (eds) (1991) *The Body: Social Process and Cultural Theory*. London: Sage.

Field, D. (1994) Palliative care and the medicalisation of death. *European Journal of Cancer Care*, 3, 58–62.

Field, D. (1996) Awareness and modern dying. *Mortality*, 1, 255–65.

Fleck, J. (2000) The artefact–activity couple: the co-evolution of artefacts, knowledge and organization in technological innovation. In J. Ziman (ed.) *Technological Innovation as an Evolutionary Process*. Cambridge: Cambridge University Press, 248–66.

Fortun, M. (2001) Mediated speculations in the genomics futures markets. *New Genetics and Society*, 20, 139–56.

Foss, L., and Rothenberg, K. (1987) *The Second Medical Revolution*. London: Shambhala.

Foucault, M. (1976) *The Birth of the Clinic*. London: Tavistock.

Foucault, M. (1979a) *Discipline and Punish: The Birth of the Prison*. Harmondsworth: Penguin.

Foucault, M. (1979b) *The History of Sexuality, Vol. 1: An Introduction*. Harmondsworth: Penguin.

Fox, R. C. (1974) *Experiment Perilous*. Philadelphia: University of Philadelphia Press.

Fox, R. C. (1988) *Essays in Medical Sociology: Journeys into the Field*. New Brunswick, NJ: Transaction.

Fox, R. C. and Swazey, J. P. (1978) *The Courage to Fail: A Social View of Organ Transplants and Dialysis*. Chicago: University of Chicago Press.

Fox, R. C. and Swazey, J. P. (1992) Leaving the field. *Hastings Centre Report*, Sept/Oct, 9–15.

Frank, R. et al. (1996) *Telemedicine: A Guide to Assessing Telecommunications for Health Care*. Washington, DC: National Academy of Science, Institute of Medicine.

Franklin, A. (1999) *Animals and Modern Cultures: A Sociology of Human–Animal Relations in Modernity*. London: Sage.

Franklin, S. (1998) Animal models: an anthropologist considers Dolly. Department of Sociology, Lancaster University; <http://www.comp.lancs.ac.uk/sociology/soc022sf.html>.

Franklin, S. (1999) What we know and what we don't about cloning and society. *New Genetics and Society*, 18, 111–20.

Franklin, S. (2001) Culturing biology: cell lines for the new millennium. *Health*, 5, 335–54.

Franklin, S. (n.d.) Are we post-genomic? Department of Sociology, Lancaster University; <http://www.comp.lancs.ac.uk/sociology/soc085sf.html>.

Franklin, S., and Roberts, C. (2002) Listening to uncertainties: preliminary findings from an ethnography of PGD. Department of Sociology, Lancaster University; <http://www.comp.lancs.ac.uk/sociology/IHT/>.

Frow, J. (1997) *Gift and Commodity: Time and Commodity Culture: Essays in Cultural Theory and Postmodernity*. Oxford: Clarendon Press.

Fudge, E. (2002) *Perceiving Animals: Humans and Beasts in Early Modern English Culture*. Urbana: University of Illinois Press.

Fujimura, J. (1987) Constructing do-able problems in cancer research: articulating alignment. *Social Studies of Science*, 17, 257–93.

Fujimura, J. (1992) Crafting science: standardised packages, boundary objects and 'translation'. In A. Pickering (ed.) *Science as Practice and Culture*. Chicago: University of Chicago Press, 168–211.

GAIC (Genetics and Insurance Committee) (2002) Decision on Huntingdon's disease, available at <http://www.doh.gov.uk/genetics/gaic/decisions.htm>.

Gallagher, C., and Laqueur, T. (1987) *The Making of the Modern Body*. Berkeley: University of California Press.

Gallagher, E. B., and Riska, E. (2001) Introduction. *Current Sociology*, 49, 3, 1–14.

Geels, F., and Schot, J. (1998) Reflexive technology: policies and socio-technical scenarios. Working paper for conference, Constructing Tomorrow: Technology Strategies for the New Millennium, Bristol Business School.

Gelijns, A., and Rosenberg, N. (1999) Diagnostic devices: an analyis of comparative advantages. In D. C. Mowery and R. Nelson (eds) *Sources of Industrial Leadership*. Cambridge: Cambridge University Press.

Gibbons, M., Limoges, C., Nowotny, H., Schwartzman, S., Scott, P., and Trow, M. (1994) *The New Production of Knowledge*. London: Sage.

Giddens, A. (1990) *The Consequences of Modernity*. Cambridge: Polity.

Giddens, A. (1994) *Beyond Left and Right*. Cambridge: Polity.

Glaser, B., and Strauss, A. (1968) *Time for Dying*. Chicago: Aldine.

Glaser, B., and Strauss, A. (1971) *Status Passage*. London: Routledge & Kegan Paul.

Gollust, S. E., Chandros Hull, S., and Wilfond, B. S. (2002) Limitations of direct-to-consumer advertising for clinical genetic testing. *Journal of the American Medical Association*, 288, 1762–7.

Goodman, J. (2000) The pharmaceutical industry in the twentieth century. In R. Cooter and J. Pickstone (eds) *Medicine in the Twentieth Century*. Amsterdam: Harwood Academic.

Goorman, E., and Berg, M. (2000) Modelling nursing activities: electronic health care records and their discontents. *Nursing Inquiry*, 7, 1, 3–9.

Gott, M., Seymour, J., Bellamy, G., Clark, D., and Ahmedzai, S. (2003) How important is dying at home to the 'good death'? Findings from a qualitative study with older people. Innovative Health Technologies Programme Working Paper, available at <www.york.ac.uk/res/iht>.

Granshaw, L. (1992) The rise of the modern hospital in Britain. In A. Wear (ed.) *Medicine in Society: Historical Essays*. Cambridge: Cambridge University Press, 197–218.

Green, J. M., Richards, M. P. M., Murton, F. E., Statham, H. E., and Hallowell, N. (1997) Family communication and genetic counselling. *Journal of Genetic Counselling*, 6, 45–60.

Grey, W. (1999) Right to die or duty to live? *Journal of Applied Philosophy*, 16, 19–31.

Grint, K., and Woolgar, S. (1997) *The Machine at Work: Technology, Work and Society*. Cambridge: Polity.

Hagendijk, R., and Nelis, A. (2002) Patient organisations in the new genetics. Paper presented at EASST Annual Conference, University of York, August.

Hale, D., and Towse, A. (1995) *Value of the Pharmaceutical Industry to the UK Economy*. London: Office of Health Economics.

Hallam, E., and Hockey, J. (2001) *Death, Memory and Material Culture*. London: Berg.

Hallowell, N., and Lawton, J. (2002) Negotiating present and future selves: managing the risk of hereditary ovarian cancer by prophylactic surgery. *Health*, 6, 423–43.

Hallowell, N., Statham, H., Murton, F., Green, J., and Richards, M. (1997) 'Talking about chance': the presentation of risk information during genetic counselling for breast and ovarian cancer. *Journal of Genetic Counselling*, 6, 269–86.

Hansen, M., Kurinczuk, J., Bower, C., and Webb, S. (2002) The risk of major birth defects after intracytoplasmic sperm injection and in vitro fertilisation. *New England Journal of Medicine*, 346, 725–30.

Haraway, D. (1989) *Primate Visions: Gender, Race, and Nature in the World of Modern Science*. New York: Routledge.

Haraway, D. (1991) *Simians, Cyborgs and Women: The Re-invention of Nature*. New York: Routledge.

Haraway, D. (1992) The promises of monsters: a regenerative politics for inappropriate/d others. In L. Grossberg, C. Nelson and P. A. Treichler (eds) *Cultural Studies*. New York: Routledge, 295–337.

Haraway, D. (1997) *Modest <u>witness@second</u> Millennium: FemaleMan meets OncomouseTM*. London: Routledge.

Harrison, S. (1996) The politics of evidence-based medicine in the United Kingdom. *Policy and Politics*, 26, 15–31.

Harrison, S., and Moran, M. (2000) Resources and rationing: managing supply and demand in health care. In G. Albrecht, R. Fitzpatrick and

S. Scrimshaw (eds) *The Handbook of Social Studies in Health and Medicine*. New York: Sage, 493–508.

Harvey, J. (1997) The technological regulation of death. *Sociology*, 31, 719–35.

Hayles, N. K. (1999) *How We Became Posthuman: Virtual Bodies in Cybernetics, Literature, and Informatics*. Chicago: University of Chicago Press.

Haynes, R. B. et al. (2002) Clinical expertise in the era of evidence-based medicine and patient choice. *Evidence-Based Medicine*, 7, 36–8.

Healy, D. (1997) *The Antidepressant Era*. Cambridge, MA: Harvard University Press.

Heath, C., Luff, P., and Svensson, M. S. (2003) Technology and medical practice. *Sociology of Health and Illness*, 25, 3, 75–96.

Heaton, J., Noyes, J., Sloper, P., and Shah, R. (2003) Technology dependent children and family life: research works. Social Policy Research Unit, University of York.

Hedgecoe, A. (1999) Reconstructing geneticization: a research manifesto. *Health Law Journal*, 7, 5–18.

Hedgecoe, A., and Martin, P. (2003) The drugs don't work: expectations and the shaping of pharmacogenetics. *Social Studies of Science*, 33, 327–64.

Helmreich, S. (1998) Recombination, rationality, reductionism, and romantic reactions: culture, computers, and the genetic algorithm. *Social Studies of Science*, 28, 39–71.

Helmreich, S. (1999) The dynamics of digitality in artificial life. Paper presented at the International Society for the History, Philosophy, and Social Study of Biology, Oaxaca, Mexico, 7–11 July.

Helmreich, S. (2000) *Silicon Second Nature: Culturing Artificial Life in a Digital World*. San Diego: University of California Press.

Hepworth, M., and Turner, B. S. (eds) *The Body: Social Process and Cultural Theory*. London: Sage.

Hevia, J. L. (1998) The archive state and the fear of pollution: from the opium wars to Fu-Manchu. *Cultural Studies*, 12, 234–64.

Hewitt, M. (1991) Bio-politics and social policy: Foucault's account of welfare. In M. Featherstone, M. Hepworth and B. Turner (eds) *The Body: Social Processes and Cultural Theory*. London: Sage, 225–55.

HGC (Human Genetics Commission) (2002) *The Supply of Genetic Tests Direct to the Public*. London: HMSO; <http://www.hgc.gov.uk/testingconsultation>.

Hirst, P., and Woolley, P. (1982) *Social Relations and Human Attributes*. London: Tavistock.

HoC (House of Commons) (2001) Science and Technology Committee 5th report on genetics and insurance, 26 March, London: HMSO.

Hockley, J., and Clark, D. (2002) *Palliative Care for Older People in Care Homes*. Milton Keynes: Open University Press.

Howson, A. (1998) Embodied obligation: health surveillance. In S. Nettleton and N. Watson (eds) *The Body in Everyday Life*. London: Routledge, 218–40.

Hughes, B. (2000) Medicalised bodies. In Hancock, P. et al. (eds) *The Body, Culture and Society*. Milton Keynes: Open University Press, 12–28.

Hughes, T. (1983) *Networks of Power: Electrification in Western Society, 1880–1930*. Baltimore: Johns Hopkins University Press.

Hughes, T. (1986) The seamless web: technology, science, etcetera, etcetera. *Social Studies of Science*, 16, 281–92.

Illich, I. (1976) *Limits to Medicine: Medical Nemesis: The Expropriation of Health*. Harmondsworth: Penguin.

Immergut, H. E. (1992) *Health Politics, Interests and Institutions in Western Europe*. Cambridge: Cambridge University Press.

The Independent (2002) Court rules out attempt to create designer baby. 21 December.

Irwin, A., and Wynne, B. (eds) (1996) *Misunderstanding Science? The Public Reconstruction of Science and Technology*. Cambridge: Cambridge University Press.

Jain, S. S. (1999) The prosthetic imagination: enabling and disabling the prosthesis trope. *Science, Technology and Human Values*, 24, 31–54.

Jamous, H., and Pelloile, B. (1970) Changes in the French university hospital system. In J. A. Jackson (ed.) *Professions and Professionalisation*. Cambridge: Cambridge University Press.

Jasanoff, S. (2002) Citizens at risk. *Science as Culture*, 11, 363–80.

Jewson, N. (1976) The disappearance of the sick man from medical cosmology 1770–1870. *Sociology*, 10, 225–44.

Jones, A., Henwood, F., and Hart, A. (2002) *EPRs and Maternity Services – The Challenge of Client Held Records and the Blurring of Boundaries*. Healthcare 2002 Conference, Harrogate.

Jones, S. (1993) *The Language of the Genes*. London: Flamingo.

Jordan, T. (1999) *The Culture and Politics of Cyberspace and the Internet*. London: Routledge.

Katz Rothman, B. (1986) *The Tentative Pregnancy: Prenatal Diagnosis and the Future of Motherhood*. Harmondsworth: Penguin.

Kember, S. (1995) Medicine's new vision and surveillance, technology and crime: the James Bulger case. In M. Lister (ed.) *The Photographic Image in Digital Culture*. London: Routledge.

Kenen, R. (1994) The Human Genome Project: creator of the potentially sick, potentially vulnerable and potentially stigmatized? In I. Robinson (ed.) *Life and Death under High Technology Medicine*. Manchester: Manchester University Press, 49–64.

Kent, J., and Faulkner, A. (2002) Regulating human implant technologies in Europe – understanding the new era in medical device regulation. *Health, Risk and Society*, 4, 190–209.

Kerr, A., and Cunningham-Burley, S. (2000) On ambivalence and risk: reflexive modernity and the new human genetics. *Sociology*, 34, 283–304.

Kerr, A., and Shakespeare, T. (2002) *Genetic Politics: From Eugenics to Genome*. Cheltenham: New Clarion Press.

Kevles, D. J., and Hood, L. (1992) *The Code of Codes: Scientific and Social Issues in the Human Genome Project*. Cambridge, MA: Harvard University Press.

Kierkegaard, S. (1944a) *The Concept of Dread*. Princeton, NJ: Princeton University Press.

Kierkegaard, S. (1944b) *Fear and Trembling and a Sickness unto Death*. Harmondsworth: Penguin.

Klein, R., Day, P., and Redmayne, S. (1996) *Managing Scarcity*. Buckingham: Open University Press.

Knight, N. (1986) The new light: X-rays and medical futurism. In J. J. Corn (ed.) *Imagining Tomorrow*. Cambridge, MA: MIT Press.

Koch, L., and Stemerding, D. (1994) The sociology of entrenchment: a cystic fibrosis test for everyone? *Social Science and Medicine*, 39, 1211–20.

Kohn, L. T., Corrigan, J. M., and Donaldson, M. S. (eds) (2000) *To Err is Human: Building a Safer Health System*. Washington, DC: National Academy Press.

Kroker, A., and Kroker, M. (1987) *Body Invaders: Panic Sex in America*. New York: St Martin's Press.

Kurzweil, R. (2001) Human cloning is the least of it. *WIRED Future*, <www.wired.com>.

Lakoff, G., and Johnson, M. (1980) *Metaphors We Live By*. Chicago: University of Chicago Press.

Lamb, D. (1996) *Organ Transplants and Ethics*. Aldershot: Avery.

Lash, S. (2002) *Critique of Information*. London: Sage.

Laslett, P. (1989) *A Fresh Map of Life: The Emergence of the Third Age*. London: Weidenfeld & Nicolson.

Latour, B. (1987) *Science in Action*. Milton Keynes: Open University Press.

Latour, B. (1988) The prince for machines as well as for machinations. In B. Elliott (ed.) *Technology and Social Process*. Edinburgh: Edinburgh University Press.

Latour, B. (1993) *We Have Never Been Modern*. Cambridge, MA: Harvard University Press.

Latour, B. (1996) *Aramis or the Love of Technology*. Cambridge, MA: Harvard University Press.

Latour, B. (1999) On recalling ANT. In J. Law and J. Hassard (eds) *Actor Network Theory and After*. Oxford: Blackwell, 15–25.

Latour, B., and Woolgar, S. (1979) *Laboratory Life*. Princeton, NJ: Princeton University Press.

Law, J. (1986) On the methods of long distance control: vessels, navigation and the Portuguese route to India. In J. Law (ed.) *Power, Action and Belief: A New Sociology of Knowledge?* London: Routledge & Kegan Paul.

Law, J. (1988) The anatomy of a socio-technical struggle: the design of the TSR2. In B. Elliott (ed.) *Technology and Social Process*. Edinburgh: Edinburgh University Press, 44–69.

Law, J. (1991) Introduction. In J. Law (ed.) *A Sociology of Monsters: Essays on Power*. London: Routledge.

Law, J., and Callon, M. (1992) The life and death of an aircraft: a network analysis of technical change. In W. E. Bijker and J. Law (eds) *Shaping Technology – Building Society: Studies in Sociotechnical Change*. Cambridge, MA: MIT Press, 21–52.

Lawton, J. (2001) *The Dying Process: Experience of Patients in Palliative Care*. London: Routledge.

Lazarou, J., Pomeranz, B. H., and Corey, P. N. (1998) Incidence of adverse drug reactions in hospitalised patients: a meta-analysis of perspective studies. *Journal of the American Medical Association*, 279, 1200–5.

Le Fanu, J. (1999) *The Rise and Fall of Modern Medicine*. London: Little, Brown & Co.

Lente, H. van (1993) *Promising Technology: The Dynamics of Expectations in Technological Developments*. Enschede: University of Twente.

Lente, H. van (2000) From promises to requirement. In N. Brown, B. Rappert and A. Webster (eds) *Contested Futures: A Sociology of Prospective Techno-Science*. Aldershot: Ashgate.

Lindsay, N. (2002) Gene talk and straight talk: the multiple framing of policy discourses in the case of genetics and insurance in the UK. Paper presented at the EASST Annual Conference, University of York, August.

Lippman, A. (1992) Led (astray) by genetic maps: the cartography of the human genome and health care. *Social Science and Medicine*, 35, 1469–76.

Lippman, A. (1994) Prenatal genetic testing and screening: constructing needs and reinforcing inequities. In A. Clarke (ed.) *Genetic Counselling: Practice and Principles*. London: Routledge.

Lock, M. (2002) *Twice Dead: Organ Transplants and the Reinvention of Death*. Berkeley: University of California Press.

Lock, M., Young, A., and Cambrosio, A. (eds) (2000) *Living and Working with New Medical Technologies*. Cambridge: Cambridge University Press.

Lower, R. ([1669] 1728) *Tractatus De Corde*. Leiden: Apud Johan.

Lundin, S. (1999a) Xenotransplantation: biotechnology and the reinvention of nature. In S. Lundin and L. Akesson, *Amalgamations: Fusing Technology and Culture*. Lund: Nordic Academic Press.

Lundin, S. (1999b) The boundless body: cultural perspectives on xenotransplantation. *Ethnos*, 64, 1, 5–31.

Lundvall, B. (2002) *Innovation, Growth and Social Cohesion*. Cheltenham: Edward Elgar.

Lupton, D. (1995) *The Imperative of Health*. London: Sage.

Lupton, D. (1999) *Risk*. London: Routledge.

Lynch, M. (2000) Against reflexivity as an academic virtue and source of privileged knowledge. *Theory, Culture and Society*, 17, 26–54.

Lyon, D. (2001) *Surveillance Society: Monitoring Everyday Life*. Milton Keynes: Open University Press.

Mackenzie, A. (2002) *Transductions: Bodies and Machines at Speed*. London: Continuum.

MacKenzie, D. (1990) *Inventing Accuracy: An Historical Sociology of Ballistic Missile Guidance*. Cambridge, MA: MIT Press.

McKeown, T. (1979) *The Role of Medicine*. Oxford: Blackwell.

McKie, L., and Watson, N. (2000) *Organising Bodies: Policy Institutions and Work*. Basingstoke: Macmillan.

McLaughlin, J., Rosen, P., Skinner, D., and Webster, A. (1998) *Valuing Technology: Organisations, Culture and Change*. London: Routledge.

Macnaghten, P., and Urry, J. (2000) Bodies of nature. *Body and Society*, 6, 3–4, 1–11.

McNeil, M., and Franklin, S. (eds) (1993) *Procreation Stories*. Special issue of *Science as Culture*.

McNeil, M., Varcoe, I., and Yearley, S. (eds) (1990) *The New Reproductive Technologies*. Basingstoke: Macmillan.

Malerba, F. (1992) The organization of the innovative process. In N. Rosenberg, R. Landau and D. C. Mowery (eds) *Technology and the Wealth of Nations*. Stanford, CA: Stanford University Press, 247–78.

Martin, E. (1989) *The Woman in the Body*. Buckingham: Open University Press.

Martin, E. (1994) *Flexible Bodies*. Boston: Beacon Press.

Martin, L. H., Gutman, H., and Hutton, P. H. (1988) *Technologies of the Self: a Seminar with Michel Foucault*. London: Tavistock.

Martin, P. A. (2001) Great expectations: the construction of markets, products and user needs during the early development of gene therapy in the USA. In R. Coombs, K. Green, A. Richards and V. Walsh (eds) *Technology and the Market: Demand, Users and Innovation*. Cheltenham: Edward Elgar.

Marvin, C. (1988) *When Old Technologies Were New*. Oxford: Oxford University Press.

Masson, J. (2002) Non-professional perceptions of 'good death': a study of the views of hospice care patients and relatives of deceased hospice care patients. *Mortality*, 7, 191–209.

Matthews, H. (1998) Better palliative care could cut euthanasia. *British Medical Journal*, 317, 1613.

Mauss, M. ([1925] 1990) *The Gift: Forms and Functions of Exchange in Archaic Societies*. New York: W. W. Norton.

May, C., and Ellis, N. T. (2001) When protocols fail: technical evaluation, biomedical knowledge and the social production of 'facts' about a tele-medicine clinic. *Social Science and Medicine*, 53, 989–1002.

May, C., Gask, L., Atkinson, T., Ellis, N., Mair, F., and Esmail, A. (2001) Resisting and promoting new technologies in clinical practice: the case of telepsychiatry. *Social Science and Medicine*, 52, 1889–1901.

May, C. et al. (2002) *What Factors Promote or Inhibit the Effective Evaluation of Telehealthcare Interventions?* ICT 032, Department of Health, London.

Meade, T. (2000) The future of Biobank. *The Lancet*, 362, 492.

Mechanic, D. (2002) Socio-cultural implications of changing organisational technologies in the provision of care. *Social Science and Medicine*, 54, 459–67.

Melia, K. M. (2001) Ethical issues and the importance of consensus for the intensive care team. *Social Science and Medicine*, 53, 707–19.

Mellor, P. (1993) Death in high modernity: the contemporary presence and absence of death. In D. Clark (ed.) *The Sociology of Death*. Oxford: Blackwell.

Mellor, P. A., and Shilling, C. (1993) Modernity, self identity and the sequestration of death. *Sociology*, 27, 411–31.

Melzer, D., and Zimmern, R. (2002) Editorial: genetics and medicalisation. *British Medical Journal*, 324, 863–4.

Merkx, F. (2002) Genetics and insurance: using positioning theory to understand the dynamics in the configuration of responsibilities: a comparative study between the Netherlands and the UK. Paper presented at the EASST Annual Conference, University of York, August.

Metcalfe, J. S., and Coombs, R. (2000) Organising for innovation: co-ordinating distributed innovation capabilities. In N. Foss and V. Mahnke (eds) *Competence, Governance and Entrepreneurship*. Oxford: Oxford University Press.

Metcalfe, J. S., and James, A. (2001) *Emergent Innovation Systems and the Delivery of Clinical Services: The Case of Intraocular Lenses*. CRIC, University of Manchester, Working Paper no. 9.

Mialet, H. (1999) Do angels have bodies? Two stories about subjectivity in science: the cases of William X and Mister H. *Social Studies of Science*, 24, 551–81.

Michael, M. (2000) *Reconnecting Culture, Nature and Technology: From Society to Heterogeneity*. London: Routledge.

Michael, M. (2001) Technoscientific bespoking: animals, publics and the new genetics. *New Genetics and Society*, 20, 205–24.

Michael, M., and Brown, N. (2000–03) *Xenotransplantation: Risk Identities and the Human/Nonhuman Interface*. Research project funded by the UK Economic and Social Research Council [L218 25 2044].

Miles, I. (1997) *Technology Foresight: Implications for Social Science*. CRIC, University of Manchester, Working Paper no. 3.

Milunsky, A. (1993) *Know Your Genes*. New York: Perseus.

Mitchell, L. M., and Georges, E. (1998) Baby's first picture: the cyborg fetus of ultrasound imaging. In R. Davis-Floyd and J. Dumit (eds) *Cyborg Babies: From Techno-sex to Techno-tots*. London: Routledge, 105–24.

Mody, C. C. M. (2001) A little dirt never hurt anyone: knowledge-making and contamination in materials science. *Social Studies of Science*, 31, 7–36.

Mol, A. (1998) Missing links, making links: the performance of some artheroscleroses. In A. Mol and M. Berg (eds) *Differences in Medicine: Unravelling Practices, Techniques and Bodies*. Durham, NC, and London: Duke University Press, 144–65.

Mol, A. (1999) Ontological politics: a word and some questions. In J. Law and J. Hassard (eds) *Actor Network Theory and After*. Oxford: Blackwell, 74–89.

Mol, A. (2002) *The Body Multiple: Ontology in Medical Practice*. Durham, NC: Duke University Press.

Moldrup, C., and Morgall, J. (2001) Risk society – reconsidered in a drug context. *Health, Risk and Society*, 3, 1, 59–74.

Moore, L. J., and Clarke, A. (2001) The traffic in cyberanatomies. *Body and Society*, 7, 1, 57–96.

Morgan, D. (2001) *Issues in Medical Law and Ethics*. London: Cavendish.

Mort, M., May, C., and Williams, T. (2003) Remote doctors and absent patients: acting at a distance in telemedicine? *Science, Technology and Human Values*, 28, 274–95.

Mort, M., May, C., Williams, T., and Mair, F. (2004) From convergence to confidence: science, technology and politics in telemedicine. In A. Gray and S. Harrison (eds) *Governing Medicine: Theory and Practice*. Buckingham: Open University Press.

Moser, I. (2000) Against normalisation: subverting norms of ability and disability. *Science as Culture*, 9, 201–40.

Moser, I., and Law, J. (1999) Good passages, bad passages. In J. Law and J. Hassard (eds) *Actor Network Theory and After*. Oxford: Blackwell, 196–219.

Moskowitz, E. H., and Nelson, J. L. (1995) The best laid plans. *Hastings Center Report*, 25, 6, S3–S5.

Mulkay, M. (1993a) Rhetorics of hope and fear in the great embryo debate. *Social Studies of Science*, 23, 721–42.

Mulkay, M. (1993b) Social death in Britain. In D. Clark (ed.) *The Sociology of Death*. Oxford: Blackwell.

Mulkay, M. (1997) *The Embryo Research Debate: Science and the Politics of Reproduction*. Cambridge: Cambridge University Press.

Murray, T. H. (1996) Organ vendors, families and the gift of life. In S. J. Youngner, R. C. Fox and J. L. O'Connell (eds) *Organ Transplantation: Meanings and Realities*. Madison: University of Wisconsin Press, 101–25.

NAE (National Academy of Engineering) (2000) Health technologies. *Greatest Engineering Achievements of the Twentieth Century, no. 16*. Washington, DC: NAE.

Navarro, V. (1976) *Medicine Under Capitalism*. London: Croom Helm.

NCHS (National Centre for Health Statistics) (2003a) *2001 National Hospital Discharge Survey*. Advance Data No. 332.

NCHS (National Centre for Health Statistics) (2003b) *Leading Causes of Death: Heart Disease & Stroke*. Washington, DC: NCHS, Centre for Disease Control and Prevention.

Nelis, A. (2000) Genetic uncertainties. In N. Brown, B. Rappert and A. Webster (eds) *Contested Futures*. Aldershot: Ashgate.

Nelkin, D. (1984) *Controversy: The Politics of Technical Decisions*. New York: Sage.

Nelkin, D., and Tancredi, L. (1994) *Dangerous Diagnostics: The Social Power of Biological Information*. Chicago: University of Chicago Press.

Ness, R. B., Cramer, D. W., and Goodman, M. T. (2002) Infertility, fertility drugs, and ovarian cancer: a pooled analysis of case-control studies. *American Journal of Epidemiology*, 155, 217–24.

Nettleton, S. (2004) The emergence of E-scaped medicine. *Sociology of Health and Illness* (in press).

Nettleton, S., and Burrows, R. (2003) E-scaped medicine? Information, reflexivity and health. *Critical Social Policy*, 23, 208–26.

Nettleton, S., and Watson, J. (eds) (1998) *The Body in Everyday Life*. London: Routledge.

Novas, C., and Rose, N. (2000) Genetic risk and the birth of the somatic individual. *Economy and Society*, 29, 484–513 [special issue on configurations of risk].

Nowotny, H. (2002) Contextualizing expertise. Plenary address at the EASST Annual Conference, University of York, 31 July–3 August.

Nowotny, H., Scott, P., and Gibbons, M. (2000) *Re-Thinking Science*. Cambridge: Polity.

Nuland, S. B. (1994) *How We Die*. London: Chatto & Windus.

Nygren, E., Johnson, M., and Henriksson, P. (1992) Reading the medical record, II: design of a human–computer interface for basic reading of computerized medical records. *Computer Methods and Programs in Biomedicine*, 39, 13–25.

ONS (Office of National Statistics) (2002) *Deaths: Age and Sex, Numbers and Rates, 1976 Onwards (England and Wales)*. Health Statistics Quarterly, 17. London: HMSO.

Ott, K. (2002) The sum of its parts. In K. Ott, D. Serlin and S. Mihm (eds) *Artificial Parts, Practical Lives: Modern Histories of Prosthetics*. New York: New York University Press.

Overall, C. (1987) *Ethics and Human Reproduction*. Boston: Unwin Hyman.

Palladino, P. (2001) Medicine yesterday, today, and tomorrow. *Social History of Medicine*, 14, 539–51.

Palsson, G. (2002) The life of family trees and the book of Icelanders. *Medical Anthropology*, 21, 337–67.

Pavitt, K. (1990) What we know about the strategic management of technology. *California Management Review*, 32, 3, 17–26.

Penley, C., and Ross, A. (1991) Cyborgs at large: interview with Donna Haraway. In C. Penley and A. Ross (eds) *Technoculture*. Minneapolis: Minnesota University Press.

Petchesky, R. P. (1987) Foetal images: the power of visual culture in the politics of reproduction. In M. Stanworth (ed.) *Reproductive Technologies*. Minneapolis: University of Minnesota Press.

Petersen, A. (1998) The new genetics and the politics of public health. *Critical Public Health*, 8, 59–72.

Pickstone, J. V. (ed.) (1992) *Medical Innovation in Historical Perspective*. London: Macmillan.

Pickstone, J. V. (1993) Ways of knowing: towards a historical sociology of science, technology and medicine. *British Journal for the History of Science*, 24, 433–58.

Pickstone, J. V. (2000a) *Ways of Knowing: A New Science, Technology and Medicine*. Manchester: Manchester University Press.

Pickstone, J. V. (2000b) Production, community and consumption: the political economy of twentieth-century medicine. In R. Cooter and J. Pickstone (eds) *Medicine in the Twentieth Century*. Amsterdam: Harwood Academic.

Pilnick, A. (2002) *Genetics and Society: An Introduction*. Buckingham: Open University Press.

Pinch, T. (1994) Cold fusion and the sociology of scientific knowledge. *Technical Communication Quarterly*, 3, 85–100.

Plein, C. (1991) Popularising biotechnology. *Science, Technology and Human Values*, 16, 474–90.

Porter, R. (1987) Introduction. In R. Porter, *Man Masters Nature: 25 Centuries of Science*. London: BBC Books, 8–15.

Porter, R. (1997) *The Greatest Benefit to Mankind*. London: Harper Collins.

Porter, R. (2001) Medical futures. *Interdisciplinary Science Reviews*, 26, 1, 35–42.

Porter, R., and Wear, A. (1987) *Problems and Methods in the History of Medicine*. London: Routledge.

Poste, G. (1998) Molecular medicine and information-based targeted healthcare. *Nature Biotechnology*, 16, 19–21.

Power, M. (1999) *The Audit Society: Rituals of Verification*. Oxford: Oxford University Press.

Prior, L. (1989) *The Social Organisation of Death*. Basingstoke: Macmillan.

Prior, L. (2001) Rationing through risk assessment in clinical genetics: all categories have wheels. *Sociology of Health and Illness*, 23, 570–93.

Prior, L., Wood, F., Gray, J., Pill, R., and Hughes, D. (2002) Making risk visible: the role of images in the assessment of cancer genetic risk. *Health Risk and Society*, 4, 241–58.

Prout, A. (1996) Actor-network theory, technology and medical sociology: an illustrative analysis of the metered dose inhaler. *Sociology of Health and Illness*, 18, 198–219.

Rabinow, P. (1992) Artificiality and enlightenment: from socio-biology to biosociality. In J. Crary and S. Kwinter (eds) *Zone 6: Incorporations*. Cambridge, MA: MIT Press.

Rabinow, P. (1996) Severing the ties: fragmentation and dignity in late modernity. In P. Rabinow, *Essays on the Anthropology of Reason*. Princeton, NJ: Princeton University Press, 129–52.

Rabinow, P. (1999) *French DNA: Trouble in Purgatory*. Chicago: University of Chicago Press.

Rapp, R. (1988) Refusing prenatal diagnosis: the multiple meanings of biotechnology in a multicultural world. *Science, Technology and Human Values*, 23, 45–70.

Rapp, R. (2000) *Testing Women, Testing the Fetus: The Social Impact of Amniocentesis in America.* New York: Routledge.

Rapp, R., and Ginsburg, F. D. (2001) Enabling disability: rewriting kinship, reimagining citizenship. *Public Culture,* 13, 533–56.

Rappert, B., and Brown, N. (2000) Putting the future in its place: comparing innovation moments in genetic diagnostics and telemedicine. *New Genetics and Society,* 19, 1, 49–75.

Raven, A. (1999) Improving the validity of economic evaluations alongside randomised controlled trials. *European Pharmaceutical Contractor,* November; <http://www.cambridgehealthcare.co.uk/EPC%20article.htm>.

Reiser, S. J. (1978) *Medicine and the Reign of Technology.* Cambridge and New York: Cambridge University Press.

Richards, M. (1996) Lay and professional knowledge about genetics and inheritance. *Public Understanding of Science,* 5, 217–30.

Richter, J. (1996) *Vaccination Against Pregnancy: Miracle or Menace?* London: Zed Books.

Riley, J. W. Jr (1983) Dyings and the meanings of death. *Annual Review of Sociology,* 9, 191–216.

Rip, A. (2001) Assessing the impacts of innovation: new developments in technology assessment. In OECD, *Social Sciences and Innovation.* Paris: OECD, 197–213.

Rip, A., and Schot, J. (2002) Identifying loci for influencing the dynamics of technological development. In R. Williams and K. Sørensen (eds) *Shaping Technology, Guiding Policy.* Cheltenham: Edward Elgar, 158–76.

Robbins, M. (1996) The donation of organs for transplantation. In G. Howarth and P. C. Jupp (eds) *Contemporary Issues in the Sociology of Death, Dying and Disposal.* Basingstoke: Macmillan.

Robertson, J. (1996) *Children of Choice: Freedom and the New Reproductive Technologies.* Princeton, NJ: Princeton University Press.

Robotham, J., and Smith, D. (2002) Abortions set to fuel stem cell research. *Sydney Morning Herald,* 5 August, 5.

Rose, H. (2001) Gendered genetics in Iceland. *New Genetics and Society,* 20, 119–38.

Rosengarten, M. (2001) A pig's tale: porcine viruses and species boundaries. In A. Bashford and C. Hooker (eds) *Contagion: Historical and Cultural Studies.* London: Routledge.

Sackett, D. L., Richardson, W. S., Rosenberg, W., and Haynes, R. B. (1997) *Evidence-Based Medicine.* Edinburgh: Churchill Livingstone.

Salter, B., and Jones, M. (2002) Regulating human genetics: the changing politics of biotechnology governance in the European Union. *Health, Risk and Society,* 4, 325–41.

Samson, C. (ed.) (1999) *Health Studies.* Oxford: Blackwell.

Scarry, E. (1985) *The Body in Pain.* New York: Oxford University Press.

Scheper-Hughes, N. (2000) The global traffic in human organs. *Current Anthropology,* 41, 2, 1–22.

Scheper-Hughes, N. (2001) Commodity fetishism in organs trafficking. *Body and Society*, 7, 2, 31–62.

Scheper-Hughes, N., and Lock, M. (1987) The mindful body. *Medical Anthropology Quarterly*, 1, 1, 6–41.

Schieber, G., Poullier, J. P., and Greenwald, L. (1994) Health system performances in OECD countries 1980–92. *Health Affairs*, 13, 100–12.

Schou, K. (1993) Awareness contexts and the construction of dying in the cancer treatment setting. In D. Clark (ed.) *The Sociology of Death*. London: Blackwell, 238–63.

Seale, C. (1995) Heroic death. *Sociology*, 29, 597–613.

Seale, C. (1998) *Constructing Death*. Cambridge: Cambridge University Press.

Seale, C., and Addington-Hall, J. (1994) Euthanasia: why people want to die earlier. *Social Science and Medicine*, 39, 647–54.

Seymour, J. E. (1999) Revisiting medicalisation and natural death. *Social Science and Medicine*, 49, 691–74.

Shachar, A. (2001) *Multicultural Jurisdictions*. Cambridge: Cambridge University Press.

Shakespeare, T. (ed.) (1998) *The Disability Reader: Social Science Perspectives*. London: Cassell.

Shanley, M. (2002) *Making Babies, Making Families*. Boston: Beacon Press.

Shapin, S., and Schaffer, S. (1985) *Leviathan and the Air Pump: Hobbes, Boyle and the Experimental Life*. Princeton, NJ: Princeton University Press.

Shilling, C. (1993) *The Body and Social Theory*. London: Sage.

Sigurdsson, S. (2001) Yin–yang genetics, or the HSD deCODE controversy. *New Genetics and Society*, 20, 103–17.

Siminoff, L. A., and Chillag, K. (1999) The fallacy of the 'gift of life'. *Hastings Centre Report*, 29, 6, 34–41.

Singleton, V., and Michael, M. (1993) Actor-networks and ambivalence: general practitioners in the UK cervical screening programme. *Social Studies of Science*, 23, 227–64.

Slevin, J. (2000) *The Internet and Society*. Oxford: Blackwell.

Smith, R. M., and Horden, P. (1998) Introduction. In R. M. Smith and P. Horden (eds) *The Locus of Care: Families, Communities, Institutions and the Provision of Welfare Since Antiquity*. London: Routledge, 1–20.

Sneddon, R. (2000) The challenge of pharmacogenetics and pharmacogenomics. *New Genetics and Society*, 19, 145–64.

Spallone, P. (1989) *Beyond Conception: The New Politics of Reproduction*. London: Bergin & Garvey.

SPRU (Science Policy Research Unit), University of Sussex (1996) *Europe's Pharmaceutical Industry: An Innovation Profile*. EIMS Publication no. 32 European Commission, DGXII, The Innovation Programme.

Stankiewicz, R., and Granberg, A. (2001) The evolving design space of technology and the public R&D system. Paper presented at NPRNet Conference, Science Policy Research Unit, University of Sussex, March.

Starzl, T. (1992) *The Puzzle People: Memoirs of a Transplant Surgeon*. Pittsburgh: University of Pittsburgh Press.

Stewart, J., and Williams, R. (1998) The co-evolution of society and multi-media technology: issues in predicting the future innovation and use of a ubiquitous technology. *Social Science Computer Review*, 16, 3 [special issue: ISTAS '97: Computers and Society at a Time of Sweeping Change].

Stone, R. A. (1995) *The War of Desire and Technology at the Close of the Mechanical Age*. Cambridge, MA: MIT Press.

Strathern, M. (1996) Enabling identity? Biology, choice and the new reproductive technologies. In S. Hall and P. du Gay (eds) *Questions of Cultural Identity*. London: Sage.

Strauss, A. (1971) *Anguish: The Case History of a Dying Trajectory*. San Francisco: Sociology Press.

Strauss, S. (2002) Evidence-based medicine in practice. *Evidence-Based Medicine*, 7, 68–9.

Strydom, P. (1999) The civilisation of the gene: biotechnological risk framed in the responsibility discourse. In P. O'Mahony (ed.) *Nature, Risk and Responsibility*. London: Macmillan.

Sudnow, D. (1967) *Passing On: The Social Organisation of the Dying*. Englewood Cliffs, NJ: Prentice Hall.

Sylvia, C., and Novak, W. (1997) *A Change of Heart*. London: Little, Brown & Co.

Tabberer, S., and Hall, C. (2000) *Teenage Pregnancy and Choice*. York: Joseph Rowntree Foundation.

Talbott, J. H. (1970) *A Biographical History of Medicine*. New York: Grune & Stratton.

Timmermans, S. (1998) Resuscitation technology in the emergency department: towards a dignified death. *Sociology of Health and Illness*, 20, 144–67.

Timmermans, S. (2002) The cause of death vs. the gift of life: boundary maintenance and the politics of expertise in death investigation. *Sociology of Health and Illness*, 24, 550–74.

Timmermans, S., and Berg, M. (2003) The practice of medical technology. *Sociology of Health and Illness*, 25, 3, 97–114.

Timmermans, S., Bowker, G., and Star, S. L. (1998) The architecture of difference: visibility, control, and comparability in building a nursing interventions classification. In M. Berg and A. Mol (eds) *Differences in Medicine: Unravelling Practices, Techniques and Bodies*. Durham, NC, and London: Duke University Press, 202–25.

Titmuss, R. (1970) *The Gift Relationship: From Human Blood to Social Policy*. New York: Pantheon.

Treichler, L., Cartwright, L., and Penley, C. (eds) (1998) *The Visible Woman: Imaging Technologies, Gender, and Science*. New York: New York University Press.

Tritter, J. Q., and Calnan, M. (2002) Cancer as a chronic illness? Reconsidering categorisation and exploring experience. *European Journal of Cancer Care*, 11, 161–5.

Turner, B. (1996) *The Body and Society*. 2nd edn, London: Sage.

Turney, J., and Balmer, B. (2000) The genetic body. In R. Cooter and J. Pickstone (eds) *Medicine in the Twentieth Century*. Amsterdam: Harwood Academic.

Tutton, R. (2002) Gift relationships in genetics research. *Science as Culture*, 11, 523–42.

Tutton, R., and Corrigan, O. (eds) (2004) *Genetic Databases: Socio-ethical Issues in the Collection and Use of DNA*. London: Routledge.

Urry, J. (2000) *Sociology Beyond Societies*. London: Routledge.

Urry, J., and Macnaghten, P. (eds) (2001) *Bodies of Nature*. London: Sage.

Van Gennep, A. (1960) *The Rites of Passage*. Chicago: University of Chicago Press.

Vaughan, D. (1999) The role of the organisation in the production of techno-scientific knowledge. *Social Studies of Science*, 29, 913–43.

Virilio, P. (2000) *The Information Bomb*. London: Verso.

Waldby, C. (1997) The body and the digital archive: the visible human project and the computerisation of medicine. *Health*, 1, 2, 77–90.

Waldby, C. (1998) Medical imaging: the biopolitics of visibility. *Health*, 2, 372–84.

Waldby, C. (2000) Fragmented bodies, incoherent medicine. *Social Studies of Science*, 30, 465–75.

Waldby, C. (2002) Stem cells, tissue cultures and the production of biovalue. *Health*, 6, 305–23.

Walter, T. (1994) *The Revival of Death*. London: Routledge.

Warnock, M. (1990) *A Question of Life*. London: HMSO [Warnock Report].

Webb, M. (1997) *The Good Death: The New American Search to Reshape the End of Life*. New York: Bantam Books.

Webster, A. (2002) Risk and innovative health technologies: calculation, interpretation and regulation. *Health, Risk and Society*, 4, 221–6.

Webster, A. (2004) Health technology assessment: a sociological commentary on reflexive innovation. *International Journal of Health Technology Assessment* (in press).

Webster, A., and Rappert, B. (2002) The commercialisation of science. *Knowledge, Economy and Society*, 45, 41–65.

Wellcome Trust, Medicine and Society Programme (1998) *Public Perspectives on Human Cloning*. London: Wellcome Trust.

Wexler, N. (1995) *Mapping Fate: A Memoire of Family Risk and Genetic Research*. New York: Random House.

Whalley, T., Earl-Slater, A., Haycox, A., and Bagust, A. (2000) An integrated national pharmaceutical policy for the United Kingdom? *British Medical Journal*, 321, 1523–6.

Wheale, P. R. (1998) Human genome research and the Human Genome Diversity Project: some ethical issues. In P. R. Wheale, R. von Schomberg and P. Glasner (eds) *The Social Management of Genetic Engineering*. Aldershot: Ashgate.

Wheale, P. R., and McNally, R. (1998) The social management of genetic engineering: an introduction. In P. R. Wheale, R. von Schomberg and

P. Glasner (eds) *The Social Management of Genetic Engineering*. Aldershot: Ashgate, 1–28.

Whitt, L. A. (1998) Biocolonialism and the commodification of knowledge. *Science as Culture*, 7, 33–68.

Williams, R., and Edge, D. (1996) The social shaping of technology. *Research Policy*, 25, 865–99.

Williams, R., Faulkner, W., and Fleck, J. (1997) *Exploring Expertise: Issues and Perspectives*. Basingstoke: Macmillan.

Williams, S. (2001) Sociological imperialism and the profession of medicine revisited. *Sociology of Health and Illness*, 23, 135–58.

Williams, S., and Bendelow, G. (1998) *The Lived Body: Sociological Themes, Embodied Issues*. London: Routledge.

Williams, S., and Calnan, M. (eds) (1996) *Modern Medicine: Lay Perspectives and Experiences*. London: University College London Press.

Williams, T., May, C., Mair, F., Mort, M., and Gask, L. (2003) Normative models of health technology assessment and the social production of evidence about telehealth care. *Health Policy*, 64, 1–16.

Wilson, R. (1995) Cyber(body)parts: prosthetic consciousness. In M. Featherstone and R. Burrows (eds) *Cyberspace/Cyberbodies/Cyberpunk: Cultures of Technological Embodiment*. London: Thousand Oaks; New Delhi: Sage, 239–59.

Woods, B., and Watson, N. (2004) When wheelchair innovation in Britain was under state control. *Technology and Disability* (in press).

Wouters, C. (2002) The quest for new rituals in dying and mourning: changes in the we–I balance. *Body and Society*, 8, 1–27.

Youngner, S. J., Fox, R. C., and O'Connell, J. L. (eds) (1996) *Organ Transplantation: Meanings and Realities*. Madison: University of Wisconsin Press.

Index